Hands-On Parallel Programming with C# 8 and .NET Core 3

Build solid enterprise software using task parallelism and multithreading

Shakti Tanwar

BIRMINGHAM - MUMBAI

Hands-On Parallel Programming with C# 8 and .NET Core 3

Copyright © 2019 Packt Publishing

All rights reserved. No part of this book may be reproduced, stored in a retrieval system, or transmitted in any form or by any means, without the prior written permission of the publisher, except in the case of brief quotations embedded in critical articles or reviews.

Every effort has been made in the preparation of this book to ensure the accuracy of the information presented. However, the information contained in this book is sold without warranty, either express or implied. Neither the author, nor Packt Publishing or its dealers and distributors, will be held liable for any damages caused or alleged to have been caused directly or indirectly by this book.

Packt Publishing has endeavored to provide trademark information about all of the companies and products mentioned in this book by the appropriate use of capitals. However, Packt Publishing cannot guarantee the accuracy of this information.

Commissioning Editor: Richa Tripathi
Acquisition Editor: Alok Dhuri
Content Development Editor: Digvijay Bagul
Senior Editor: Rohit Singh
Technical Editor: Pradeep Sahu
Copy Editor: Safis Editing
Project Coordinator: Francy Puthiry
Proofreader: Safis Editing
Indexer: Priyanka Dhadke
Production Designer: Jyoti Chauhan

First published: December 2019

Production reference: 1191219

Published by Packt Publishing Ltd.
Livery Place
35 Livery Street
Birmingham
B3 2PB, UK.

ISBN 978-1-78913-241-0

www.packt.com

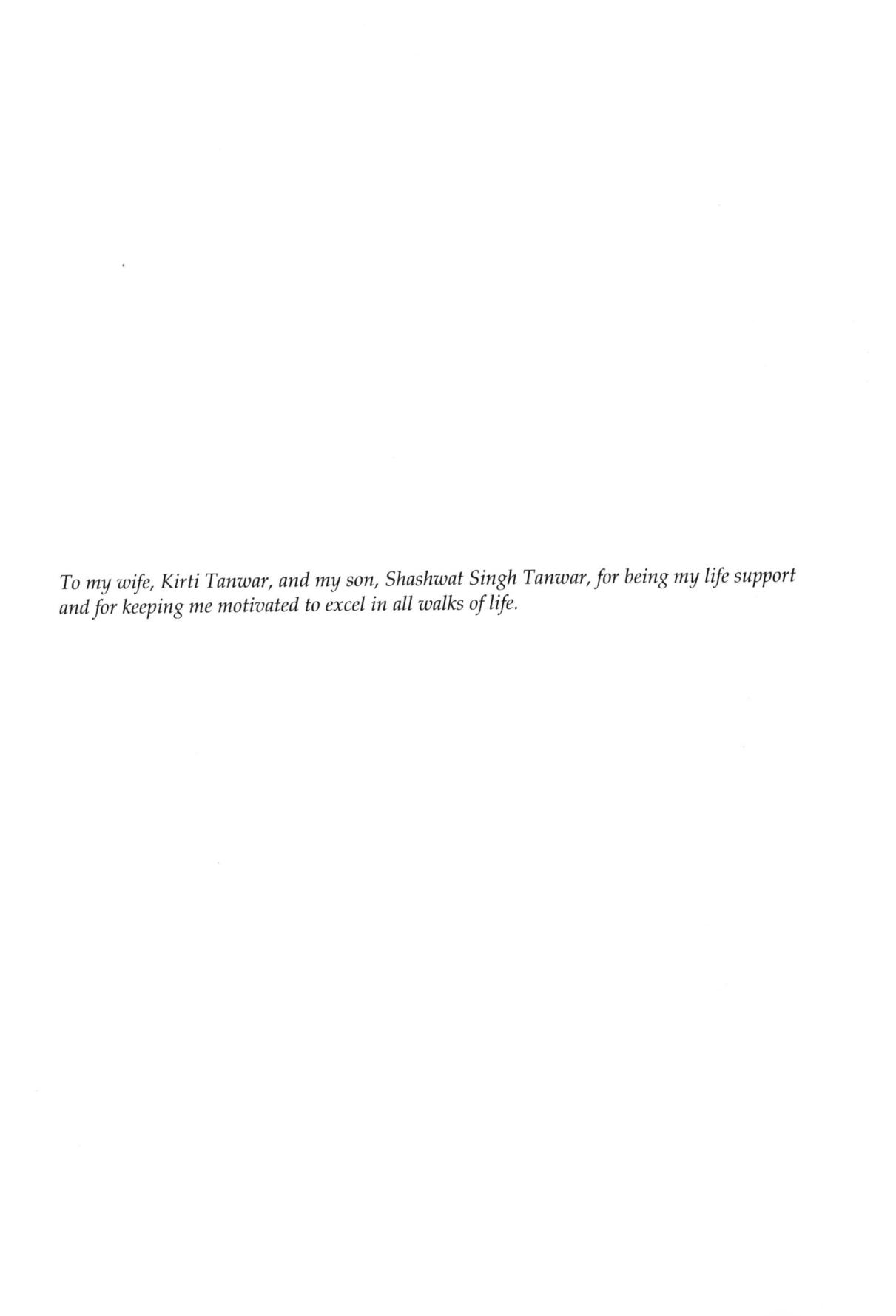

To my wife, Kirti Tanwar, and my son, Shashwat Singh Tanwar, for being my life support and for keeping me motivated to excel in all walks of life.

Packt.com

Subscribe to our online digital library for full access to over 7,000 books and videos, as well as industry leading tools to help you plan your personal development and advance your career. For more information, please visit our website.

Why subscribe?

- Spend less time learning and more time coding with practical eBooks and Videos from over 4,000 industry professionals

- Improve your learning with Skill Plans built especially for you

- Get a free eBook or video every month

- Fully searchable for easy access to vital information

- Copy and paste, print, and bookmark content

Did you know that Packt offers eBook versions of every book published, with PDF and ePub files available? You can upgrade to the eBook version at www.packt.com and as a print book customer, you are entitled to a discount on the eBook copy. Get in touch with us at customercare@packtpub.com for more details.

At www.packt.com, you can also read a collection of free technical articles, sign up for a range of free newsletters, and receive exclusive discounts and offers on Packt books and eBooks.

Contributors

About the author

Shakti Tanwar is the CEO of Techpro Compsoft Pvt Ltd, a global provider of consulting in information technology services. He is a technical evangelist and software architect with more than 15 years of experience in software development and corporate training. Shakti is a Microsoft Certified Trainer and has been conducting training in association with Microsoft in the Middle East. His areas of expertise include .NET; Azure Machine Learning; artificial intelligence; applications of pure functional programming to build fault-tolerant, reactive systems; and parallel computing. His love for teaching led him to start a special "train the professors" program for the betterment of colleges in India.

> *This book would not have been possible without the sacrifices of my wife, Kirti, and son, Shashwat. They stood by me through every struggle and every success. It was their smiles and motivation during tough times that kept me going.*
>
> *I'm also eternally grateful to my parents and my siblings, who always motivated me to scale new heights of success.*
>
> *Many thanks to my friends, mentors, and team Packt, who guided me throughout this journey.*

About the reviewers

Alvin Ashcraft is a developer living near Philadelphia. He has spent his 23-year career building software with C#, Visual Studio, WPF, ASP.NET, and more. He has been awarded, nine times, the Microsoft MVP title. You can read his daily links for .NET developers on his blog, *Morning Dew*. He works as a principal software engineer for Allscripts, building healthcare software. He has previously been employed by software companies, including Oracle. He has reviewed other titles for Packt Publishing, such as *Mastering ASP.NET Core 2.0*, *Mastering Entity Framework Core 2.0*, and *Learning ASP.NET Core 2.0*.

> *I would like to thank wonderful wife, Stelene, and our three amazing daughters for their support. They were very understanding when I was reading and reviewing these chapters on evenings and weekends to help deliver a useful, high-quality book for .NET developers.*

Vidya Vrat Agarwal is an avid reader, speaker, published author for Apress, and technical reviewer of over a dozen books for Apress, Packt, and O'Reilly. He is a hands-on architect with 20 years of experience in architecting, designing, and developing distributed software solutions for large enterprises. At T-Mobile as a principal architect, he has worked with B2C and B2B teams where he continues to partner with other domain architects to establish the solution vision and architecture roadmaps for various T-Mobile initiatives to positively impact millions of T-Mobile customers. He sees software development as a craft, and he is a big proponent of software architecture and clean code practices.

Packt is searching for authors like you

If you're interested in becoming an author for Packt, please visit `authors.packtpub.com` and apply today. We have worked with thousands of developers and tech professionals, just like you, to help them share their insight with the global tech community. You can make a general application, apply for a specific hot topic that we are recruiting an author for, or submit your own idea.

Table of Contents

Preface   1

Section 1: Fundamentals of Threading, Multitasking, and Asynchrony

Chapter 1: Introduction to Parallel Programming   9
  Technical requirements   10
  Preparing for multi-core computing   10
    Processes   10
      Some more information about the OS   11
    Multitasking   11
    Hyper-threading   11
      Flynn's taxonomy   13
    Threads   14
      Types of threads   14
        Apartment state   14
    Multithreading   17
      Thread class   19
        Advantages and disadvantages of threads   23
      The ThreadPool class   23
        Advantages, disadvantages, and when to avoid using ThreadPool   26
      BackgroundWorker   27
        Advantages and disadvantages of using BackgroundWorker   31
    Multithreading versus multitasking   31
  Scenarios where parallel programming can come in handy   32
  Advantages and disadvantages of parallel programming   32
  Summary   33
  Questions   34

Chapter 2: Task Parallelism   35
  Technical requirements   36
  Tasks   36
  Creating and starting a task   37
    The System.Threading.Tasks.Task class   37
      Using lambda expressions syntax   38
      Using the Action delegate   38
      Using delegate   38
    The System.Threading.Tasks.Task.Factory.StartNew method   39
      Using lambda expressions syntax   39
      Using the Action delegate   39
      Using delegate   39
    The System.Threading.Tasks.Task.Run method   40

Table of Contents

       Using lambda expressions syntax   40
       Using the Action delegate   40
       Using delegate   40
   The System.Threading.Tasks.Task.Delay method   41
   The System.Threading.Tasks.Task.Yield method   42
   The System.Threading.Tasks.Task.FromResult<T> method   45
   The System.Threading.Tasks.Task.FromException and System.Threading.Tasks.Task.FromException<T> methods   46
   The System.Threading.Tasks.Task.FromCanceled and System.Threading.Tasks.Task.FromCanceled<T> methods   46
Getting results from finished tasks   47
How to cancel tasks   48
   Creating a token   49
   Creating a task using tokens   49
       Polling the status of the token via the IsCancellationRequested property   49
       Registering for a request cancellation using the Callback delegate   50
How to wait on running tasks   52
   Task.Wait   53
   Task.WaitAll   54
   Task.WaitAny   54
   Task.WhenAll   55
   Task.WhenAny   55
Handling task exceptions   56
   Handling exception from single tasks   56
   Handling exceptions from multiple tasks   57
   Handling task exceptions with a callback function   58
Converting APM patterns into tasks   59
Converting EAPs into tasks   61
More on tasks   63
   Continuation tasks   63
       Continuing tasks using the Task.ContinueWith method   63
       Continuing tasks using Task.Factory.ContinueWhenAll and Task.Factory.ContinueWhenAll<T>   65
       Continuing tasks using Task.Factory.ContinueWhenAny and Task.Factory.ContinueWhenAny<T>   65
   Parent and child tasks   66
   Creating a detached task   66
   Creating an attached task   67
Work-stealing queues   68
Summary   71

Chapter 3: Implementing Data Parallelism   73
Technical requirements   73
Moving from sequential loops to parallel loops   74
   Using the Parallel.Invoke method   75
   Using the Parallel.For method   77

Using the Parallel.ForEach method	78
Understanding the degree of parallelism	**79**
Creating a custom partitioning strategy	**81**
Range partitioning	82
Chunk partitioning	82
Canceling loops	**83**
Using the Parallel.Break method	84
Using ParallelLoopState.Stop	86
Using CancellationToken to cancel loops	86
Understanding thread storage in parallel loops	**88**
Thread local variable	89
Partition local variable	90
Summary	**91**
Questions	**92**
Chapter 4: Using PLINQ	**93**
Technical requirements	**93**
LINQ providers in .NET	**94**
Writing PLINQ queries	**95**
Introducing the ParallelEnumerable class	95
Our first PLINQ query	96
Preserving order in PLINQ while doing parallel executions	**97**
Sequential execution using the AsUnOrdered() method	98
Merge options in PLINQ	**99**
Using the NotBuffered merge option	99
Using the AutoBuffered merge option	100
Using the FullyBuffered merge option	101
Throwing and handling exceptions with PLINQ	**103**
Combining parallel and sequential LINQ queries	**106**
Canceling PLINQ queries	**107**
Disadvantages of parallel programming with PLINQ	**108**
Understanding the factors that affect the performance of PLINQ (speedups)	**109**
Degree of parallelism	109
Merge option	109
Partitioning type	109
Deciding when to stay sequential with PLINQ	110
Order of operation	110
ForAll versus calling ToArray() or ToList()	111
Forcing parallelism	111
Generating sequences	111
Summary	**112**
Questions	**112**

[iii]

Table of Contents

Section 2: Data Structures that Support Parallelism in .NET Core

Chapter 5: Synchronization Primitives — 117
- Technical requirements — 118
- What are synchronization primitives? — 118
- Interlocked operations — 119
  - Memory barriers in .NET — 120
  - What is reordering? — 121
  - Types of memory barriers — 122
  - Avoiding code reordering using constructs — 123
- Introduction to locking primitives — 124
  - How locking works — 124
  - Thread state — 125
  - Blocking versus spinning — 126
  - Lock, mutex, and semaphore — 127
    - Lock — 127
    - Mutex — 130
    - Semaphore — 132
      - Local semaphore — 133
      - Global semaphore — 134
  - ReaderWriterLock — 134
- Introduction to signaling primitives — 134
  - Thread.Join — 135
  - EventWaitHandle — 136
    - AutoResetEvent — 136
    - ManualResetEvent — 137
  - WaitHandles — 140
- Lightweight synchronization primitives — 143
  - Slim locks — 143
    - ReaderWriterLockSlim — 144
    - SemaphoreSlim — 146
    - ManualResetEventSlim — 146
- Barrier and countdown events — 147
  - A case study using Barrier and CountDownEvent — 147
- SpinWait — 150
  - SpinLock — 151
- Summary — 152
- Questions — 153

Chapter 6: Using Concurrent Collections — 155
- Technical requirements — 155
- An introduction to concurrent collections — 156
  - Introducing IProducerConsumerCollection<T> — 156
    - Using ConcurrentQueue<T> — 157
      - Using queues to solve a producer-consumer problem — 158

[iv]

Solving problems using concurrent queues	159
Performance consideration – Queue<T> versus ConcurrentQueue<T>	160
Using ConcurrentStack<T>	161
Creating a concurrent stack	161
Using ConcurrentBag<T>	162
Using BlockingCollection<T>	164
Creating BlockingCollection<T>	164
A multiple producer-consumer scenario	**166**
Using ConcurrentDictionary<TKey,TValue>	167
Summary	**169**
Questions	**170**

Chapter 7: Improving Performance with Lazy Initialization — 171
Technical requirements — 171
Introducing lazy initialization concepts — 172
Introducing System.Lazy<T> — 175
    Construction logic encapsulated inside a constructor — 175
    Construction logic passed as a delegate to Lazy<T> — 177
Handling exceptions with the lazy initialization pattern — 178
    No exceptions occur during initialization — 178
    Random exception while initialization with exception caching — 178
    Not caching exceptions — 181
Lazy initialization with thread-local storage — 182
Reducing the overhead with lazy initializations — 184
Summary — 187
Questions — 188

Section 3: Asynchronous Programming Using C#

Chapter 8: Introduction to Asynchronous Programming — 191
Technical requirements — 191
Types of program execution — 192
    Understanding synchronous program execution — 192
    Understanding asynchronous program execution — 194
When to use asynchronous programming — 195
    Writing asynchronous code — 195
        Using the BeginInvoke method of the Delegate class — 196
        Using the Task class — 197
        Using the IAsyncResult interface — 198
When not to use asynchronous programming — 200
    In a single database without connection pooling — 200
    When it is important that the code is easy to read and maintain — 200
    For simple and short-running operations — 200
    For applications with lots of shared resources — 201
Problems you can solve using asynchronous code — 201
Summary — 202

Table of Contents

Questions	203
Chapter 9: Async, Await, and Task-Based Asynchronous Programming Basics	205
Technical requirements	206
Introducing async and await	206
The return type of async methods	210
Async delegates and lambda expressions	211
Task-based asynchronous patterns	212
The compiler method, using the async keyword	212
Implementing the TAP manually	212
Exception handling with async code	213
A method that returns Task and throws an exception	213
An async method from outside a try-catch block without the await keyword	214
An async method from inside the try-catch block without the await keyword	216
Calling an async method with the await keyword from outside the try-catch block	218
Methods returning void	219
Async with PLINQ	220
Measuring the performance of async code	221
Guidelines for using async code	224
Avoid using async void	224
Async chain all the way	224
Using ConfigureAwait wherever possible	225
Summary	226
Questions	226

Section 4: Debugging, Diagnostics, and Unit Testing for Async Code

Chapter 10: Debugging Tasks Using Visual Studio	231
Technical requirements	232
Debugging with VS 2019	232
How to debug threads	232
Using Parallel Stacks windows	236
Debugging using Parallel Stacks windows	236
Threads view	237
Tasks view	238
Debugging using the Parallel Watch window	239
Using Concurrency Visualizer	241
Utilization view	242
Threads view	243
Cores view	244
Summary	244
Questions	245

[vi]

Further reading	245

Chapter 11: Writing Unit Test Cases for Parallel and Asynchronous Code — 247

Technical requirements	248
Unit testing with .NET Core	248
Understanding the problems with writing unit test cases for async code	250
Writing unit test cases for parallel and async code	253
Checking for a successful result	253
Checking for an exception result when the divisor is 0	254
Mocking the setup for async code using Moq	254
Testing tools	257
Summary	258
Questions	258
Further reading	259

Section 5: Parallel Programming Feature Additions to .NET Core

Chapter 12: IIS and Kestrel in ASP.NET Core — 263

Technical requirements	263
IIS threading model and internals	264
Starvation Avoidance	265
Hill Climbing	265
Kestrel threading model and internals	266
ASP.NET Core 1.x	267
ASP.NET Core 2.x	268
Introducing the best practices of threading in microservices	269
Single thread-single process microservices	269
Single thread-multiple process microservices	270
Multiple threads-single process	270
Asynchronous services	270
Dedicated thread pools	270
Introducing async in ASP.NET MVC core	271
Async streams	275
Summary	278
Questions	279

Chapter 13: Patterns in Parallel Programming — 281

Technical requirements	281
The MapReduce pattern	282
Implementing MapReduce using LINQ	282
Aggregation	285
The fork/join pattern	287

[vii]

The speculative processing pattern	287
The lazy pattern	289
Shared state pattern	292
Summary	292
Questions	293
Chapter 14: Distributed Memory Management	295
Technical requirements	296
Introduction to distributed systems	296
Shared versus distributed memory model	297
Shared memory model	298
Distributed memory model	300
Types of communication network	301
Static communication networks	301
Dynamic communication networks	302
Properties of communication networks	302
Topology	302
Routing algorithms	303
Switching strategy	304
Flow control	304
Exploring topologies	305
Linear and ring topologies	305
Linear arrays	305
Ring or torus	306
Meshes and tori	306
2D mesh	307
2D torus	308
Programming distributed memory machines using message passing	308
Why MPI?	309
Installing MPI on Windows	309
Sample program using MPI	309
Basic send/receive use	310
Collectives	312
Summary	312
Questions	313
Assessments	315
Other Books You May Enjoy	319
Index	323

Preface

Packt first contacted me about writing this book nearly a year ago. It's been a long journey, harder than I anticipated at times, and I've learned a lot. The book you hold now is the culmination of many long days, and I'm proud to finally present it.

Having written this book about C# means a lot to me as it has always been a dream of mine to write about the language that I started my career with. C# has really grown in leaps and bounds since it was first introduced. .NET Core has actually enhanced the power and reputation of C# within the developer community.

To make this book meaningful to a wide audience, we will cover both the classic threading model and the **Task Parallel Library** (**TPL**), using code to explain them. We'll first look at the basic concepts of the OS that make it possible to write multithreaded code. We'll then look closely at the differences between classic threading and the TPL.

In this book, I take care to approach parallel programming in the context of modern-day best programming practices. The examples have been kept short and simple so as to ease your understanding. The chapters have been written in a way that makes the topics easy to learn even if you don't have much prior knowledge of them.

I hope you enjoy reading this book as much as I enjoyed writing it.

Who this book is for

This book is for C# programmers who want to learn multithreading and parallel programming concepts and want to use them in enterprise applications built using .NET Core. It is also designed for students and professionals who simply want to learn about how parallel programming works with modern-day hardware.

It is assumed that you already have some familiarity with the C# programming language and some basic knowledge of how OSes work.

Preface

What this book covers

Chapter 1, *Introduction to Parallel Programming*, introduces the important concepts of multithreading and parallel programming. This chapter includes coverage of how OSes have evolved to support modern-day parallel programming constructs.

Chapter 2, *Task Parallelism*, demonstrates how to divide your program into tasks for the efficient utilization of CPU resources and high performance.

Chapter 3, *Implementing Data Parallelism*, focuses on implementing data parallelism using parallel loops. This chapter also covers extension methods to help in achieving parallelism, as well as partitioning strategies.

Chapter 4, *Using PLINQ*, explains how to take advantage of PLINQ support. This includes ordering queries and canceling queries, as well as the pitfalls of using PLINQ.

Chapter 5, *Synchronization Primitives*, covers the synchronization constructs available in C# for working with shared resources in multithreaded code.

Chapter 6, *Using Concurrent Collections*, describes how to take advantage of concurrent collections available in .NET Core without worrying about the effort of manual synchronization coding.

Chapter 7, *Improving Performance with Lazy Initialization*, explores how to implement built-in constructs utilizing lazy patterns.

Chapter 8, *Introduction to Asynchronous Programming*, explores how to write asynchronous code in earlier versions of .NET.

Chapter 9, *Async, Await, and Task-Based Asynchronous Programming Basics*, covers how to take advantage of the new constructs in .NET Core to implement asynchronous code.

Chapter 10, *Debugging Tasks Using Visual Studio*, focuses on the various tools available in Visual Studio 2019 that makes debugging parallel tasks easier.

Chapter 11, *Writing Unit Test Cases for Parallel and Asynchronous Code*, covers the various ways to write unit test cases in Visual Studio and .NET Core.

Chapter 12, *IIS and Kestrel in ASP.NET Core*, introduces the concepts of IIS and Kestrel. The chapter also looks at support for asynchronous streams.

Chapter 13, *Patterns in Parallel Programming*, explains the various patterns that are already implemented in the C# language. This also includes custom pattern implementations.

Chapter 14, *Distributed Memory Management*, explores how memory is shared in distributed programs.

To get the most out of this book

You need to have Visual Studio 2019 installed on your system along with .NET Core 3.1. Basic knowledge of C# and OS concepts is recommended as well.

Download the example code files

You can download the example code files for this book from your account at www.packt.com. If you purchased this book elsewhere, you can visit www.packtpub.com/support and register to have the files emailed directly to you.

You can download the code files by following these steps:

1. Log in or register at www.packt.com.
2. Select the **Support** tab.
3. Click on **Code Downloads**.
4. Enter the name of the book in the **Search** box and follow the onscreen instructions.

Once the file is downloaded, please make sure that you unzip or extract the folder using the latest version of:

- WinRAR/7-Zip for Windows
- Zipeg/iZip/UnRarX for Mac
- 7-Zip/PeaZip for Linux

The code bundle for the book is also hosted on GitHub at https://github.com/PacktPublishing/Hands-On-Parallel-Programming-with-C-8-and-.NET-Core-3. In case there's an update to the code, it will be updated on the existing GitHub repository.

We also have other code bundles from our rich catalog of books and videos available at https://github.com/PacktPublishing/. Check them out!

Download the color images

We also provide a PDF file that has color images of the screenshots/diagrams used in this book. You can download it here: `https://static.packt-cdn.com/downloads/9781789132410_ColorImages.pdf`.

Conventions used

There are a number of text conventions used throughout this book.

`CodeInText`: Indicates code words in text, database table names, folder names, filenames, file extensions, pathnames, dummy URLs, user input, and Twitter handles. Here is an example: "Mount the downloaded `WebStorm-10*.dmg` disk image file as another disk in your system."

A block of code is set as follows:

```
private static void PrintNumber10Times()
{
    for (int i = 0; i < 10; i++)
        {
        Console.Write(1);
        }
    Console.WriteLine();
}
```

When we wish to draw your attention to a particular part of a code block, the relevant lines or items are set in bold:

```
private static void PrintNumber10Times()
{
    for (int i = 0; i < 10; i++)
        {
        Console.Write(1);
        }
    Console.WriteLine();
}
```

Bold: Indicates a new term, an important word, or words that you see on screen. For example, words in menus or dialog boxes appear in the text like this. Here is an example: "Rather than finding the optimal number of threads ourselves, we can leave it to the **Common Language Runtime**."

Preface

 Warnings or important notes appear like this.

 Tips and tricks appear like this.

Get in touch

Feedback from our readers is always welcome.

General feedback: If you have questions about any aspect of this book, mention the book title in the subject of your message and email us at customercare@packtpub.com.

Errata: Although we have taken every care to ensure the accuracy of our content, mistakes do happen. If you have found a mistake in this book, we would be grateful if you would report this to us. Please visit www.packtpub.com/support/errata, selecting your book, clicking on the Errata Submission Form link, and entering the details.

Piracy: If you come across any illegal copies of our works in any form on the internet, we would be grateful if you would provide us with the location address or website name. Please contact us at copyright@packt.com with a link to the material.

If you are interested in becoming an author: If there is a topic that you have expertise in and you are interested in either writing or contributing to a book, please visit authors.packtpub.com.

Reviews

Please leave a review. Once you have read and used this book, why not leave a review on the site that you purchased it from? Potential readers can then see and use your unbiased opinion to make purchase decisions, we at Packt can understand what you think about our products, and our authors can see your feedback on their book. Thank you!

For more information about Packt, please visit packt.com.

Section 1: Fundamentals of Threading, Multitasking, and Asynchrony

In this section, you will become familiar with the concepts of threading, multitasking, and asynchronous programming.

This section comprises the following chapters:

- `Chapter 1`, *Introduction to Parallel Programming*
- `Chapter 2`, *Task Parallelism*
- `Chapter 3`, *Implementing Data Parallelism*
- `Chapter 4`, *Using PLINQ*

Introduction to Parallel Programming

Parallel programming has been supported in .NET since the start and it has gained a strong footing since the introduction of the **Task Parallel Library** (**TPL**) from .NET framework 4.0 onward.

Multithreading is a subset of parallel programming and is one of the least understood aspects of programming; it's one that many new developers struggle to understand. C# has evolved significantly since its inception. It has very strong support, not only for multithreading but also for asynchronous programming. Multithreading in C# goes way back to C# version 1.0. C# is primarily synchronous, but with the strong async support that has been added from C# 5.0 onward, it has become the first choice for application programmers. Whereas multithreading only deals with how to parallelize within processes, parallel programming also deals with inter-process communication scenarios.

Prior to the introduction of the TPL, we relied on `Thread`, `BackgroundWorker`, and `ThreadPool` to provide us with multithreading capabilities. At the time of C# v1.0, it relied on threads to split up work and free up the **user interface** (**UI**), thereby allowing the user to develop responsive applications. This model is now referred to as classic threading. With time, this model made way for another model of programming, called TPL, which relies on tasks and still uses threads internally.

In this chapter, we will learn about various concepts that will help you learn about writing multithreaded code from scratch.

We will cover the following topics:

- Basic concepts of multi-core computing, starting with an introduction to the concepts and processes related to the **operating system** (**OS**)
- Threads and the difference between multithreading and multitasking
- Advantages and disadvantages of writing parallel code and scenarios in which parallel programming is useful

Technical requirements

All the examples demonstrated in this book have been created in Visual Studio 2019 using C# 8. All the source code can be found on GitHub at `https://github.com/PacktPublishing/Hands-On-Parallel-Programming-with-C-8-and-.NET-Core-3/tree/master/Chapter01`.

Preparing for multi-core computing

In this section, we will introduce the core concepts of the OS, starting with the process, which is where threads live and run. Then, we will consider how multitasking evolved with the introduction of hardware capabilities, which make parallel programming possible. After that, we will try to understand the different ways of creating a thread with code.

Processes

In layman's terms, the word *process* refers to a program in execution. In terms of the OS, however, a process is an address space in the memory. Every application, whether it is a Windows, web, or mobile application, needs processes to run. Processes provide security for programs against other programs that run on the same system so that data that's allocated to one cannot be accidentally accessed by another. They also provide isolation so that programs can be started and stopped independently of each other and independently of the underlying OS.

Some more information about the OS

The performance of applications largely depends on the quality and configuration of the hardware. This includes the following:

- CPU speed
- Amount of RAM
- Hard disk speed (5400/7200 RPM)
- Disk type, that is, HDD or SSD

Over the last few decades, we have seen huge jumps in hardware technology. For example, microprocessors used to have a single core, which is a chip with one **central processing unit** (**CPU**). By the turn of the century, we saw the advent of multi-core processors, which are chips with two or more processors, each with its own cache.

Multitasking

Multitasking refers to the ability of a computer system to run more than one process (application) at a time. The number of processes that can be run by a system is directly proportional to the number of cores in that system. Therefore, a single-core processor can only run one task at a time, a dual-core processor can run two tasks at a time, and a quad-core processor can run four tasks at a time. If we add the concept of CPU scheduling to this, we can see that the CPU runs more applications at a time by scheduling or switching them based on CPU scheduling algorithms.

Hyper-threading

Hyper-threading (**HT**) technology is a proprietary technology that was developed by Intel that improves the parallelization of computations that are performed on x86 processors. It was first introduced in Xeon server processors in 2002. HT-enabled single-processor chips run with two virtual (logical) cores and are capable of executing two tasks at a time. The following diagram shows the difference between single- and multi-core chips:

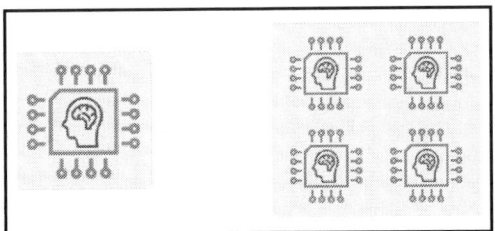

Introduction to Parallel Programming

The following are a few examples of processor configurations and the number of tasks that they can perform:

- **A single processor with a single-core chip**: One task at a time
- **A single processor with an HT-enabled single-core chip**: Two tasks at a time
- **A single processor with a dual-core chip**: Two tasks at a time
- **A single processor with an HT-enabled dual-core chip**: Four tasks at a time
- **A single processor with a quad-core chip**: Four tasks at a time
- **A single processor with an HT-enabled quad-core chip**: Eight tasks at a time

The following is a screenshot of a CPU resource monitor for an HT-enabled quad-core processor system. On the right-hand side, you can see that there are eight available CPUs:

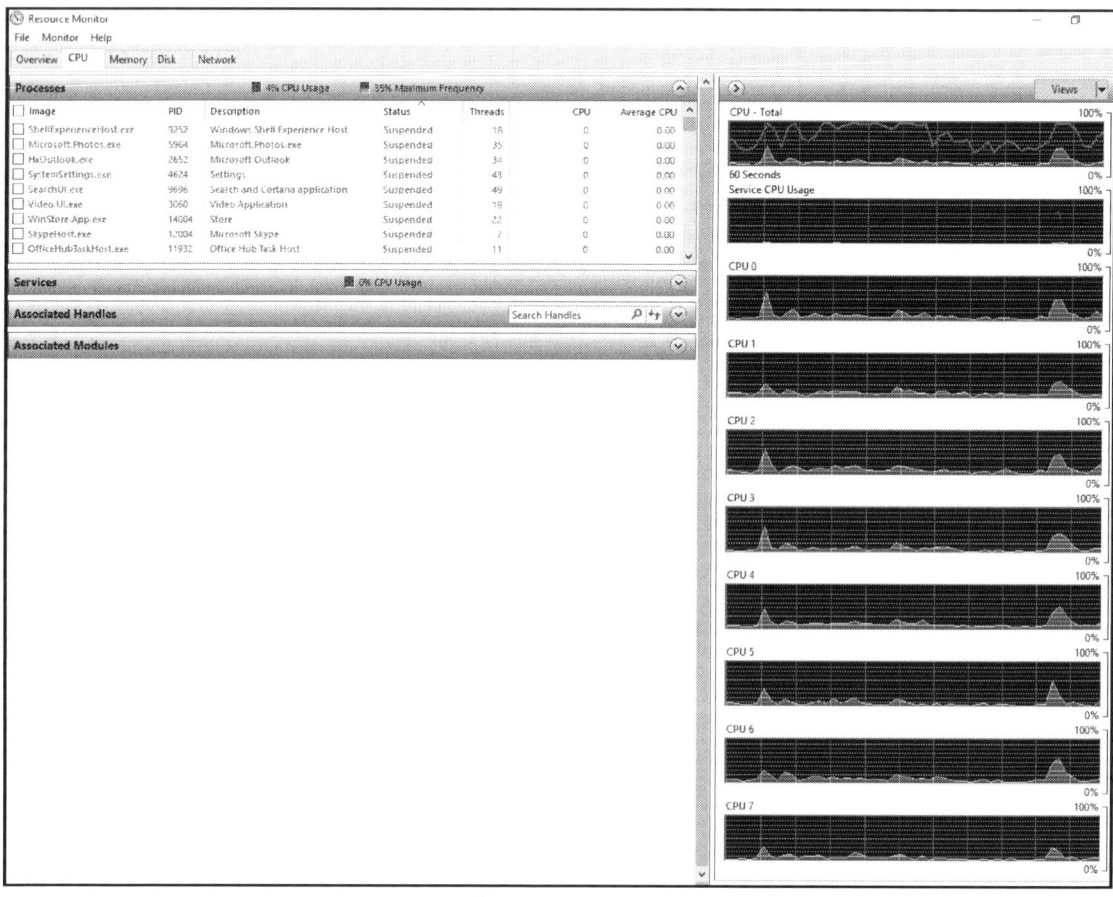

[12]

You might be wondering how much you can improve the performance of your computer simply by moving from a single-core to a multi-core processor. At the time of writing, most of the fastest supercomputers are built on the **Multiple Instruction, Multiple Data (MIMD)** architecture, which was one of the classifications of computer architecture proposed by Michael J. Flynn in 1966.

Let's try to understand this classification.

Flynn's taxonomy

Flynn classified computer architectures into four categories based on the number of concurrent instruction (or control) streams and data streams:

- **Single Instruction, Single Data (SISD)**: In this model, there is a single control unit and a single instruction stream. These systems can only execute one instruction at a time without any parallel processing. All single-core processor machines are based on the SISD architecture.
- **Single Instruction, Multiple Data (SIMD)**: In this model, we have a single instruction stream and multiple data streams. The same instruction stream is applied to multiple data streams in parallel. This is handy in speculative-approach scenarios where we have multiple algorithms for data and we don't know which one will be faster. It provides the same input to all the algorithms and runs them in parallel on multiple processors.
- **Multiple Instructions, Single Data (MISD)**: In this model, multiple instructions operate on one data stream. Therefore, multiple operations can be applied in parallel on the same data source. This is generally used for fault tolerance and in space shuttle flight control computers.
- **Multiple Instructions, Multiple Data (MIMD)**: In this model, as the name suggests, we have multiple instruction streams and multiple data streams. Due to this, we can achieve true parallelism, where each processor can run different instructions on different data streams. Nowadays, this architecture is used by most computer systems.

Now that we've covered the basics, let's move our discussion to threads.

Introduction to Parallel Programming

Threads

A thread is a unit of execution inside a process. At any point, a program may consist of one or more threads for better performance. GUI-based Windows applications, such as legacy **Windows Forms (WinForms)** or **Windows Presentation Foundation (WPF)**, have a dedicated thread for managing the UI and handling user actions. This thread is also called the UI thread, or the **foreground thread**. It owns all the controls that are created as part of the UI.

Types of threads

There are two different types of managed threads, that is, a foreground thread and a background thread. The difference between these is as follows:

- **Foreground threads:** These have a direct impact on an application's lifetime. The application keeps running until there is a foreground thread.
- **Background threads:** These have no impact on the application's lifetime. When the application exits, all the background threads are killed.

An application may comprise any number of foreground or background threads. While active, a foreground thread keeps the application running; that is, the application's lifetime depends on the foreground thread. The application stops completely when the last foreground thread is stopped or aborted. When the application exits, the system stops all the background threads.

Apartment state

Another important aspect of threads to understand is the apartment state. This is the area inside a thread where **Component Object Model (COM)** objects reside.

COM is an object-oriented system for creating binary software that the user can interact with and is distributed and cross-platform. COM has been used to create Microsoft OLE and ActiveX technologies.

As you may be aware, all Windows forms controls are wrapped over COM objects. Whenever you create a .NET WinForms application, you are actually hosting COM components. A thread apartment is a distinct area inside the application process where COM objects are created. The following diagram demonstrates the relationship between the thread apartment and COM objects:

Chapter 1

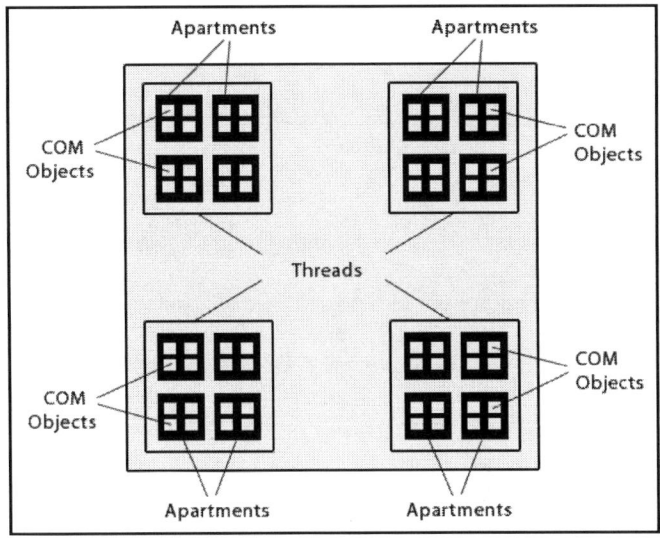

As you can see from the preceding diagram, every thread has thread apartments where COM objects reside.

A thread can belong to one of two apartment states:

- **Single-Threaded Apartment (STA)**: The underlying COM object can be accessed via a single thread only
- **Multi-Threaded Apartment (MTA)**: The underlying COM object can be accessed via multiple threads at a time

The following list highlights some important points regarding thread apartment states:

- Processes can have multiple threads, either foreground or background.
- Each thread can have one apartment, either STA or MTA.
- Every apartment has a concurrency model, either single-threaded or multithreaded. We can change the thread state programmatically as well.
- An application process may have more than one STA, but a maximum of one MTA.
- An example of an STA application is a Windows application, and an example of an MTA application is a web application.
- COM objects are created in apartments. One COM object can only lie in one thread apartment, and apartments cannot be shared.

Introduction to Parallel Programming

An application can be forced to start in STA mode by using the `STAThread` attribute over the main methods. The following is an example of the `Main` method of a legacy WinForm:

```
static class Program
{
    /// <summary>
    /// The main entry point for the application.
    /// </summary>
    [STAThread]
    static void Main()
    {
        Application.EnableVisualStyles();
        Application.SetCompatibleTextRenderingDefault(false);
        Application.Run(new Form1());
    }
}
```

The `STAThread` attribute is also present in WPF but is hidden from users. The following is the code for the compiled `App.g.cs` class, which can be found in the `obj/Debug` directory of your WPF project after compilation:

```
/// <summary>
/// App
/// </summary>
public partial class App : System.Windows.Application {

    /// <summary>
    /// InitializeComponent
    /// </summary>
    [System.Diagnostics.DebuggerNonUserCodeAttribute()]
    [System.CodeDom.Compiler.GeneratedCodeAttribute(
     "PresentationBuildTasks", "4.0.0.0")]
    public void InitializeComponent() {

        #line 5 "..\..\App.xaml"
        this.StartupUri = new System.Uri("MainWindow.xaml",
         System.UriKind.Relative);

        #line default
        #line hidden
    }

    /// <summary>
    /// Application Entry Point.
    /// </summary>
    [System.STAThreadAttribute()]
    [System.Diagnostics.DebuggerNonUserCodeAttribute()]
```

```
[System.CodeDom.Compiler.GeneratedCodeAttribute(
  "PresentationBuildTasks", "4.0.0.0")]
public static void Main() {
    WpfApp1.App app = new WpfApp1.App();
    app.InitializeComponent();
    app.Run();
  }
}
```

As you can see, the `Main` method is decorated with the `STAThread` attribute.

Multithreading

Parallel execution of code in .NET is achieved through multithreading. A process (or application) can utilize any number of threads, depending on its hardware capabilities. Every application, including console, legacy WinForms, WPF, and even web applications, is started by a single thread by default. We can easily achieve multithreading by creating more threads programmatically as and when they are required.

Multithreading typically functions using a scheduling component known as a **thread scheduler**, which keeps track of when a thread should run out of active threads inside a process. Every thread that's created is assigned a `System.Threading.ThreadPriority`, which can have one of the following valid values. `Normal` is the default priority that's assigned to any thread:

- `Highest`
- `AboveNormal`
- `Normal`
- `BelowNormal`
- `Lowest`

Every thread that runs inside a process is assigned a time slice by the OS based on the thread priority scheduling algorithm. Every OS can have a different scheduling algorithm for running threads, so the order of execution may vary in different operating systems. This makes it more difficult to troubleshoot threading errors. The most common scheduling algorithm is as follows:

1. Find the threads with the highest priority and schedule them to run.
2. If there is more than one thread with the highest priority, each thread is assigned a fixed time slices in which they can execute.

3. Once the highest-priority threads finish executing, the lower-priority threads start to be allocated to time slices in which it can begin executing.
4. If a new highest-priority thread is created, low-priority threads are pushed back again.

Time slicing refers to switching the execution between the active threads. It can vary, depending on the hardware configuration. A single-core processor machine can only run one thread at a time, so the thread scheduler carries out the time slicing. The time slice largely depends on the clock speed of the CPU, but there still aren't many performance gains that can be achieved via multithreading in such systems. Moreover, context switching comes with performance overheads. If the work that's allocated to a thread spans multiple time slices, then the thread needs to be switched in and out of memory. Every time it switches out, it needs to bundle and save its state (data) and reload it when it switches back in.

Concurrency is a concept that's primarily used in the context of multi-core processors. A multi-core processor has a higher number of CPUs available, as we discussed previously, and therefore different threads can be run simultaneously on different CPUs. A higher number of processors means a higher degree of concurrency.

There are multiple ways that threads can be created in programs. These include the following:

- The `Thread` class
- The `ThreadPool` Class
- The `BackgroundWorker` Class
- Asynchronous delegates
- TPL

We will cover asynchronous delegates and TPL in depth during the course of this book, but in this chapter, we will provide an explanation of the remaining three methods.

Thread class

The simplest and easiest way of creating threads is via the `Thread` class, which is defined in the `System.Threading` namespace. This approach has been used since the arrival of .NET version 1.0 and it works with .NET core as well. To create a thread, we need to pass a method that the thread needs to execute. The method can either be parameter-less or parameterized. There are two delegates that are provided by the framework to wrap these functions:

- `System.Threading.ThreadStart`
- `System.Threading.ParameterizedThreadStart`

We will learn both of these through examples. Before showing you how to create a thread, I will try to explain how a synchronous program works. Later on, we will introduce multithreading so that we understand the asynchronous way of execution. An example of *how to create a thread* is as follows:

```
using System;
namespace Ch01
{
    class _1Synchronous
    {
        static void Main(string[] args)
        {
            Console.WriteLine("Start Execution!!!");

            PrintNumber10Times();
            Console.WriteLine("Finish Execution");
            Console.ReadLine();
        }
        private static void PrintNumber10Times()
        {
            for (int i = 0; i < 10; i++)
            {
                Console.Write(1);
            }
            Console.WriteLine();
        }
    }
}
```

Introduction to Parallel Programming

In the preceding code, everything runs in the main thread. We have called the `PrintNumber10Times` method from within the `Main` method, and since the `Main` method is invoked by the main GUI thread, the code runs synchronously. This can cause unresponsive behavior if the code runs for a long time as the main thread will be busy during execution.

The output of the code is as follows:

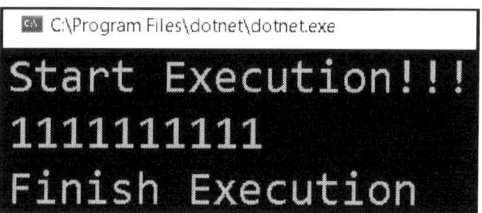

In the following timeline, we can see that everything happens in the **Main Thread**:

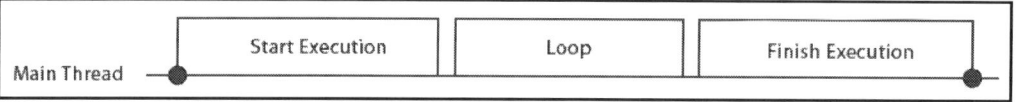

The preceding diagram shows sequential code execution on the `Main` thread.

Now, we can make the program multithreaded by creating a thread to do the printing. The main thread prints the statements that are written in the `Main` method:

```
using System;
namespace Ch01
{
    class _2ThreadStart
    {
        static void Main(string[] args)
        {
            Console.WriteLine("Start Execution!!!");
            //Using Thread without parameter
            CreateThreadUsingThreadClassWithoutParameter();
            Console.WriteLine("Finish Execution");
            Console.ReadLine();
        }
        private static void CreateThreadUsingThreadClassWithoutParameter()
        {
            System.Threading.Thread thread;
            thread = new System.Threading.Thread(new
              System.Threading.ThreadStart(PrintNumber10Times));
```

Chapter 1

```
        thread.Start();
    }
    private static void PrintNumber10Times()
    {
        for (int i = 0; i < 10; i++)
        {
            Console.Write(1);
        }
        Console.WriteLine();
    }
  }
}
```

In the preceding code, we have delegated the execution of `PrintNumber10Times()` to a new thread that has been created via the `Thread` class. The `Console.WriteLine` statements in the `Main` method are still executed via the main thread, but `PrintNumber10Times` is not called via the child thread.

The output of the code is as follows:

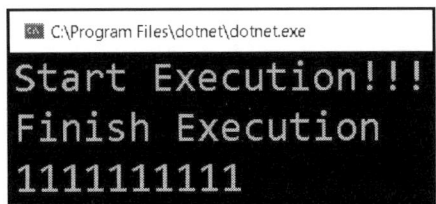

The timeline for this process is as follows. You can see that `Console.WriteLine` executes on the **Main Thread** and that the loop executes on the **Child Thread**:

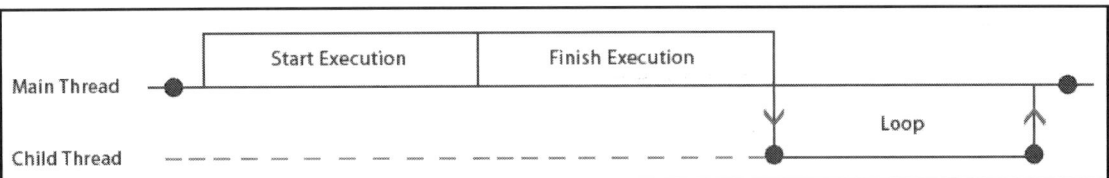

The preceding diagram is an example of multithreaded execution.

If we compare the outputs, we can see that the program finishes everything in the main thread and then starts to print the number 10 times. The operations in this example are very small and thus work in a deterministic manner. If there are time-consuming statements in the main thread before **Finish Execution** is printed, however, the results can vary. We will look at how multithreading works and how it is related to CPU speed and numbers later on in this chapter in order to fully understand this idea.

Here is another example to show you how to pass data to the thread using the System.Threading.ParameterizedThreadStart delegate:

```
using System;
namespace Ch01
{
    class _3ParameterizedThreadStart
    {
        static void Main(string[] args)
        {
            Console.WriteLine("Start Execution!!!");
            //Using Thread with parameter
            CreateThreadUsingThreadClassWithParameter();
            Console.WriteLine("Finish Execution");
            Console.ReadLine();
        }
        private static void CreateThreadUsingThreadClassWithParameter()
        {
            System.Threading.Thread thread;
            thread = new System.Threading.Thread(new
              System.Threading.ParameterizedThreadStart(PrintNumberNTimes));
            thread.Start(10);
        }
        private static void PrintNumberNTimes(object times)
        {
            int n = Convert.ToInt32(times);
            for (int i = 0; i < n; i++)
            {
                Console.Write(1);
            }
            Console.WriteLine();
        }
    }
}
```

The output of the preceding code is as follows:

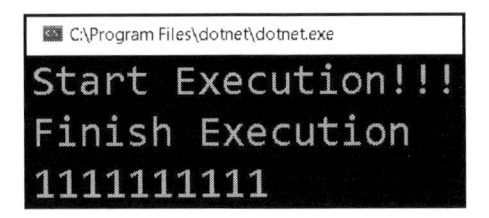

```
C:\Program Files\dotnet\dotnet.exe
Start Execution!!!
Finish Execution
1111111111
```

Using the `Thread` class has some advantages and disadvantages. Let's try to understand them.

Advantages and disadvantages of threads

The `Thread` class has the following advantages:

- Threads can be utilized to free up the main thread.
- Threads can be used to break up a task into smaller units that can be executed concurrently.

The `Thread` class has the following disadvantages:

- With more threads, the code becomes difficult to debug and maintain.
- Thread creation puts a load on the system in terms of memory and CPU resources.
- We need to do exception handling inside the worker method as any unhandled exceptions can result in the program crashing.

The ThreadPool class

Thread creation is an expensive operation in terms of both memory and CPU resources. On average, every thread consumes around 1 MB of memory and a few hundred microseconds of CPU time. Application performance is a relative concept, so it will not necessarily improve by creating a large number of threads. Conversely, creating a large number of threads can sometimes decrease application performance drastically. We should always aim to create an optimal number of threads, depending on the target system's CPU load, that is, other programs running on the system. This is because every program gets a time slice by the CPU, which is then distributed among the threads inside the application. If you create too many threads, they may not be able to do any constructive work before being swapped out of memory to give the time slice other similar-priority threads.

finding the optimal number of threads can be tricky as it can vary from one system to another, depending on the configuration and the number of applications that are running concurrently on the system. What may be an optimal number on one system may cause a negative impact on another. Rather than finding the optimal number of threads ourselves, we can leave it to the **Common Language Runtime** (**CLR**). The CLR has an algorithm to determine the optimal number based on the CPU load at any point in time. It maintains a pool of threads, known as the `ThreadPool`. The `ThreadPool` resides in a process and each application has its own pool of threads. The advantage of thread pooling is that it maintains an optimal number of threads and assigns them to a task. When the work is finished, the threads are returned to the pool, where they can be assigned to the next work item, thereby preventing the cost of creating and destroying threads.

The following is a list of the optimal number of threads that can be created in different frameworks inside `ThreadPool`:

- 25 per core in .NET Framework 2.0
- 250 per core in .NET Framework 3.5
- 1,023 in .NET Framework 4.0 in a 32-bit environment
- 32,768 in .NET Framework 4.0 onward, as well as in .NET core in a 64-bit environment

> While working with an investment bank, we came across a scenario where a trade process was taking almost 1,800 seconds to book close to 1,000 trades synchronously. After trying various optimal numbers, we finally switched to `ThreadPool` and made the process multithreaded. With .NET Framework version 2.0, the application finished in close to 72 seconds. With version 3.5, the same application finished in just a few seconds. This is a typical example of using the framework that's been provided rather than reinventing the wheel. You can get much-needed performance gains just by updating the framework.

We can create a thread via `ThreadPool` by calling `ThreadPool.QueueUserWorkItem`, as shown in the following example.

Here is the method that we want to call in parallel:

```
private static void PrintNumber10Times(object state)
{
    for (int i = 0; i < 10; i++)
    {
        Console.Write(1);
    }
    Console.WriteLine();
}
```

Here is how we can create a thread using `ThreadPool.QueueUserWorkItem` while passing the `WaitCallback` delegate:

```
private static void CreateThreadUsingThreadPool()
{
    ThreadPool.QueueUserWorkItem(new WaitCallback(PrintNumber10Times));
}
```

Here is a call from the `Main` method:

```
using System;
using System.Threading;

namespace Ch01
{
    class _4ThreadPool
    {
        static void Main(string[] args)
        {
            Console.WriteLine("Start Execution!!!");
            CreateThreadUsingThreadPool();
            Console.WriteLine("Finish Execution");
            Console.ReadLine();
        }
    }
}
```

The output of the preceding code is as follows:

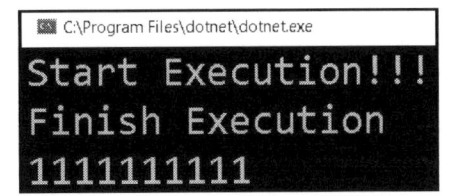

```
Start Execution!!!
Finish Execution
1111111111
```

Every thread pool maintains a minimum and a maximum number of threads. These values can be modified by calling the following static methods:

- `ThreadPool.SetMinThreads`
- `ThreadPool.SetMaxThreads`

> A thread is created via `System.Threading`. The `Thread` class doesn't belong to the `ThreadPool`.

Let's take a look at the advantages and disadvantages associated with using the `ThreadPool` class and when to avoid using it.

Advantages, disadvantages, and when to avoid using ThreadPool

The advantages of the `ThreadPool` are as follows:

- Threads can be utilized to free up the main thread.
- Threads are created and maintained in an optimal way by CLR.

The disadvantages of the `ThreadPool` are as follows:

- With more threads, the code becomes difficult to debug and maintain.
- We need to do exception handling inside the worker method as any unhandled exception can result in the program crashing.
- Progress reporting, cancellations, and completion logic need to be written from scratch.

The following are the reasons when we should avoid `ThreadPool`:

- When we need a foreground thread.
- When we need to set an explicit priority to a thread.
- When we have long-running or blocking tasks. Having a large number of blocked threads in the pool will prevent new tasks from starting due to the limited number of threads that are available per process in `ThreadPool`.
- If we need STA threads since `ThreadPool` threads are MTA by default.
- If we need to dedicate a thread to a task by providing it a distinct identity since we cannot name a `ThreadPool` thread.

BackgroundWorker

`BackgroundWorker` is a construct provided by .NET to create more manageable threads from a `ThreadPool`. When explaining GUI-based applications, we saw that the `Main` method was decorated with the `STAThread` attribute. This attribute guarantees control safety as controls are created in the apartment owned by the thread and cannot be shared with other threads. In Windows applications, there is the main thread of execution that owns the UI and controls, which is created when the application starts. It is responsible for accepting user inputs and painting or repainting the UI based on the actions of the user. For a great user experience, we should try to make the UI as thread-free as possible and delegate all time-consuming tasks to worker threads. Some common tasks that are usually assigned to worker threads are as follows:

- Downloading images from a server
- Interacting with a database
- Interacting with a filesystem
- Interacting with web services
- Complex local computations

As you can see, most of these are **input/output (I/O)** operations. I/O operations are carried out by the CPU. The moment we call a piece of code that encapsulates an I/O operation, the execution is passed from the thread to the CPU, which performs the task. When it is complete, the result of the operation is returned to the caller thread. This period from passing the baton and receiving results is a period of inactivity for the thread as it just has to wait for the operation to complete. If this occurs in the main thread, the application becomes unresponsive. For this reason, it makes sense to delegate these tasks to the worker threads. There are still several challenges to overcome with regard to responsive applications. Let's look at an example.

Case study:

We need to fetch data from a service that streams data. We would like to update the user with the percentage completion of work. Once the work is complete, we need to update the user with all the data.

Challenges:

The service call takes time, so we need to delegate the call in a worker thread to avoid UI freeze.

Introduction to Parallel Programming

Solution:

`BackgroundWorker` is a class provided in `System.ComponentModel` that can be used to create a worker thread utilizing `ThreadPool`, as we discussed previously. This means that it works in an efficient way. `BackgroundWorker` also supports progress reporting and cancellations, apart from notifying the result of the operation.

This scenario can be further explained with the following code:

```csharp
using System;
using System.ComponentModel;
using System.Text;
using System.Threading;

namespace Ch01
{
    class _5BackgroundWorker
    {
        static void Main(string[] args)
        {
            var backgroundWorker = new BackgroundWorker();
            backgroundWorker.WorkerReportsProgress = true;
            backgroundWorker.WorkerSupportsCancellation = true;
            backgroundWorker.DoWork += SimulateServiceCall;
            backgroundWorker.ProgressChanged += ProgressChanged;
            backgroundWorker.RunWorkerCompleted +=
               RunWorkerCompleted;
            backgroundWorker.RunWorkerAsync();
            Console.WriteLine("To Cancel Worker Thread Press C.");
            while (backgroundWorker.IsBusy)
            {
                if (Console.ReadKey(true).KeyChar == 'C')
                {
                    backgroundWorker.CancelAsync();
                }
            }
        }
        // This method executes when the background worker finishes
        // execution
        private static void RunWorkerCompleted(object sender,
           RunWorkerCompletedEventArgs e)
        {
            if (e.Error != null)
            {
                Console.WriteLine(e.Error.Message);
            }
            else
```

```csharp
                    Console.WriteLine($"Result from service call
                      is {e.Result}");
    }

    // This method is called when background worker want to
    // report progress to caller
    private static void ProgressChanged(object sender,
        ProgressChangedEventArgs e)
    {
        Console.WriteLine($"{e.ProgressPercentage}% completed");
    }

    // Service call we are trying to simulate
    private static void SimulateServiceCall(object sender,
        DoWorkEventArgs e)
    {
        var worker = sender as BackgroundWorker;
        StringBuilder data = new StringBuilder();
        //Simulate a streaming service call which gets data and
        //store it to return back to caller
        for (int i = 1; i <= 100; i++)
        {
            //worker.CancellationPending will be true if user
            //press C
            if (!worker.CancellationPending)
            {
                data.Append(i);
                worker.ReportProgress(i);
                Thread.Sleep(100);
                //Try to uncomment and throw error
                //throw new Exception("Some Error has occurred");
            }
            else
            {
                //Cancels the execution of worker
                worker.CancelAsync();
            }
        }
        e.Result = data;
    }
  }
}
```

`BackgroundWorker` provides an abstraction over raw threads, which gives more control and options to the user. The best part about using `BackgroundWorker` is that it uses an **Event-Based Asynchronous Pattern (EAP)**, which means it is able to interact with the code more efficiently than raw threads. The code is more or less self-explanatory. In order to raise progress reporting and cancellation events, you need to set the following properties to `true`:

```
backgroundWorker.WorkerReportsProgress = true;
backgroundWorker.WorkerSupportsCancellation = true;
```

You need to subscribe to the `ProgressChanged` event to receive progress, the `DoWork` event to pass a method that needs to be invoked by the thread, and the `RunWorkerCompleted` event to receive either the final results or any error messages from the thread's execution:

```
backgroundWorker.DoWork += SimulateServiceCall;
backgroundWorker.ProgressChanged += ProgressChanged;
backgroundWorker.RunWorkerCompleted += RunWorkerCompleted;
```

Once this has been set up, you can invoke the worker by calling the following command:

```
backgroundWorker.RunWorkerAsync();
```

At any point in time, you can cancel the execution of the thread by calling the `backgroundWorker.CancelAsync()` method, which sets the `CancellationPending` property on the worker thread. We need to write some code that keeps checking this flag and exits gracefully.

If there are no exceptions, the result of the thread's execution can be returned to the caller by setting the following:

```
e.Result = data;
```

If there are any unhandled exceptions in the program, they are returned to the caller gracefully. We can do this by wrapping it into `RunWorkerCompletedEventArgs` and passing it as a parameter to the `RunWorkerCompleted` event handler.

We will look at the advantages and disadvantages of using `BackgroundWorker` in the next section.

Advantages and disadvantages of using BackgroundWorker

The advantages of using `BackgroundWorker` are as follows:

- Threads can be utilized to free up the main thread.
- Threads are created and maintained in an optimal way by the `ThreadPool` class's CLR.
- Graceful and automatic exception handling.
- Supports progress reporting, cancellation, and completion logic using events.

The disadvantage of using `BackgroundWorker` is that, with more threads, the code becomes difficult to debug and maintain.

Multithreading versus multitasking

We have seen how both multithreading and multitasking work. Both have advantages and disadvantages and you can use either, depending on your specific use case. The following are some examples where multithreading can come in handy:

- **If you need a system that is easy to set up and terminate**: Multithreading can be useful when you have a process that has a large overhead. With threads, all you need to do is copy the thread stack. Creating a duplicate process, however, means recreating the entire data process in a separate memory space.
- **If you require fast task switching**: The CPU caches and program context can be easily maintained between threads in a process. If you have to switch the CPU to a different process, however, it has to be reloaded.
- **If you need to share data with other threads**: All the threads inside a process share the same memory pool, which makes it easier for them to share data to compare processes. If processes want to share data, they need I/O operation and transport protocols, which is expensive.

In this section, we have discussed the basics of multithreading and multitasking, alongside various approaches that were used to create threads in older versions of .NET. In the next section, we will try to understand some scenarios where you can utilize parallel programming techniques.

Scenarios where parallel programming can come in handy

The following are the scenarios in which parallel programming can be useful:

- **Creating a responsive UI for GUI-based applications**: We can delegate all of the heavy lifting and time-consuming tasks to the worker thread, thereby allowing the UI thread to process user interactions and the UI repainting tasks.
- **Processing simultaneous requests**: In server-side programming scenarios, we need to process a large number of concurrent users. We can create a separate thread to process each request. For example, we can use an ASP.NET request model, which makes use of `ThreadPool` and assigns a thread to every request that hits the server. Then, the thread takes care of processing the request and returning a response to the client. In a client-side scenario, we can call multiple mutually exclusive API calls via multithreading to save time.
- **Making efficient use of CPU**: With multi-core processors, only one core is generally utilized without multithreading and is overburdened. We can make full use of CPU resources by creating multiple threads, each running on separate CPUs. Sharing the burden in this way results in improved performance. This is useful for long-running and complex calculations, which can be performed faster using a divide-and-conquer strategy.
- **Speculative approaches**: Scenarios involving more than one algorithm, such as for an input set of numbers, where we want to get a sorted set as quickly as possible. The only way to do this is to pass the input to all the algorithms and run them in parallel, and whichever finishes first is accepted, while the rest are canceled.

Advantages and disadvantages of parallel programming

Multithreading leads to parallelism, which has its own programming and pitfalls. Now that we have grasped the basic concepts of parallel programming, it is important to understand its advantages and disadvantages.

The following are the benefits of parallel programming:

- **Enhanced performance**: We can achieve better performance since tasks are distributed across threads that run in parallel.
- **Improved GUI responsiveness**: Since tasks perform non-blocking I/O, this means the GUI thread is always free to accept user inputs. This results in better responsiveness.
- **The simultaneous and parallelized occurrence of tasks**: Since tasks run in parallel, we can simultaneously run different programming logic.
- Better use of cache storage by utilizing resources and better use of CPU resources. Tasks can run on different cores, thereby ensuring maximizing throughput.

Parallel programming also has the following disadvantages:

- **Complex debugging and testing processes**: It's not easy to debug threads without good multithreading tool support as different threads runs in parallel.
- **Context switching overheads**: Every thread works on a slice of time that's been allocated to it. Once the time slice expires, context switching happens, which also wastes resources.
- **High chance of deadlock occurrence**: If multiple threads work on a shared resource, we need to apply locks to achieve thread-safety. This can lead to deadlocks if multiple threads are simultaneously locking and waiting for shared resources.
- **Difficult to program**: With code branching, parallel programs can be difficult to write compared to synchronous versions.
- **Unpredictable results**: Since parallel programming relies on CPU cores, we can get different results on different configuration machines.

We should always understand that parallel programming is a relative concept and that something that worked for others may or may not work for you. You are advised to implement this approach and validate it yourself.

Summary

In this chapter, we discussed the scenarios, benefits, and pitfalls of parallel programming. Computer systems have evolved over the last few decades from single-core processors to multi-core processors. The hardware in chips has become HT-enabled, thereby increasing the performance of modern systems.

Before embarking on your journey in parallel programming, it's a good idea to understand the basic concepts related to the OS, such as processes, tasks, and the difference between multithreading and multitasking.

In the next chapter, we will focus our discussion entirely on the TPL and its associated implementations. In the real world, however, there is a lot of legacy code that still relies on older constructs, so knowledge of these will be handy.

Questions

1. Multithreading is a superset of parallel programming.
    1. True
    2. False
2. How many cores will there be in a single-processor dual-core machine with hyper-threading enabled?
    1. 2
    2. 4
    3. 8
3. When an application exits, all the foreground threads are killed as well. There is no separate logic required to close foreground threads on an application's exit.
    1. True
    2. False
4. Which exception is thrown when a thread has tried to access controls it has not owned/created?
    1. `ObjectDisposedException`
    2. `InvalidOperationException`
    3. `CrossThreadException`
5. Which of these provides cancellation support and progress reporting?
    1. `Thread`
    2. `BackgroundWorker`
    3. `ThreadPool`

2
Task Parallelism

In the previous chapter, we introduced the concept of parallel programming. In this chapter, we will move on to discussing TPL and task parallelism.

One of the major goals of .NET as a programming framework is to make a developer's life easier by wrapping up all the commonly required tasks as APIs. As we have already seen, threads have existed since the earliest versions of .NET, but they were initially very complex and were associated with a lot of overhead. Microsoft has introduced a lot of new parallel primitives that make it easier to write, debug, and maintain parallel programs from scratch, without having to deal with the complexities that are involved with legacy threading.

The following topics will be covered in this chapter:

- Creating and starting a task
- Getting results from finished tasks
- How to cancel tasks
- How to wait on running tasks
- Handling task exceptions
- Converting **Asynchronous Programming Model (APM)** patterns into tasks
- Converting **Event-Based Asynchronous Patterns (EAPs)** into tasks
- More on tasks:
    - Continuation tasks
    - Parent and child tasks
    - Local and global queues and storage
    - Work-stealing queues

Technical requirements

To complete this chapter, you should have a good understanding of C# and some advanced concepts such as delegates.

The source code for this chapter is available on GitHub at `https://github.com/PacktPublishing/Hands-On-Parallel-Programming-with-C-8-and-.NET-Core-3/tree/master/Chapter02`.

Tasks

Tasks are abstractions in .NET that provide units of asynchrony, just like promises in JavaScript. In initial versions of .NET, we had to rely on threads only, which were created either directly or using the `ThreadPool` class. The `ThreadPool` class provided a managed abstraction layer over threads but developers still relied on the `Thread` class for better control. By creating a thread via the `Thread` class, we gained access to the underlying object, which we can wait for, cancel, or move to the foreground or background. In real time, however, we required threads to perform work continuously. This required us to write lots of code, which was difficult to maintain. The `Thread` class was also unmanaged, which put a high burden on both the memory and the CPU. We needed the best of both worlds, which is where tasks come to the rescue. A task is nothing but a wrapper over a thread, which is created via `ThreadPool`. Tasks provide features such as await, cancellation, and continuation, and these run after a task has finished.

Tasks have the following important features:

- Tasks are executed by a `TaskScheduler` and the default scheduler simply runs on `ThreadPool`.
- We can return values from tasks.
- Tasks let you know when they finish, unlike `ThreadPool` or threads.
- A task can be run in continuation using the `ContinueWith()` construct.
- We can wait on tasks by calling `Task.Wait()`. This blocks the calling thread until it has finished.
- Tasks make the code much more readable compared to legacy threads or `ThreadPool`. They also paved the way to the introduction of the asynchronous programming construct in C# 5.0.

- We can establish a parent/child relationship when one task is started from another task.
- We can propagate child task exceptions to parent tasks.
- A task can be canceled using the `CancellationToken` class.

Creating and starting a task

There are many ways in which we can create and run a task using the TPL. In this section, we will try to understand all of these approaches and do a comparative analysis wherever we can. First, you need to add a reference to the `System.Threading.Tasks` namespace:

```
using System.Threading.Tasks;
```

We will try to create a task using the following approaches:

- The `System.Threading.Tasks.Task` class
- The `System.Threading.Tasks.Task.Factory.StartNew` method
- The `System.Threading.Tasks.Task.Run` method
- `System.Threading.Tasks.Task.Delay`
- `System.Threading.Tasks.Task.Yield`
- `System.Threading.Tasks.Task.FromResult<T>` Method
- `System.Threading.Tasks.Task.FromException` and `Task.FromException<T>`
- `System.Threading.Tasks.Task.FromCancelled` and `Task.FromCancelled<T>`

The System.Threading.Tasks.Task class

A task class is a way of executing work asynchronously as a `ThreadPool` thread and is based on the **Task-Based Asynchronous Pattern (TAP)**. The non-generic `Task` class doesn't return results, so whenever we need to return values from a task, we need to use the generic version, `Task<T>`. The tasks that are created via the `Task` class are not scheduled to run until we call the `Start` method.

We can create a task using the `Task` class in various ways, all of which we'll cover in the following subsections.

Using lambda expressions syntax

In the following code, we are creating a task by calling the `Task` constructor and passing a lambda expression containing the method we want to execute:

```
Task task = new Task (() => PrintNumber10Times ());
task.Start();
```

Using the Action delegate

In the following code, we are creating a task by calling the `Task` constructor and passing a delegate containing the method we want to execute:

```
Task task = new Task (new Action (PrintNumber10Times));
task.Start();
```

Using delegate

In the following code, we are creating a `task` object by calling the `Task` constructor and passing an anonymous `delegate` containing the method we want to execute:

```
Task task = new Task (delegate {PrintNumber10Times ();});
task.Start();
```

In all of these cases, the output will be as follows:

```
1111111111
```

All the preceding methods do the same thing – they just have different syntaxes.

> **TIP**
> We can only call the `Start` method on tasks that have not run previously. If you need to rerun a task that has already been completed, you need to create a new task and call the `Start` method on that.

The System.Threading.Tasks.Task.Factory.StartNew method

We can also create a task using the `StartNew` method of the `TaskFactory` class, as follows. In this approach, the task is created and scheduled for execution inside the `ThreadPool` and a reference of that `Task` is returned to the caller.

We can create a task using the `Task.Factory.StartNew` method. We'll go over this in the following subsections.

Using lambda expressions syntax

In the following code, we are creating a `Task` by calling the `StartNew()` method on `TaskFactory` and passing a lambda expression containing the method we want to execute:

```
Task.Factory.StartNew(() => PrintNumber10Times());
```

Using the Action delegate

In the following code, we are creating a `Task` by calling the `StartNew()` method on `TaskFactory` and passing a delegate wrapping method that we want to execute:

```
Task.Factory.StartNew(new Action( PrintNumber10Times));
```

Using delegate

In the following code, we are creating a `Task` by calling the `StartNew()` method on `TaskFactory` and passing the `delegate` wrapping method we want to execute:

```
Task.Factory.StartNew(delegate { PrintNumber10Times(); });
```

All the preceding methods do the same thing – they just have different syntaxes.

The System.Threading.Tasks.Task.Run method

We can also create a task using the `Task.Run` method. This works just like the `StartNew` method and returns a `ThreadPool` thread.

We can create a `Task` using the `Task.Run` method in the following ways, all of which will be discussed in the following subsections.

Using lambda expressions syntax

In the following code, we are creating a `Task` by calling the static `Run()` method on `Task` and passing a lambda expression containing the method we want to execute:

```
Task.Run(() => PrintNumber10Times ());
```

Using the Action delegate

In the following code, we are creating a `Task` by calling the static `Run()` method on `Task` and passing a delegate containing the method we want to execute:

```
Task.Run(new Action (PrintNumber10Times));
```

Using delegate

In the following code, we are creating a `Task` by calling the static `Run()` method on `Task` and passing a `delegate` containing the method we want to execute:

```
Task.Run(delegate {PrintNumber10Times ();});
```

The System.Threading.Tasks.Task.Delay method

We can create a task that completes after a specified interval of time or that can be canceled at any time by the user using the `CancellationToken` class. In the past, we used the `Thread.Sleep()` method of the `Thread` class to create blocking constructs to wait on other tasks. The problem with this approach, however, was that it still used CPU resources and ran synchronously. `Task.Delay` provides a better alternative to waiting on tasks without utilizing CPU cycles. It also runs asynchronously:

```
Console.WriteLine("What is the output of 20/2. We will show result in 2
seconds.");
Task.Delay(2000);
Console.WriteLine("After 2 seconds delay");
Console.WriteLine("The output is 10");
```

The preceding code asks the user a question and then waits for two seconds before presenting the answer. During those two seconds, the main thread doesn't have to wait but has to carry out other tasks to improve the user's experience. The code runs asynchronously on the system clock and, once the time expires, the rest of the code is executed.

The output of the preceding code is as follows:

```
C:\Program Files\dotnet\dotnet.exe
What is the output of 20/2. We will show result in 2 seconds.
After 2 seconds delay
The output is 10
```

Before looking at the other methods we can use to create a task, we'll take a look at two asynchronous programming constructs that were introduced in C# 5.0: the `async` and `await` keywords.

`async` and `await` are code markers that make it easier for us to write asynchronous programs. We will learn about these keywords in depth in Chapter 9, *Async, Await, and Task-Based Asynchronous Programming Basics*. As the name suggests, we can wait on any asynchronous call using the `await` keyword. The moment the executing thread encounters the `await` keyword inside a method, it returns to `ThreadPool`, marks the rest of the method as a continuation delegate, and starts executing the other queued tasks. Once the asynchronous task finishes, any available thread from `ThreadPool` finishes the rest of the method.

The System.Threading.Tasks.Task.Yield method

This is another way of creating an `await` task. The underlying task is not directly accessible to the caller but is used in some scenarios involving asynchronous programming that are related to program execution. It is more like a promise than a task. Using `Task.Yield`, we can force our method to be asynchronous and return control to the OS. When the rest of the method executes at a later point in time, it may still run as asynchronous code. We can achieve the same effect using the following code:

```
await Task.Factory.StartNew(() => {},
    CancellationToken.None,
    TaskCreationOptions.None,
    SynchronizationContext.Current != null?
    TaskScheduler.FromCurrentSynchronizationContext():
    TaskScheduler.Current);
```

This approach can be used to make UI applications responsive by providing control to the UI thread from time to time inside long-running tasks. However, this is not the preferred approach for UI applications. There are better alternatives, which are available in the form of `Application.DoEvents()` in WinForms and `Dispatcher.Yield(DispatcherPriority.ApplicationIdle)` in WPF:

```
private async static void TaskYield()
{
    for (int i = 0; i < 100000; i++)
    {
        Console.WriteLine(i);
        if (i % 1000 == 0)
            await Task.Yield();
    }
}
```

In the case of console or web applications, when we run the code and apply a breakpoint on the task's yield, we will see random thread pool threads switching context to run the code. The following screenshots depict various threads controlling execution at various stages.

Chapter 2

The following screenshot shows all the threads executing at the same time in the program flow. We can see that the current thread ID is **1664**:

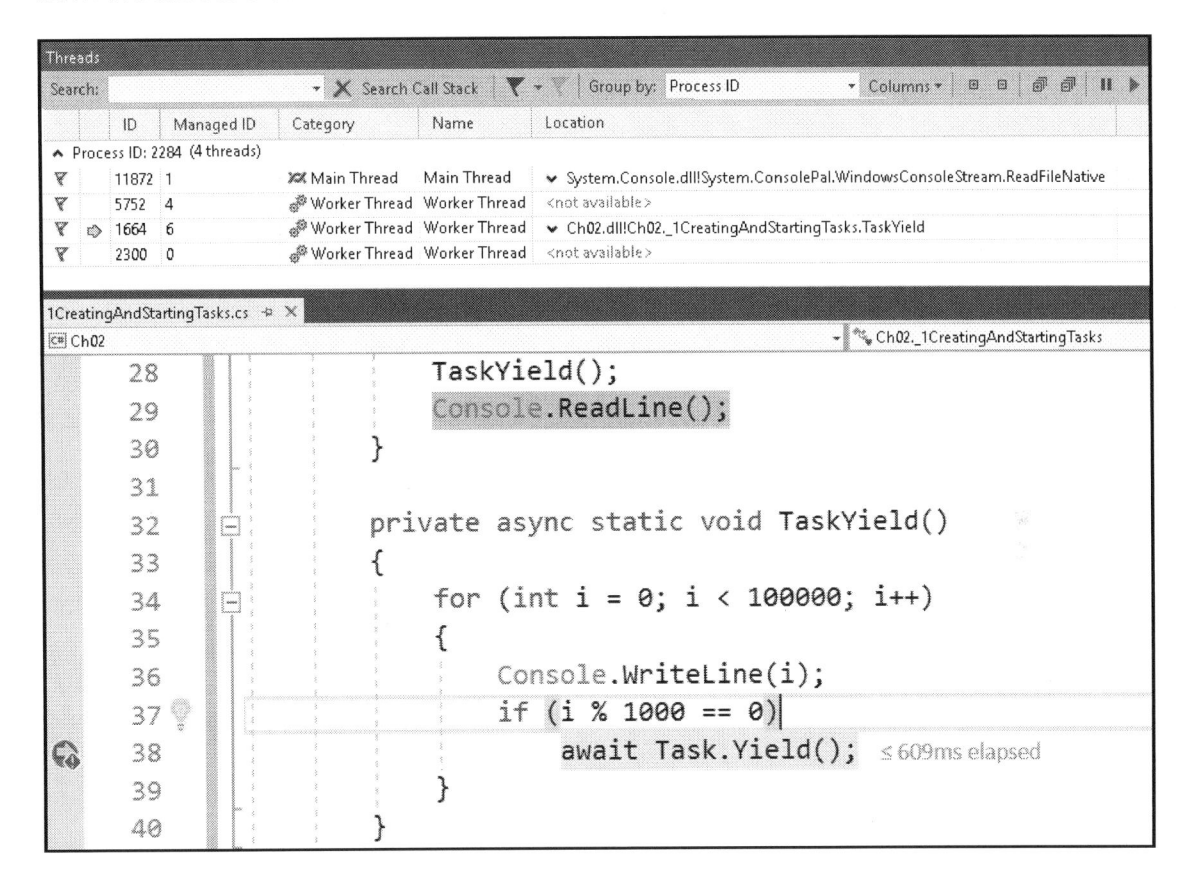

```
Threads
Search:                          X Search Call Stack    Group by: Process ID    Columns

       ID      Managed ID   Category        Name           Location
  Process ID: 2284 (4 threads)
       11872   1            Main Thread     Main Thread    System.Console.dll!System.ConsolePal.WindowsConsoleStream.ReadFileNative
       5752    4            Worker Thread   Worker Thread  <not available>
   ⇨   1664    6            Worker Thread   Worker Thread  Ch02.dll!Ch02._1CreatingAndStartingTasks.TaskYield
       2300    0            Worker Thread   Worker Thread  <not available>
```

```csharp
28              TaskYield();
29              Console.ReadLine();
30          }
31
32          private async static void TaskYield()
33          {
34              for (int i = 0; i < 100000; i++)
35              {
36                  Console.WriteLine(i);
37                  if (i % 1000 == 0)
38                      await Task.Yield();   ≤ 609ms elapsed
39              }
40          }
```

[43]

Task Parallelism

If we press *F5* and allow the breakpoint to get hit for another value of i, we will see that the code is now being executed by another thread with an ID of **10244**:

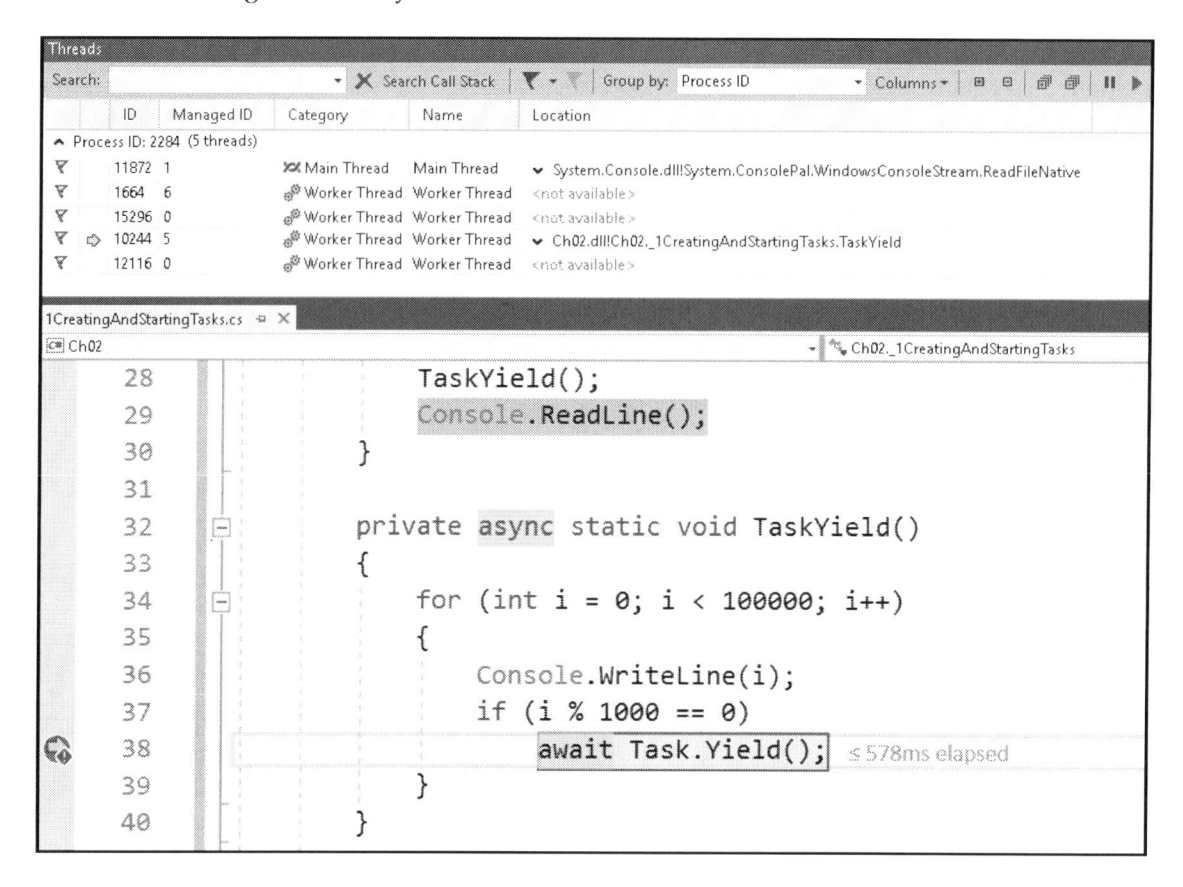

ID	Managed ID	Category	Name	Location
11872	1	Main Thread	Main Thread	System.Console.dll!System.ConsolePal.WindowsConsoleStream.ReadFileNative
1664	6	Worker Thread	Worker Thread	<not available>
15296	0	Worker Thread	Worker Thread	<not available>
10244	5	Worker Thread	Worker Thread	Ch02.dll!Ch02._1CreatingAndStartingTasks.TaskYield
12116	0	Worker Thread	Worker Thread	<not available>

```
28              TaskYield();
29              Console.ReadLine();
30          }
31
32          private async static void TaskYield()
33          {
34              for (int i = 0; i < 100000; i++)
35              {
36                  Console.WriteLine(i);
37                  if (i % 1000 == 0)
38                      await Task.Yield();  ≤ 578ms elapsed
39              }
40          }
```

We will learn more about thread windows and debugging techniques in Chapter 11, *Writing Unit Test Cases for Parallel and Asynchronous Code*.

The System.Threading.Tasks.Task.FromResult<T> method

This approach, which was introduced recently in .NET framework 4.5, is very much underrated. We can return a completed task with results via this approach, as shown here:

```
static void Main(string[] args)
{
    StaticTaskFromResultUsingLambda();
}
private static void StaticTaskFromResultUsingLambda()
{
    Task<int> resultTask = Task.FromResult<int>( Sum(10));
    Console.WriteLine(resultTask.Result);
}
private static int Sum (int n)
{
    int sum=0;
    for (int i = 0; i < 10; i++)
    {
        sum += i;
    }
    return sum;
}
```

As you can see from the preceding code, we have actually converted a synchronous Sum method to return results in an asynchronous manner using the Task.FromResult<int> class. This approach is frequently used in TDD for mocking asynchronous methods, as well as inside asynchronous methods to return default values based on conditions. We will explain these approaches in Chapter 11, *Writing Unit Test Cases for Parallel and Asynchronous Code*.

The System.Threading.Tasks.Task.FromException and System.Threading.Tasks.Task.FromException<T> methods

These methods create tasks that have completed with a predefined exception and are used to throw exceptions from asynchronous tasks, as well as in TDD. We will explain this approach further in Chapter 11, *Writing Unit Test Cases for Parallel and Asynchronous Code*:

```
return Task.FromException<long>(
new FileNotFoundException("Invalid File name."));
```

As you can see in the preceding code, we are wrapping `FileNotFoundException` as a task and returning it to the caller.

The System.Threading.Tasks.Task.FromCanceled and System.Threading.Tasks.Task.FromCanceled<T> methods

These methods are used to create tasks that have completed as a result of cancellation via the cancellation token:

```
CancellationTokenSource source = new CancellationTokenSource();
var token = source.Token;
source.Cancel();
Task task = Task.FromCanceled(token);
Task<int> canceledTask = Task.FromCanceled<int>(token);
```

As shown in the preceding code, we created a cancellation token using the `CancellationTokenSource` class. Then, we created a task from that token. The important thing to consider here is that the token needs to be canceled before we can use it with the `Task.FromCanceled` method.

This approach is useful if we want to return values from asynchronous methods, as well as in TDD.

Getting results from finished tasks

To return values from tasks, TPL provides a generic variant of all of the classes that we defined previously:

- Task<T>
- Task.Factory.StartNew<T>
- Task.Run<T>

Once a task finishes, we should be able to get results from it by accessing the Task.Result property. Let's try to understand this using some code examples. We will create various tasks and try to return values from them on completion:

```csharp
using System;
using System.Threading.Tasks;
namespace Ch02
{
    class _2GettingResultFromTasks
    {
        static void Main(string[] args)
        {
            GetResultsFromTasks();
            Console.ReadLine();
        }
        private static void GetResultsFromTasks()
        {
            var sumTaskViaTaskOfInt = new Task<int>(() => Sum(5));
            sumTaskViaTaskOfInt.Start();
            Console.WriteLine($"Result from sumTask is 
              {sumTaskViaTaskOfInt.Result}" );
            var sumTaskViaFactory = Task.Factory.StartNew<int>(() => 
              Sum(5));
            Console.WriteLine($"Result from sumTask is 
              {sumTaskViaFactory.Result}");
            var sumTaskViaTaskRun = Task.Run<int>(() => Sum(5));
            Console.WriteLine($"Result from sumTask is 
              {sumTaskViaTaskRun.Result}");
            var sumTaskViaTaskResult = Task.FromResult<int>(Sum(5));
            Console.WriteLine($"Result from sumTask is 
              {sumTaskViaTaskResult.Result}");
        }
        private static int Sum(int n)
        {
            int sum = 0;
            for (int i = 0; i < n; i++)
            {
```

```
            sum += i;
        }
        return sum;
    }
  }
}
```

As shown in the preceding code, we have created tasks using generic variants. Once they finished, we were able to get the results using the result property:

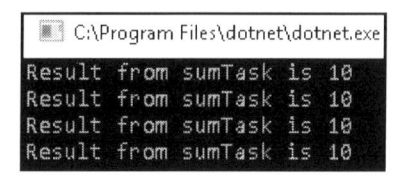

```
C:\Program Files\dotnet\dotnet.exe
Result from sumTask is 10
Result from sumTask is 10
Result from sumTask is 10
Result from sumTask is 10
```

In the next section, we will learn about how we can cancel tasks.

How to cancel tasks

Another important function of the TPL is to equip developers with ready-made data structures to cancel running tasks. Those of you that have a classic threading background will be aware of how difficult it used to be to make threads support canceling with all the custom home-grown logic, but this is no longer the case. The .NET Framework provides two classes to support task cancellation:

- `CancellationTokenSource`: This class is responsible for creating cancellation tokens and passing the cancellation request to all the tokens that were created via the source
- `CancellationToken`: This class is used by listeners to monitor the current state of a request

To create tasks that can be canceled, we need to perform the following steps:

1. Create an instance of the `System.Threading.CancellationTokenSource` class, which further provides a `System.Threading.CancellationToken` via the `Token Property`.
2. Pass the token while creating the task.
3. When required, call the `Cancel()` method on the `CancellationTokenSource`.

Let's try to understand how to create a token and how to pass it to the task.

Creating a token

Tokens can be created using the following code:

```
CancellationTokenSource tokenSource = new CancellationTokenSource();
CancellationToken token = tokenSource.Token;
```

First, we created a `tokenSource` using the `CancellationTokenSource` constructor. Then, we got our token using the token property of `tokenSource`.

Creating a task using tokens

We can create a task by passing `CancellationToken` as the second argument to the task constructor, as follows:

```
var sumTaskViaTaskOfInt = new Task<int>(() => Sum(5), token);
var sumTaskViaFactory = Task.Factory.StartNew<int>(() => Sum(5), token);
var sumTaskViaTaskRun = Task.Run<int>(() => Sum(5), token);
```

In the classic threading model, we used to call the `Abort()` method on a thread that was non-deterministic. This would stop the thread abruptly, thereby leaking memory if resources were unmanaged. With TPL, we can call the `Cancel` method, which is a cancellation token source that will, in turn, set up the `IsCancellationRequested` property on the token. The underlying method that's being executed by the task should watch for this property and should exit gracefully if it is set.

There are various ways of keeping a watch of whether the token source has requested a cancellation:

- Polling the status of the `IsCancellationRequested` property on the token
- Registering for a request cancellation callback

Polling the status of the token via the IsCancellationRequested property

This approach is handy in scenarios that involve recursive methods or methods that contain long-running computational logic via loops. Within our method or loops, we write code that polls `IsCancellationRequested` at certain optimal intervals. If it is set, it breaks the loop by calling the `ThrowIfCancellationRequested` method of the `token` class.

The following code is an example of canceling a task by polling the token:

```
private static void CancelTaskViaPoll()
{
    CancellationTokenSource cancellationTokenSource =
      new CancellationTokenSource();
    CancellationToken token = cancellationTokenSource.Token;
    var sumTaskViaTaskOfInt = new Task(() =>
      LongRunningSum(token), token);
    sumTaskViaTaskOfInt.Start();
    //Wait for user to press key to cancel task
    Console.ReadLine();
    cancellationTokenSource.Cancel();
}
private static void LongRunningSum(CancellationToken token)
{
    for (int i = 0; i < 1000; i++)
    {
        //Simulate long running operation
        Task.Delay(100);
        if (token.IsCancellationRequested)
            token.ThrowIfCancellationRequested();
    }
}
```

In the preceding code, we created a cancellation token via the `CancellationTokenSource` class. Then, we created a task by passing the token. The task executes a long-running method, `LongRunningSum` (simulated), which keeps polling for the `IsCancellationRequested` property of the token. It throws an exception if the user has called `cancellationTokenSource.Cancel()` before the method finishes.

> **TIP**
> Polling doesn't come with any significant performance overhead and can be used according to your requirements. Use it when you have full control over the work that's performed by the task, such as if it's core logic that you wrote yourself.

Registering for a request cancellation using the Callback delegate

This approach makes use of a `Callback` delegate that gets invoked when the cancellation is requested by the underlying token. We should use this with operations that are blocked in a way that makes it not possible to check the value of `CancellationToken` in a regular fashion.

Let's have a look at the following code, which downloads files from a remote URL:

```
private static void DownloadFileWithoutToken()
{
    WebClient webClient = new WebClient();
    webClient.DownloadStringAsync(new
     Uri("http://www.google.com"));
    webClient.DownloadStringCompleted += (sender, e) =>
      {
         if (!e.Cancelled)
            Console.WriteLine("Download Complete.");
         else
            Console.WriteLine("Download Cancelled.");
      };
}
```

As you can see from the preceding method, once we call the `DownloadStringAsync` method of `WebClient`, the control leaves the user. Although the `WebClient` class allows us to cancel the task via the `webClient.CancelAsync()` method, we don't have any control over when to invoke that.

The preceding code can be modified to make use of a `Callback` delegate so that we can gain more control over task cancellation, as follows:

```
static void Main(string[] args)
{
    CancellationTokenSource cancellationTokenSource = new
     CancellationTokenSource();
    CancellationToken token = cancellationTokenSource.Token;
    DownloadFileWithToken(token);
    //Random delay before we cancel token
    Task.Delay(2000);
    cancellationTokenSource.Cancel();
    Console.ReadLine();
}
private static void DownloadFileWithToken(CancellationToken token)
{
    WebClient webClient = new WebClient();
    //Here we are registering callback delegate that will get called
    //as soon as user cancels token
    token.Register(() => webClient.CancelAsync());
    webClient.DownloadStringAsync(new
     Uri("http://www.google.com"));
    webClient.DownloadStringCompleted += (sender, e) => {
    //Wait for 3 seconds so we have enough time to cancel task
    Task.Delay(3000);
    if (!e.Cancelled)
```

```
        Console.WriteLine("Download Complete.");
    else
        Console.WriteLine("Download Cancelled.");};
}
```

As you can see, in this modified version, we passed a cancellation token and subscribed to the cancellation callback via the `Register` method.

As soon as the user calls the `cancellationTokenSource.Cancel()` method, it will cancel the download operation by calling `webClient.CancelAsync()`.

> **TIP**
> `CancellationTokenSource` works well with the legacy `ThreadPool.QueueUserWorkItem` as well.

Here is code that creates a `CancellationTokenSource` that can be passed to `ThreadPool` to support cancellation:

```
// Create the token source.
CancellationTokenSource cts = new CancellationTokenSource();
// Pass the token to the cancellable operation.
ThreadPool.QueueUserWorkItem(new WaitCallback(DoSomething), cts.Token);
```

In this section, we discussed various ways of canceling tasks. Canceling tasks can really save us a lot of CPU time in cases where tasks may have become redundant. For example, say we have created multiple tasks to sort a list of numbers using different algorithms. Although all the algorithms will return the same result (a sorted list of numbers), we are interested in getting results as fast as we can. We will accept the result for the first (fastest) algorithm and cancel the rest to improve system performance. In the next section, we will discuss how to wait on running tasks.

How to wait on running tasks

In the previous examples, we called the `Task.Result` property to get a result from a completed task. This blocks the calling thread until a result is available. TPL provides another way for us to wait on one or more tasks.

There are various APIs available in TPL so that we can wait on one or more tasks. These are as follows:

- `Task.Wait`
- `Task.WaitAll`
- `Task.WaitAny`
- `Task.WhenAll`
- `Task.WhenAny`

These APIs will be defined in the following subsections.

Task.Wait

This is an instance method that can be used to wait on a single task. We can specify the maximum amount of time for which the caller will wait for the task to complete before unblocking itself with a timeout exception. We can also have full control over monitoring events that have been canceled by passing a cancellation token to the method. The calling method will be blocked until the thread either completes, is canceled, or throws an exception:

```
var task = Task.Factory.StartNew(() => Console.WriteLine("Inside Thread"));
//Blocks the current thread until task finishes.
task.Wait();
```

There are five overloaded versions of the `Wait` method:

- `Wait()`: Waits indefinitely for the task to finish. The calling thread is blocked until the child thread has finished.
- `Wait(CancellationToken)`: Waits for the task to finish execution indefinitely or when the cancellation token is canceled.
- `Wait(int)`: Waits for the task to finish execution within a specified period of time, in milliseconds.
- `Wait(TimeSpan)`: Waits for the task to finish execution within a specified time interval.
- `Wait(int, CancellationToken)`: Waits for the task to finish execution within a specified period of time, in milliseconds, or when the cancellation token is canceled.

Task.WaitAll

This is a static method that is defined in the Task class and used to wait on multiple tasks. The tasks are passed as an array to the method and the caller is blocked until all the tasks are completed. This method also supports timeout and cancellation tokens. Some example code that uses this method is as follows:

```
Task taskA = Task.Factory.StartNew(() =>
 Console.WriteLine("TaskA finished"));
Task taskB = Task.Factory.StartNew(() =>
 Console.WriteLine("TaskB finished"));
Task.WaitAll(taskA, taskB);
Console.WriteLine("Calling method finishes");
```

The output of the preceding code is as follows:

```
TaskB finished
TaskA finished
Calling method finishes
```

As you can see, the **Calling method finishes** statement is executed when both tasks have finished executing.

An example use case of this method might be when we need data from multiple sources (we have one task for each source) and we want to combine the data from all the tasks so that they can be displayed on the UI.

Task.WaitAny

This is another static method that is defined in the Task class. Just like WaitAll, WaitAny is used to wait on multiple tasks, but the caller is unblocked as soon as any of the tasks that are passed as arrays to the method finish executing. Like the other methods, WaitAny supports the timeout and cancellation tokens. Some example code that uses this method is as follows:

```
Task taskA = Task.Factory.StartNew(() =>
 Console.WriteLine("TaskA finished"));
Task taskB = Task.Factory.StartNew(() =>
 Console.WriteLine("TaskB finished"));
Task.WaitAny(taskA, taskB);
Console.WriteLine("Calling method finishes");
```

In the preceding code, we started two tasks and waited on them using `WaitAny`. This method blocks the current thread. As soon as any of the tasks complete, the calling thread is unblocked.

An example use case of this method might be when the data we require is available from different sources and we need it as quickly as possible. Here, we create tasks that make requests to different sources. As soon as any of the tasks finish, we will unblock the calling thread and get the result from the finished task.

Task.WhenAll

This is a non-blocking variant of the `WaitAll` method. It returns a task that represents a waiting action for all of the specified tasks. Unlike `WaitAll`, which blocks the calling thread, `WhenAll` can be awaited inside an asynchronous method, thus freeing up the calling thread to perform other operations. Some example code that uses this method is as follows:

```
Task taskA = Task.Factory.StartNew(() =>
  Console.WriteLine("TaskA finished"));
Task taskB = Task.Factory.StartNew(() =>
  Console.WriteLine("TaskB finished"));
Task.WhenAll(taskA, taskB);
Console.WriteLine("Calling method finishes");
```

This code works the same way as `Task.WaitAll`, apart from the fact that the calling thread returns to the `ThreadPool` instead of being blocked.

Task.WhenAny

This is a non-blocking variant of `WaitAny`. It returns a task that encapsulates a waiting action on a single underlying task. Unlike `WaitAny`, it doesn't block the calling thread. The calling thread can call await on it inside an asynchronous method. Some example code that uses this method is as follows:

```
Task taskA = Task.Factory.StartNew(() =>
  Console.WriteLine("TaskA finished"));
Task taskB = Task.Factory.StartNew(() =>
  Console.WriteLine("TaskB finished"));
Task.WhenAny(taskA, taskB);
Console.WriteLine("Calling method finishes");
```

Task Parallelism

This code works the same way as `Task.WaitAny`, apart from the fact that the calling thread returns to the `ThreadPool` instead of being blocked.

In this section, we discussed how to write efficient code while working with multiple threads without code branching. Code flow looks synchronous though it works in parallel wherever required. In the next section, we will learn about how tasks deal with exceptions.

Handling task exceptions

Exception handling is one of the most important aspects of parallel programming. All good clean code practitioners focus on handling exceptions efficiently. This becomes even more important with parallel programming as any unhandled exceptions in threads or tasks can cause the application to crash abruptly. Fortunately, TPL provides a nice, efficient design to handle and manage exceptions. Any unhandled exceptions that occur in a task are deferred and then propagated to a joining thread, which observes the task for exceptions.

Any exception that occurs inside a task is always wrapped under the `AggregateException` class and returned to the caller that is observing the exceptions. If the caller is waiting on a single task, the inner exception property of the `AggregateException` class will return the original exception. If the caller is waiting for multiple tasks, however, such as `Task.WaitAll`, `Task.WhenAll`, `Task.WaitAny`, or `Task.WhenAny`, all the exceptions that occur from tasks are returned to the caller as a collection. They are accessible via the `InnerExceptions` property.

Now, let's look at the various ways we can handle exceptions inside tasks.

Handling exception from single tasks

In the following code, we're creating a simple task that tries to divide a number by 0, thereby causing a `DivideByZeroException`. The exception is returned to the caller and handled inside the catch block. Since it's a single task, the exception object is wrapped under the `InnerException` property of the `AggregateException` object:

```
class _4HandlingExceptions
{
    static void Main(string[] args)
    {
        Task task = null;
        try
        {
            task = Task.Factory.StartNew(() =>
```

```
            {
                int num = 0, num2 = 25;
                var result = num2 / num;
            });
            task.Wait();
        }
        catch (AggregateException ex)
        {
            Console.WriteLine($"Task has finished with
              exception {ex.InnerException.Message}");
        }
        Console.ReadLine();
    }
}
```

The following is the output when we run the preceding code:

```
C:\Program Files\dotnet\dotnet.exe
Task has finished with exception Attempted to divide by zero.
```

Handling exceptions from multiple tasks

Now, we'll create multiple tasks and then try to throw exceptions from them. Then, we'll learn how to list different exceptions from different tasks from the caller:

```
static void Main(string[] args)
{
    Task taskA = Task.Factory.StartNew(()=> throw
      new DivideByZeroException());
    Task taskB = Task.Factory.StartNew(()=> throw
      new ArithmeticException());
    Task taskC = Task.Factory.StartNew(()=> throw
      new NullReferenceException());
    try
    {
        Task.WaitAll(taskA, taskB, taskC);
    }
    catch (AggregateException ex)
    {
        foreach (Exception innerException in ex.InnerExceptions)
        {
            Console.WriteLine(innerException.Message);
        }
    }
```

```
        Console.ReadLine();
    }
```

Here is the output when we run the preceding code:

```
Attempted to divide by zero.
Overflow or underflow in the arithmetic operation.
Object reference not set to an instance of an object.
```

In the preceding code, we created three tasks that throw different exceptions and all threads are awaited using `Task.WaitAll`. As you can see, the exceptions are observed by calling `WaitAll` and not just by starting the task, which is why we wrapped `WaitAll` inside the `try` block. The `WaitAll` method will return when all the tasks that have been passed to it have faulted by throwing exceptions and the corresponding `catch` block is executed. We can find all the exceptions that originated from all the tasks by iterating over the `InnerExceptions` property of the `AggregateException` class.

Handling task exceptions with a callback function

Another option to find out about these exceptions is to use the callback function to access and handle the exceptions that originate from tasks:

```
static void Main(string[] args)
    {
        Task taskA = Task.Factory.StartNew(() => throw
         new DivideByZeroException());
        Task taskB = Task.Factory.StartNew(() => throw
         new ArithmeticException());
        Task taskC = Task.Factory.StartNew(() => throw
         new NullReferenceException());
        try
        {
            Task.WaitAll(taskA, taskB, taskC);
        }
        catch (AggregateException ex)
        {
            ex.Handle(innerException =>
            {
                Console.WriteLine(innerException.Message);
                return true;
            });
        }
```

```
        Console.ReadLine();
    }
```

Here is the output when we run the preceding code in Visual Studio:

```
C:\Program Files\dotnet\dotnet.exe
Attempted to divide by zero.
Overflow or underflow in the arithmetic operation.
Object reference not set to an instance of an object.
```

As shown in the preceding code, rather than integrating over `InnerExceptions`, we have subscribed to the handle callback function on `AggregateException`. This is fired for all the tasks that throw the exception and we can return `true`, indicating that the exception has been handled gracefully.

Converting APM patterns into tasks

The legacy APM approach used the `IAsyncResult` interface to create asynchronous methods with a design pattern using two methods: `BeginMethodName` and `EndMethodName`. Let's try to understand the journey of a program from being synchronous, to an APM, and then to a task.

Here is a synchronous method that reads data from a text file:

```
private static void ReadFileSynchronously()
{
    string path = @"Test.txt";
    //Open the stream and read content.
    using (FileStream fs = File.OpenRead(path))
    {
        byte[] b = new byte[1024];
        UTF8Encoding encoder = new UTF8Encoding(true);
        fs.Read(b, 0, b.Length);
        Console.WriteLine(encoder.GetString(b));
    }
}
```

Task Parallelism

There is nothing fancy in the preceding code. First, we created a `FileStream` object and called the `Read` method, which reads the file from the disk synchronously into a buffer and then writes the buffer to the console. We converted the buffer into a string using the `UTF8Encoding` class. The problem with this approach, however, is that the moment a call to `Read` is made, the thread is blocked until the read operation has finished. I/O operations are managed by the CPU using CPU cycles, so there is no point in keeping the thread waiting for the I/O operation to complete. Let's try to understand the APM way of doing this:

```
private static void ReadFileUsingAPMAsyncWithoutCallback()
    {
        string filePath = @"Test.txt";
        //Open the stream and read content.
        using (FileStream fs = new FileStream(filePath,
         FileMode.Open, FileAccess.Read, FileShare.Read,
         1024, FileOptions.Asynchronous))
        {
           byte[] buffer = new byte[1024];
           UTF8Encoding encoder = new UTF8Encoding(true);
           IAsyncResult result = fs.BeginRead(buffer, 0,
            buffer.Length, null, null);
           Console.WriteLine("Do Something here");
           int numBytes = fs.EndRead(result);
           fs.Close();
           Console.WriteLine(encoder.GetString(buffer));
        }
    }
```

As shown in the preceding code, we have replaced the synchronous `Read` method with an asynchronous version, that is, `BeginRead`. The moment the compiler encounters `BeginRead`, an instruction is sent to the CPU to start reading the file and the thread is unblocked. We can perform other tasks in the same method before blocking the thread again by calling `EndRead` to wait for the `Read` operation to finish and collect the result. This is a simple yet efficient approach in order to make responsive applications, though we are also blocking the thread to fetch results. Rather than calling `EndRead` in the same method, we can make use of `Overload`, which accepts a callback method that gets called automatically when the read operation finishes, to avoid blocking the thread. The signature of this method is as follows:

```
public override IAsyncResult BeginRead(
       byte[] array,
       int offset,
       int numBytes,
       AsyncCallback userCallback,
       object stateObject)
```

Here, we have seen how we moved from a synchronous method to APM. Now, we are going to convert the APM implementation into a task. This is demonstrated in the following code:

```
private static void ReadFileUsingTask()
{
    string filePath = @"Test.txt";
    //Open the stream and read content.
    using (FileStream fs = new FileStream(filePath, FileMode.Open,
     FileAccess.Read, FileShare.Read, 1024,
     FileOptions.Asynchronous))
    {
        byte[] buffer = new byte[1024];
        UTF8Encoding encoder = new UTF8Encoding(true);
        //Start task that will read file asynchronously
        var task = Task<int>.Factory.FromAsync(fs.BeginRead,
         fs.EndRead, buffer, 0, buffer.Length,null);
        Console.WriteLine("Do Something while file is read
          asynchronously");
        //Wait for task to finish
        task.Wait();
        Console.WriteLine(encoder.GetString(buffer));
    }
}
```

As shown in the preceding code, we replaced the `BeginRead` method with `Task<int>.Factory.FromAsync`. This is a way of implementing a TAP. The method returns a task, which runs in the background while we continue doing other work in the same method, before blocking the thread again to get the results using `task.Wait()`. This is how you can easily convert any APM code into TAP.

Converting EAPs into tasks

EAPs are used to create components that wrap expensive and time-consuming operations. Due to this, they need to be made asynchronous. This pattern has been used in the .NET Framework to create components such as `BackgroundWorker` and `WebClient`.

Methods that implement this pattern carry out long-running tasks asynchronously in the background but keep notifying the user of their progress and status via events, which is why they are known as event-based.

Task Parallelism

The following code shows an implementation of a component that uses EAP:

```
private static void EAPImplementation()
{
    var webClient = new WebClient();
    webClient.DownloadStringCompleted += (s, e) =>
    {
        if (e.Error != null)
            Console.WriteLine(e.Error.Message);
        else if (e.Cancelled)
            Console.WriteLine("Download Cancel");
        else
            Console.WriteLine(e.Result);
    };
    webClient.DownloadStringAsync(new
     Uri("http://www.someurl.com"));
}
```

In the preceding code, we subscribed to the `DownloadStringCompleted` event, which gets fired once `webClient` has downloaded the file from the URL. As you can see, we tried to read various result options, such as exception, cancellation, and result, using the if-else construct. Converting EAP into TAP is tricky compared to APM as it requires a good understanding of the internal nature of EAP components because we need to plug the new code into the correct events to make it work. Let's take a look at the converted implementation:

```
private static Task<string> EAPToTask()
{
    var taskCompletionSource = new TaskCompletionSource<string>();
    var webClient = new WebClient();
    webClient.DownloadStringCompleted += (s, e) =>
    {
        if (e.Error != null)
            taskCompletionSource.TrySetException(e.Error);
        else if (e.Cancelled)
            taskCompletionSource.TrySetCanceled();
        else
            taskCompletionSource.TrySetResult(e.Result);
    };
    webClient.DownloadStringAsync(new
     Uri("http://www.someurl.com"));
    return taskCompletionSource.Task;
}
```

The simplest way of converting EAP into TAP is via the `TaskCompletionSource` class. We have plugged in all the scenarios and set the result, exception, or cancellation results to the instance of the `TaskCompletionSource` class. Then, we returned the wrapped implementation as a task to the user.

More on tasks

Now, let's learn some more important concepts about tasks that might come in handy. Up until now, we have created tasks that are independent. To create more complex solutions, however, we sometimes need to define relationships between tasks. We can create subtasks, child tasks, as well as continuation tasks to do this. Let's try to understand each of these with examples. Later in this section, we will learn about thread storage and queues.

Continuation tasks

Continuation tasks work more like promises. We can make use of them when we need to chain multiple tasks. The second task starts when the first one finishes and the result of the first task or the exceptions are passed to the child task. We can chain more than one task to create a long chain of tasks, or we can create a selective continuation chain with the methods provided by TPL. The following constructs are provided by TPL for task continuation:

- `Task.ContinueWith`
- `Task.Factory.ContinueWhenAll`
- `Task.Factory.ContinueWhenAll<T>`
- `Task.Factory.ContinueWhenAny`
- `Task.Factory.ContinueWhenAny<T>`

Continuing tasks using the Task.ContinueWith method

The continuation of a task can be easily achieved using the `ContinueWith` method that's provided by TPL.

Let's try to understand simple chaining with an example:

```
var task = Task.Factory.StartNew<DataTable>(() =>
    {
        Console.WriteLine("Fetching Data");
        return FetchData();
```

Task Parallelism

```
}).ContinueWith(
    (e) => {
        var firstRow = e.Result.Rows[0];
        Console.WriteLine("Id is {0} and Name is {0}",
          firstRow["Id"], firstRow["Name"]);
});
```

In the preceding example, we need to fetch and display data. The **primary task** calls the `FetchData` method. When it has finished, the result is passed as input to the **continuation task**, which takes care of printing the data. The output is as follows:

```
Fetching Data
Id is 1 and Name is 1
```

We can chain multiple tasks as well, thereby creating a chain of tasks, as shown here:

```
var task = Task.Factory.StartNew<int>(() => GetData()).
        .ContinueWith((i) => GetMoreData(i.Result)).
        .ContinueWith((j) => DisplayData(j.Result)));
```

We can control when the continuation task will run by passing the `System.Threading.Tasks.TaskContinuationOptions` enumeration as a parameter that has the following options:

- `None`: This is the default option. The continuation task will run when the primary task has completed.
- `OnlyOnRanToCompletion`: The continuation task will run when the primary task has completed successfully, meaning it has not canceled or faulted.
- `NotOnRanToCompletion`: The continuation task will run when the primary task has been canceled or faulted.
- `OnlyOnFaulted`: The continuation task will run only when the primary task has faulted.
- `NotOnFaulted`: The continuation task will run only when the primary task has not faulted.
- `OnlyOnCancelled`: The continuation task will run only when the primary task has been canceled.
- `NotOnCancelled`: The continuation task will run only when the primary task has not been canceled.

Continuing tasks using Task.Factory.ContinueWhenAll and Task.Factory.ContinueWhenAll<T>

We can wait for multiple tasks and chain a continuation code that will only run when all the tasks are completed successfully. Let's look at an example:

```
private async static void ContinueWhenAll()
{
    int a = 2, b = 3;
    Task<int> taskA = Task.Factory.StartNew<int>(() => a * a);
    Task<int> taskB = Task.Factory.StartNew<int>(() => b * b);
    Task<int> taskC = Task.Factory.StartNew<int>(() => 2 * a * b);
    var sum = await Task.Factory.ContinueWhenAll<int>(new Task[]
      { taskA, taskB, taskC }, (tasks)
       =>tasks.Sum(t => (t as Task<int>).Result));
    Console.WriteLine(sum);
}
```

In the preceding code, we want to calculate a*a + b*b +2 *a *b. We break down the task into three units: a*a, b*b, and 2*a*b. Each of these units is executed by three different threads: taskA, taskB, and taskC. Then, we wait for all the tasks to finish and pass them as a first parameter to the ContinueWhenAll method. When all the threads finish executing, the continuation delegate executes, which is specified by the second parameter to the ContinueWhenAll method. The continuation delegate sums the result of the execution from all the threads and returns them to the caller, which is printed in the next line.

Continuing tasks using Task.Factory.ContinueWhenAny and Task.Factory.ContinueWhenAny<T>

We can wait for multiple tasks and chains in continuation code that will run when any of the tasks are completed successfully:

```
private static void ContinueWhenAny()
{
    int number = 13;
    Task<bool> taskA = Task.Factory.StartNew<bool>(() =>
     number / 2 != 0);
    Task<bool> taskB = Task.Factory.StartNew<bool>(() =>
     (number / 2) * 2 != number);
    Task<bool> taskC = Task.Factory.StartNew<bool>(() =>
     (number & 1) != 0);
```

[65]

```
            Task.Factory.ContinueWhenAny<bool>(new Task<bool>[]
              { taskA, taskB, taskC }, (task) =>
              {
                  Console.WriteLine((task as Task<bool>).Result);
              }
            );
        }
```

As shown in the preceding code, we have three different pieces of logic to find out whether a number is odd. Let's assume that we don't know which of these pieces of logic is going to be the fastest. To calculate the result, we create three tasks, each of which encapsulates a different odd-number-finding logic, and run them concurrently. Since a number can be either odd or even at a time, the result from all the threads will be the same and will differ in terms of their speed of execution. Due to this, it makes sense to just get the first result and discard the rest. This is what we have achieved using the `ContinueWhenAny` method.

Parent and child tasks

Another type of relationship that can occur between threads is a parent-child relationship. The child task is created as a nested task inside the body of the parent task. The child task can be created either as attached or detached. Both types of tasks are created inside the parent task and, by default, the created tasks are detached. We can make an attached task by setting the `AttachedToParent` property of the task to `true`. You may want to consider creating an attached task in any of the following scenarios:

- All the exceptions that are thrown in the child task need to be propagated to the parent
- The status of the parent task is dependent on the child task
- The parent needs to wait for the child task to finish

Creating a detached task

The code to create a detached class is as follows:

```
    Task parentTask = Task.Factory.StartNew(() =>
      {
              Console.WriteLine(" Parent task started");
              Task childTask = Task.Factory.StartNew(() => {
                  Console.WriteLine(" Child task started");
              });
              Console.WriteLine(" Parent task Finish");
        });
```

```
//Wait for parent to finish
parentTask.Wait();
Console.WriteLine("Work Finished");
```

As you can see, we have created another task within the body of a task. By default, the child or nested task is created as detached. We waited for the parent task to finish by calling `parentTask.Wait()`. In the following output, you can see that the parent task doesn't wait for the child task to finish and finishes first, followed by the child task starting:

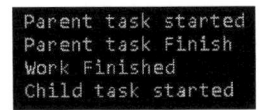

```
Parent task started
Parent task Finish
Work Finished
Child task started
```

Creating an attached task

An attached task is created similarly to a detached one. The only difference is that we set the `AttachedParent` property of the task to `true`. This is demonstrated in the following snippet:

```
Task parentTask = Task.Factory.StartNew(() =>
    {
        Console.WriteLine("Parent task started");
        Task childTask = Task.Factory.StartNew(() => {
            Console.WriteLine("Child task started");
        },TaskCreationOptions.AttachedToParent);
        Console.WriteLine("Parent task Finish");
    });
//Wait for parent to finish
parentTask.Wait();
Console.WriteLine("Work Finished");
```

The output is as follows:

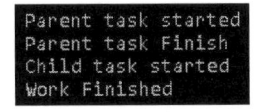

```
Parent task started
Parent task Finish
Child task started
Work Finished
```

Here, you can see that the parent task does not finish until the child task has finished executing.

In this section, we discussed advanced aspects of tasks, including creating relationships among tasks. In the next section, we will dig more into working internally on tasks by understanding the concept of work queues and how tasks deal with them.

Work-stealing queues

Work-stealing is a performance optimization technique for a thread pool. Every thread pool maintains a single global queue of tasks that are created inside a process. In `Chapter 1`, *Introduction to Parallel Programming*, we learned that the thread pool maintains an optimal number of worker threads to work on tasks. The `ThreadPool` also maintains a thread global queue, where it queues all the work items before they can be assigned to available threads. Since this is a single queue and we work in multithreaded scenarios, we need to implement thread-safety using synchronization primitives. With a single global queue, synchronization leads to performance loss.

The .NET Framework works around this performance loss by introducing the concept of local queues, which are managed by threads. Each thread has access to a global queue and also maintains its own thread-local queue to store work items in. Parent tasks can be scheduled inside the global queue. When tasks execute and need to create subtasks, they can be stacked up on local queues and processed using the FIFO algorithm as soon as the thread finishes executing.

The following diagram depicts the relationship between a global queue, a local queue, the thread, and the `Threadpool`:

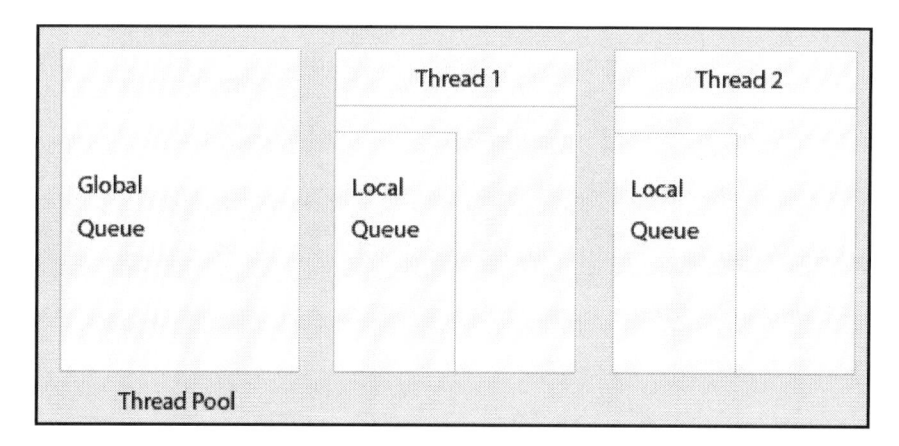

Let's say that the main thread creates a set of tasks. All of these tasks are queued to the global queue to be executed later based on the availability of the thread inside the thread pool. The following diagram depicts the global queue with all the queued tasks:

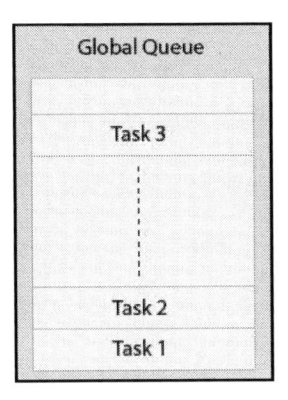

```
            Global Queue
           ┌──────────────┐
           │   Task 3     │
           │      ┆       │
           │      ┆       │
           │   Task 2     │
           │   Task 1     │
           └──────────────┘
```

Let's say **Task 1** is scheduled on **Thread 1**, **Task 2** on **Thread 2**, and so on, as shown in the following diagram:

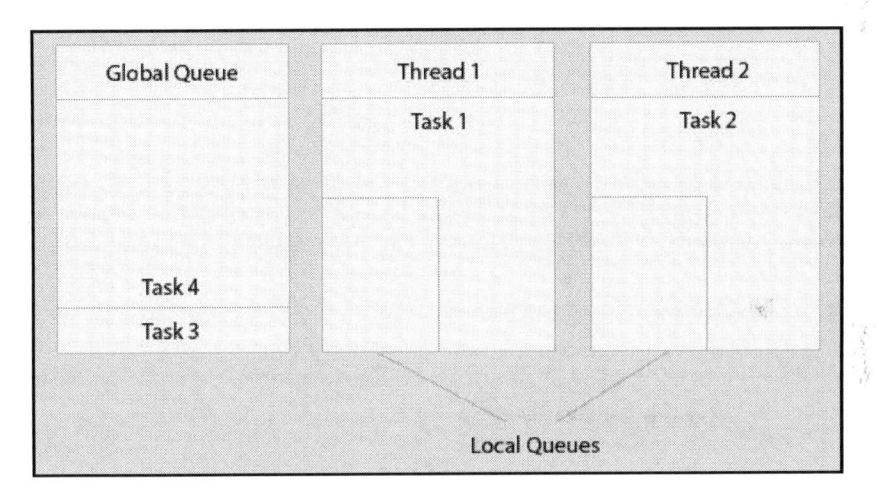

```
┌─────────────────┬──────────────┬──────────────┐
│ Global Queue    │  Thread 1    │  Thread 2    │
│                 │   Task 1     │   Task 2     │
│                 │              │              │
│   Task 4        │              │              │
│   Task 3        │              │              │
│                 └──────┬───────┴──────┬───────┘
│                        Local Queues           │
└───────────────────────────────────────────────┘
```

Task Parallelism

If **Task 1** and **Task 2** generate more tasks, the new tasks will be stored in the thread-local queue, as shown in the following diagram:

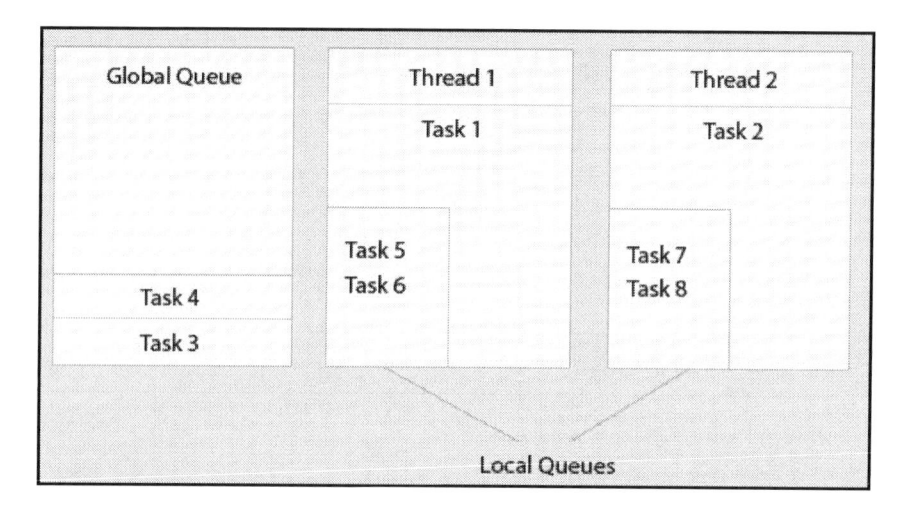

```
┌─────────────────────────────────────────────────────────────────┐
│  Global Queue        Thread 1              Thread 2             │
│                        Task 1                Task 2             │
│                                                                 │
│                        Task 5                Task 7             │
│    Task 4              Task 6                Task 8             │
│    Task 3                                                       │
│                                                                 │
│                              Local Queues                       │
└─────────────────────────────────────────────────────────────────┘
```

Similarly, if more tasks are created by these child tasks, they will go inside the local queue instead of the global queue. Once **Thread 1** has finished with **Task 1**, it will look into its local queues and pick up the last task (LIFO). There is a high chance that the last task may still be in the cache and so it doesn't need to be reloaded. Again, this improves performance.

Once a thread (T1) exhausts its local queue, it will search in the global queue. If there are no items in the global queue, it will search in the local queues for other threads (say T2). This technique is called work-stealing and is an optimization technique. This time, it doesn't pick the last task (LIFO) from T2 since the last item may still be in the T2 thread's cache. Instead, it picks up the first task (FIFO) since there is a high chance that the thread has moved out of T2's cache. This technique improves performance by making cached tasks available to the local thread and out-of-cache tasks to other threads.

Summary

In this chapter, we have discussed how to break up tasks into smaller units so that each unit can be handled independently by a thread. We have also learned about various ways we can create tasks by utilizing `ThreadPool`. We introduced various techniques related to the internal workings of tasks, including the concepts of work-stealing and task creation or cancellation. We will be utilizing the knowledge we gained in this chapter in the rest of this book.

In the next chapter, we will introduce the concepts of data parallelism. This will include working with parallel loops and handling exceptions in them.

Implementing Data Parallelism

So far, we have learned about the basics of parallel programming, tasks, and task parallelism. In this chapter, we will cover another important aspect of parallel programming, which deals with the parallel execution of data: data parallelism. While task parallelism creates a separate unit of work for each participating thread, data parallelism creates a common task that is executed by every participating thread in a source collection. This source collection is partitioned so that multiple threads can work on it concurrently. Therefore, it is important to understand data parallelism to get the maximum performance out of loops/collections.

In this chapter, we will discuss the following topics:

- Handling exceptions in parallel loops
- Creating custom partitioning strategies in parallel loops
- Canceling loops
- Understanding thread storage in parallel loops

Technical requirements

To complete this chapter, you should have a good understanding of the TPL and C#. The source code for this chapter is available on GitHub at `https://github.com/PacktPublishing/Hands-On-Parallel-Programming-with-C-8-and-.NET-Core-3/tree/master/Chapter03`.

Moving from sequential loops to parallel loops

The TPL supports data parallelism through the `System.Threading.Tasks.Parallel` class, which provides parallel implementation of the `For` and `Foreach` loops. As a developer, you don't need to worry about synchronization or creating tasks as this is handled by the parallel class. This syntactic sugar allows you to easily write parallel loops in a way that's similar to how you have been writing sequential loops.

Here is an example of a sequential `for` loop that books a trade by posting the trade object to the server:

```
foreach (var trade in trades)
{
    Book(trade);
}
```

Since the loop is sequential, the total time that it takes to finish the loop is the time it takes to book one trade multiplied by the total number of trades. This means that the loop slows down as the number of trades increases, although the trade booking time remains the same. Here, we are dealing with large numbers. Since we are going to be booking trades on a server and all the servers support multiple requests, it makes sense to convert this loop from a sequential loop into a parallel loop as that will give us significant performance gains.

The previous code can be converted so that it's parallel as follows:

```
Parallel.ForEach(trades, trade => Book(trade));
```

While running a parallel loop, the TPL partitions the source collection so that the loop can execute on multiple parts concurrently. The partitioning of tasks is done by the `TaskScheduler` class, which takes the system resources and the load into consideration while creating partitions. We can also create a **custom partitioner** or **scheduler**, as we will see later in this chapter in the *Creating a custom partitioning strategy* section.

Data parallelism performs better if the partitioning units are independent. With minimal performance overhead, we can also create dependency partitioning units using a technique called reduction, which reduces a series of operations to a scalar value. There are three ways to convert sequential code into parallel code:

- Using the `Parallel.Invoke` method
- Using the `Parallel.For` method
- Using the `Parallel.ForEach` method

Let's try to understand the various ways in which the `Parallel` class can be utilized to exhibit data parallelism.

Using the Parallel.Invoke method

This is the most basic way of executing a set of operations in parallel and forms the basis for parallel `for` and `foreach` loops. The `Parallel.Invoke` method accepts an array of actions as a parameter and executes them, though it never guarantees that the actions will be executed in parallel. There are some important points to remember when using `Parallel.Invoke`:

- Parallelism is not guaranteed. Whether the actions are executed in parallel or in sequence will depend on the `TaskScheduler`.
- `Parallel.Invoke` doesn't guarantee the order of operations for passed actions.
- It blocks the calling thread until all the actions are completed.

The syntax of `Parallel.Invoke` is as follows:

```
public static void Invoke(
  params Action[] actions
)
```

Implementing Data Parallelism

We can either pass an action or a lambda expression, as demonstrated in the following example:

```
try
{
    Parallel.Invoke(() => Console.WriteLine("Action 1"),
        new Action(() => Console.WriteLine("Action 2")));
}
catch(AggregateException aggregateException)
{
    foreach (var ex in aggregateException.InnerExceptions)
    {
        Console.WriteLine(ex.Message);
    }
}
Console.WriteLine("Unblocked");
Console.ReadLine();
```

The `Invoke` method behaves like an attached child task as it is blocked until all the actions are completed. All the exceptions are stacked together inside `System.AggregateException` and thrown to the caller. In the preceding code, since there is no exception, we will see the following output:

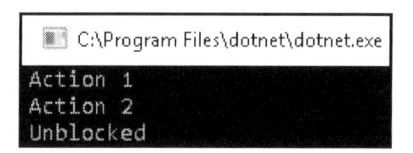

```
C:\Program Files\dotnet\dotnet.exe
Action 1
Action 2
Unblocked
```

We can achieve a similar effect using the `Task` class, although this may look like very complex code in comparison to how `Parallel.Invoke` works:

```
Task.Factory.StartNew(() => {
    Task.Factory.StartNew(() => Console.WriteLine("Action 1"),
        TaskCreationOptions.AttachedToParent);
    Task.Factory.StartNew(new Action(() => Console.WriteLine("Action 2"))
            , TaskCreationOptions.AttachedToParent);
    });
```

The `Invoke` method behaves like an attached child task as it is blocked until all the actions are completed. All the exceptions are stacked together inside `System.AggregateException` and thrown to the caller.

Using the Parallel.For method

`Parallel.For` is a variant of the sequential `for` loop, with the difference that the iterations run in parallel. `Parallel.For` returns an instance of the `ParallelLoopResult` class, which provides the loop competition status once the loop has finished execution. We can also check the `IsCompleted` and `LowestBreakIteration` properties of `ParallelLoopResult` to find out if the method has completed or canceled, or if break has been called by the users. Here are the possible scenarios:

IsCompleted	LowestBreakIteration	**Reason**
True	N/A	Run to completion
False	Null	Loop stopped pre-matching
False	Non-null integral value	Break called on the loop

The basic syntax of the `Parallel.For` method is as follows:

```
public static ParallelLoopResult For
{
    Int fromIncalme,
    Int toExclusiveme,
    Action<int> action
}
```

An example of this is as follows:

```
Parallel.For (1, 100, (i) => Console.WriteLine(i));
```

This approach can be useful if you don't want to cancel, break, or maintain any thread local state and the order of execution is not important. For example, imagine that we want to count the number of files in a directory that have been created today. The code for this is as follows:

```
int totalFiles = 0;
var files = Directory.GetFiles("C:\\");
Parallel.For(0, files.Length, (i) =>
    {
        FileInfo fileInfo = new FileInfo(files[i]);
        if (fileInfo.CreationTime.Day == DateTime.Now.Day)
          Interlocked.Increment(ref totalFiles);
    });
Console.WriteLine($"Total number of files in C: drive are {files.Count()} and {totalFiles} files were created today.");
```

Implementing Data Parallelism

This code iterates all the files in the C: drive and counts all the files that were created today. The following is the output on my machine:

```
Total number of files in C: drive are 91 and  0 files were created today.
```

In the next section, we will try to understand the `Parallel.ForEach` method, which provides a parallel variant of the `ForEach` loop.

> **TIP**: For some collections, sequential executions work faster, depending on the syntax of the loop and the type of work that's being done.

Using the Parallel.ForEach method

This is a variation of the `ForEach` loop wherein iterations may run in parallel. The source collection is partitioned and then the work is scheduled to run multiple threads. `Parallel.ForEach` works on generic collections and, just like the `for` loop, returns `ParallelLoopResult`.

The basic syntax of the `Parallel.ForEach` loop is as follows:

```
Parallel.ForEach<TSource>(
    IEnumerable<TSource> Source,
    Action<TSource> body
)
```

An example of this is as follows. We have a list of ports that we need to monitor. We also need to update their statuses:

```
List<string> urls = new List<string>() {"www.google.com" ,
"www.yahoo.com","www.bing.com" };
Parallel.ForEach(urls, url =>
{
    Ping pinger = new Ping();
     Console.WriteLine($"Ping Url {url} status is {pinger.Send(url).Status}
      by Task {Task.CurrentId}");
});
```

In the preceding code, we used the `System.Net.NetworkInformation.Ping` class to ping a part and display a status to the console. Since the parts are independent, we can achieve great performance if the code is made parallel and the order is also not important.

The following screenshot shows the output of the preceding code:

```
C:\Program Files\dotnet\dotnet.exe
Ping Url www.google.com status is Success by Task 1
Ping Url www.bing.com status is Success by Task 3
Ping Url www.yahoo.com status is Success by Task 2
```

Parallelism can make applications slow on single-core processors. We can control how many cores can be utilized in a parallel operation by using the degree of parallelism, which we will cover next.

Understanding the degree of parallelism

So far, we have learned how data parallelism gives us the advantage of running loops in parallel on multiple cores of a system, thereby making efficient use of the available CPU resources. You should be aware that there is another important concept that you can use in order to control how many tasks you want to create in your loops. This concept is called the degree of parallelism. It's a number that specifies the maximum number of tasks that can be created by your parallel loops. You can set the degree of parallelism via a property called `MaxDegreeOfParallelism`, which is part of the `ParallelOptions` class. The following is the syntax of `Parallel.For`, wherein you can pass the `ParallelOptions` instance:

```
public static ParallelLoopResult For(
        int fromInclusive,
        int toExclusive,
        ParallelOptions parallelOptions,
        Action<int> body
)
```

The following is the syntax of the `Parallel.For` and `Parallel.ForEach` methods, wherein you can pass the `ParallelOptions` instance:

```
public static ParallelLoopResult ForEach<TSource>(
        IEnumerable<TSource> source,
        ParallelOptions parallelOptions,
        Action<TSource> body
)
```

The default value for the degree of parallelism is 64, which means that the parallel loops can utilize up to 64 processors in a system by creating that many tasks. We can modify this value to limit the number of tasks. Let's try to understand this concept with a few examples.

Implementing Data Parallelism

Let's look at an example of a `Parallel.For` loop with `MaxDegreeOfParallelism` set to 4:

```
Parallel.For(1, 20, new ParallelOptions { MaxDegreeOfParallelism = 4 },
index =>
            {
                Console.WriteLine($"Index {index} executing on Task Id
                    {Task.CurrentId}");
            });
```

The output is as follows:

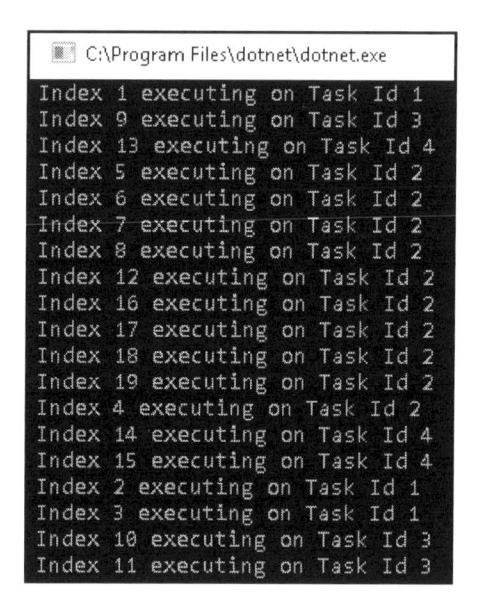

```
Index 1 executing on Task Id 1
Index 9 executing on Task Id 3
Index 13 executing on Task Id 4
Index 5 executing on Task Id 2
Index 6 executing on Task Id 2
Index 7 executing on Task Id 2
Index 8 executing on Task Id 2
Index 12 executing on Task Id 2
Index 16 executing on Task Id 2
Index 17 executing on Task Id 2
Index 18 executing on Task Id 2
Index 19 executing on Task Id 2
Index 4 executing on Task Id 2
Index 14 executing on Task Id 4
Index 15 executing on Task Id 4
Index 2 executing on Task Id 1
Index 3 executing on Task Id 1
Index 10 executing on Task Id 3
Index 11 executing on Task Id 3
```

As you can see, the loop was executed by four tasks denoted by the task IDs 1, 2, 3, and 4.

Here is an example of a `Parallel.ForEach` loop with `MaxDegreeOfParallelism` set to 4:

```
var items = Enumerable.Range(1, 20);
Parallel.ForEach(items, new ParallelOptions { MaxDegreeOfParallelism = 4 },
item =>
            {
                Console.WriteLine($"Index {item} executing on Task Id
                    {Task.CurrentId}");
            });
```

The output is as follows:

```
C:\Program Files\dotnet\dotnet.exe
Index 3 executing on Task Id 4
Index 4 executing on Task Id 3
Index 2 executing on Task Id 2
Index 1 executing on Task Id 1
Index 8 executing on Task Id 1
Index 9 executing on Task Id 1
Index 5 executing on Task Id 4
Index 12 executing on Task Id 4
Index 13 executing on Task Id 4
Index 14 executing on Task Id 4
Index 10 executing on Task Id 1
Index 11 executing on Task Id 1
Index 6 executing on Task Id 3
Index 19 executing on Task Id 3
Index 20 executing on Task Id 3
Index 15 executing on Task Id 4
Index 16 executing on Task Id 4
Index 17 executing on Task Id 1
Index 18 executing on Task Id 1
Index 7 executing on Task Id 2
```

As you can see, this loop was executed by four tasks denoted by the task IDs 1, 2, 3, and 4.

We should modify this setting for advanced scenarios where we are aware that a running algorithm cannot span more than a certain number of processors. We should also modify this setting if we are running multiple algorithms in parallel and we want to restrict each algorithm to only utilize a certain number of processors. Next, we will learn how to make custom partitions in collections by introducing the concept of partitioning strategies.

Creating a custom partitioning strategy

Partitioning is another important concept in data parallelism. To achieve parallelism in the source collection, it needs to be partitioned into smaller sections called ranges or chunks, which can be concurrently accessed by various threads. Without partitioning, the loop will execute serially. Partitioners can be classified into two categories and we can create custom partitioners as well. These categories are as follows:

- Range partitioning
- Chunk partitioning

Let's discuss these in detail.

Range partitioning

This type of partitioning is primarily used with collections where the length is known in advance. As the name suggests, every thread gets a range of elements to process or the start and end index of a source collection. This is the simplest form of partitioning and very efficient in the sense that every thread executes its range without overwriting other threads. There is no synchronization overhead, though some bits of performance are lost initially while creating ranges. This type of partitioning works best in scenarios where the number of elements in each range is the same so that they will take a similar length of time to finish. With a different number of elements, some tasks may finish early and sit idle, whereas other tasks may have a lot of pending elements in the range to process.

Chunk partitioning

This type of partitioning is primarily used with collections such as `LinkedList`, where the length isn't known in advance. Chunk partitioning provides more load balancing in case you have uneven collections. Every thread picks up a chunk of elements, processes them, and then comes back to pick up another chunk that hasn't been picked up by other threads yet. The size of the chunk depends on the partitioner's implementation and there is synchronization overhead to make sure that the chunks that are allocated to two threads don't contain duplicates.

We can change the default partitioning strategy of the `Parallel.ForEach` loop to perform custom chunk partitioning, as shown in the following example:

```
var source = Enumerable.Range(1, 100).ToList();
OrderablePartitioner<Tuple<int,int>> orderablePartitioner=
Partitioner.Create(1, 100);
Parallel.ForEach(orderablePartitioner, (range, state) =>
        {
            var startIndex = range.Item1;
            var endIndex = range.Item2;
            Console.WriteLine($"Range execution finished on task
              {Task.CurrentId} with range
              {startRange}-{endRange}");
        });
```

In the preceding code, we created chunked partitioners using the `OrderablePartitioner` class on a range of items (here, from `1` to `100`). We passed partitioners to the `ForEach` loop, where each chunk is passed to a thread and executed. The output is as follows:

```
Select C:\Program Files\dotnet\dotnet.exe
Range execution finished on task 2 with range 5-9
Range execution finished on task 4 with range 13-17
Range execution finished on task 1 with range 1-5
Range execution finished on task 3 with range 9-13
Range execution finished on task 3 with range 49-53
Range execution finished on task 3 with range 53-57
Range execution finished on task 3 with range 57-61
Range execution finished on task 3 with range 61-65
Range execution finished on task 3 with range 65-69
Range execution finished on task 7 with range 25-29
Range execution finished on task 3 with range 69-73
Range execution finished on task 3 with range 77-81
Range execution finished on task 3 with range 81-85
Range execution finished on task 3 with range 85-89
Range execution finished on task 3 with range 89-93
Range execution finished on task 3 with range 93-97
Range execution finished on task 3 with range 97-100
Range execution finished on task 1 with range 45-49
Range execution finished on task 5 with range 17-21
Range execution finished on task 4 with range 41-45
Range execution finished on task 6 with range 21-25
Range execution finished on task 7 with range 73-77
Range execution finished on task 8 with range 29-33
Range execution finished on task 9 with range 33-37
Range execution finished on task 2 with range 37-41
```

So far, we have a good understanding of how parallel loops work. Now, we need to discuss some advanced concepts in order to find out more about how we can control loop execution; that is, how to stop a loop as needed.

Canceling loops

We have used constructs such as `break` and `continue` in sequential loops; `break` is used to break out of a loop by finishing the current iteration and skipping the rest, whereas `continue` skips the current iteration and moves to the rest of the iterations. These constructs can be used because the sequential loops are executed by a single thread. In the case of parallel loops, we cannot use the `break` and `continue` keywords since they run on multiple threads or tasks. To break a parallel loop, we need to make use of the `ParallelLoopState` class. To cancel a loop, we need to make use of the `CancellationToken` and `ParallelOptions` classes.

Implementing Data Parallelism

In this section, we will discuss the options that you require to cancel loops:

- `Parallel.Break`
- `ParallelLoopState.Stop`
- `CancellationToken`

Let's get started!

Using the Parallel.Break method

`Parallel.Break` tries to mimic the results of a sequential execution. Let's have a look at how to `break` from a parallel loop. In the following code, we need to search a list of numbers for a specific number. We need to break the loop's execution when a match is found:

```
var numbers = Enumerable.Range(1, 1000);
int numToFind = 2;
Parallel.ForEach(numbers, (number, parallelLoopState) =>
{
    Console.Write(number + "-");
    if (number == numToFind)
    {
        Console.WriteLine($"Calling Break at {number}");
        parallelLoopState.Break();
    }
});
```

As shown in the preceding code, the loop is supposed to run until the number 2 is found. With a sequential loop, it will break exactly on the second iteration. With parallel loops, since iterations run on multiple tasks, it will actually print values more than 2, as shown in the following output:

```
Select C:\Program Files\dotnet\dotnet.exe
1-6-8-4-7-3-2-14-16-17-18-19-20-21-9-23-24-25-22-27-28-29-30-31-32-33-34-35-36-37-Calling Break at 2
39-5-38-40-15-10-12-13-26-11-
```

To break out of the loop, we called `parallelLoopState.Break()`, which tries to mimic the behavior of the actual `break` keyword in a sequential loop. When the `Break()` method is encountered by any of the cores, it will set an iteration number in the `LowestBreakIteration` property of the `ParallelLoopState` object. This becomes the maximum number or the last iteration that can be executed. All the other tasks will continue iterating until this number is reached.

Subsequent calls to the Break method by running iterations in parallel further reduces LowestBreakIteration, as shown in the following code:

```
var numbers = Enumerable.Range(1, 1000);
Parallel.ForEach(numbers, (i, parallelLoopState) =>
{
    Console.WriteLine($"For i={i} LowestBreakIteration =
      {parallelLoopState.LowestBreakIteration} and
      Task id ={Task.CurrentId}");
    if (i >= 10)
    {
        parallelLoopState.Break();
    }
});
```

When we run the preceding code in Visual Studio, we get the following output:

```
C:\Program Files\dotnet\dotnet.exe
For i=3 LowestBreakIteration= and Task id =8
For i=7 LowestBreakIteration= and Task id =2
For i=5 LowestBreakIteration= and Task id =3
For i=6 LowestBreakIteration= and Task id =7
For i=1 LowestBreakIteration= and Task id =4
For i=4 LowestBreakIteration= and Task id =6
For i=8 LowestBreakIteration= and Task id =9
For i=2 LowestBreakIteration= and Task id =1
For i=9 LowestBreakIteration= and Task id =5
For i=18 LowestBreakIteration= and Task id =5
For i=19 LowestBreakIteration=17 and Task id =5
For i=11 LowestBreakIteration=17 and Task id =2
For i=20 LowestBreakIteration=10 and Task id =2
For i=13 LowestBreakIteration=10 and Task id =7
For i=10 LowestBreakIteration=10 and Task id =8
For i=22 LowestBreakIteration=9 and Task id =8
For i=12 LowestBreakIteration=9 and Task id =3
For i=17 LowestBreakIteration=9 and Task id =1
For i=14 LowestBreakIteration=9 and Task id =4
For i=16 LowestBreakIteration=9 and Task id =9
For i=15 LowestBreakIteration=9 and Task id =6
For i=21 LowestBreakIteration=9 and Task id =10
```

Here, we run the code on a multi-core processor. As you can see, a lot of iterations get a null value for LowestBreakIteration as the code is being executed on multiple cores. On iteration 17, one core calls the Break() method and sets the value of LowestBreakIteration to 17. On iteration 10, another core calls Break() and further reduces the number to 10. Later, on iteration 9, another core calls Break(), and further reduces the number to 9.

Using ParallelLoopState.Stop

If you don't want to mimic the results of sequential loops and want to exit the loop as soon as possible, you can call `ParallelLoopState.Stop`. Just like we did with the `Break()` method, all the iterations running in parallel finish before the loop exits:

```
var numbers = Enumerable.Range(1, 1000);
Parallel.ForEach(numbers, (i, parallelLoopState) =>
        {
                Console.Write(i + " ");
                if (i % 4 == 0)
                {
                    Console.WriteLine($"Loop Stopped on {i}");
                    parallelLoopState.Stop();
                }
        });
```

The following is the output when we run the preceding code in Visual Studio:

```
C:\Program Files\dotnet\dotnet.exe
6 7 2 5 4 8 Loop Stopped on 4
1 9 Loop Stopped on 8
11 14 13 12 Loop Stopped on 12
3 10
```

As you can see, one core called `Stop` on iteration 4, another core called `Stop` on iteration 8, and a third core called `Stop` on iteration 12. Iterations 3 and 10 still execute since they were already scheduled for execution.

Using CancellationToken to cancel loops

Just like normal tasks, we can use the `CancellationToken` class to cancel the `Parallel.For` and `Parallel.ForEach` loops. When we cancel the token, the loop will finish the current iterations that may be running in parallel but will not start new iterations. Once the existing iterations finish, the parallel loops throw `OperationCanceledException`.

Let's look at this with an example. First, we'll create a cancellation token source:

```
CancellationTokenSource cancellationTokenSource = new
CancellationTokenSource();
```

Then, we'll create a task that cancels the token after five seconds:

```
Task.Factory.StartNew(() =>
{
    Thread.Sleep(5000);
    cancellationTokenSource.Cancel();
    Console.WriteLine("Token has been cancelled");
});
```

After that, we'll create a parallel options object by passing the cancellation token:

```
ParallelOptions loopOptions = new ParallelOptions()
{
    CancellationToken = cancellationTokenSource.Token
};
```

Next, we'll run the loop with an operation that will last for more than five seconds:

```
try
{
    Parallel.For(0, Int64.MaxValue, loopOptions, index =>
    {
        Thread.Sleep(3000);
        double result = Math.Sqrt(index);
        Console.WriteLine($"Index {index}, result {result}");
    });
}
catch (OperationCanceledException)
{
    Console.WriteLine("Cancellation exception caught!");
}
```

The following is the output when we run the preceding code in Visual Studio:

```
C:\Program Files\dotnet\dotnet.exe
Index 1152921504606846975, result 1073741824
Index 0, result 0
Index 2305843009213693950, result 1518500249.98802
Index 3458764513820540925, result 1859775393.37968
Index 4611686018427387900, result 2147483648
Index 5764607523034234875, result 2400959708.74862
Index 6917529027641081850, result 2630119584.2853
Index 8070450532247928825, result 2840853838.59289
Index 9223372036854775800, result 3037000499.97605
Index 1, result 1
Token has been cancelled
Index 1152921504606846976, result 1073741824
Index 1152921504606846977, result 1073741824
Index 2, result 1.4142135623731
Index 2305843009213693951, result 1518500249.98802
Index 3458764513820540926, result 1859775393.37968
Index 4611686018427387901, result 2147483648
Index 5764607523034234876, result 2400959708.74862
Index 6917529027641081851, result 2630119584.2853
Index 8070450532247928826, result 2840853838.59289
Index 2305843009213693953, result 1518500249.98802
Index 9223372036854775801, result 3037000499.97605
Index 3458764513820540928, result 1859775393.37968
Index 4, result 2
Cancellation exception caught!
```

As you can see, the scheduled iterations are still executed, even after the canceling token has been called. I hope this gives you a good idea of how we can cancel loops based on program requirements. Another important aspect of parallel programming is the concept of storage. We'll discuss this in the next section.

Understanding thread storage in parallel loops

By default, all parallel loops have access to a global variable. However, there is a synchronization overhead associated with accessing global variables, and because of this, it makes sense to use thread-scoped variables wherever possible. We can create either a **thread local** or a **partition local** variable to be used in parallel loops.

Thread local variable

Thread local variables are like global variables for a particular task. They have a lifetime that spans the number of iterations the loop is going to execute.

In the following example, we are going to look at thread local variables using the `for` loop. In the case of the `Parallel.For` loop, multiple tasks are created to run the iterations. Let's say we need to find out the sum of 60 numbers via a parallel loop.

As an example, say there are four tasks, each of which has 15 iterations. One way of achieving this is to create a global variable. After every iteration, the running task should update the global variable. This would require synchronization overhead. For four tasks, there would be four thread local variables that are private to each task. The variable will be updated by the task and the last updated value can be returned to the caller program, which can then be used to update the global variable.

Here are the steps to be followed:

1. Create a collection of 60 numbers, with each item having a value equal to the index:

   ```
   var numbers = Enumerable.Range(1, 60);
   ```

2. Create a finished action that will execute once the task has finished all its allocated iterations. The method will receive the final result of the thread local variable and add that to the global variable, that is, `sumOfNumbers`:

   ```
   long sumOfNumbers = 0;
   Action<long> taskFinishedMethod = (taskResult) =>
   {
       Console.WriteLine($"Sum at the end of all task iterations for task
           {Task.CurrentId} is {taskResult}");
       Interlocked.Add(ref sumOfNumbers, taskResult);
   };
   ```

3. Create a `For` loop. The first two parameters are `startIndex` and `endIndex`. The third parameter is a delegate that provides a seed value for the thread local variable. It is an action that needs to be performed by the task. In our case, we are just assigning the index to `subtotal`, which is our thread local variable.

Implementing Data Parallelism

Let's say there is a task, *TaskA*, which gets the iterations with an index from 1 to 5. *TaskA* will add up these iterations as 1+2+3+4+5. This equals 15, which will be returned as the task's result and passed to `taskFinishedMethod` as a parameter:

```
Parallel.For(0,numbers.Count(),
                    () => 0,
                    (j, loop, subtotal) =>
                    {
                        subtotal += j;
                        return subtotal;
                    },
                    taskFinishedMethod
);
Console.WriteLine($"The total of 60 numbers is {sumOfNumbers}");
```

Here is the output when we run the preceding code in Visual Studio:

```
C:\Program Files\dotnet\dotnet.exe
Sum at the end of all task iterations for task 4 is 21
Sum at the end of all task iterations for task 2 is 0
Sum at the end of all task iterations for task 1 is 1735
Sum at the end of all task iterations for task 3 is 14
The total of 60 numbers is 1770
```

Remember that the output may be different on different machines, depending on the number of available cores.

Partition local variable

This is similar to the thread local variable but works with partitions. As you are aware, the `ForEach` loop divides the source collection into a number of partitions. Each partition will have its own copy of the partition local variable. With the thread local variable, there is a single copy of the variable per thread. Here, however, we can have multiple copies per thread since multiple partitions can be run on a single thread.

First, we need to create a `ForEach` loop. The first parameter is a source collection, which means numbers. The second parameter is a delegate that provides a seed value for the thread local variable. The third parameter is an action that needs to be performed by the task. In our case, we are just assigning the index to the `subtotal`, which is our thread local variable.

For the sake of understanding, let's say there is a task, *TaskA*, that gets iterations with indexes from 1 to 5. *TaskA* will add up these iterations, which is 1+2+3+4+5. This equals 15, which will be returned as the task's result and passed to `taskFinishedMethod` as a parameter.

The code for this is as follows:

```
Parallel.ForEach<int, long>(numbers,
    () => 0, // method to initialize the local variable
    (j, loop, subtotal) => // Action performed on each iteration
    {
        subtotal += j; //Subtotal is Thread local variable
        return subtotal; // value to be passed to next iteration
    },
    taskFinishedMethod);
Console.WriteLine($"The total of 60 numbers is {sumOfNumbers}");
```

Again, in this case, the output will be different on different machines, depending on the number of available cores.

Summary

In this chapter, we elaborated on achieving task parallelism using TPL. We started by introducing how to move sequential loops to parallel using some built-in methods provided by TPL, such as `Parallel.Invoke`, `Parallel.For`, and `Parallel.ForEach`. Next, we discussed how to get maximum utilization out of the available CPU resources by understanding the degree of parallelism and partitioning strategies. Then, we discussed how to cancel and break out of parallel loops using built-in constructs such as cancellation tokens, `Parallel.Break`, and `ParallelLoopState.Stop`. At the end of this chapter, we discussed various thread storage options that are available in TPL.

The TPL provides a few very exciting options that we can use to achieve data parallelism through the parallel implementation of `For` and `ForEach` loops. Along with features such as `ParallelOptions` and `ParallelLoopState`, we can achieve significant performance benefits and control without losing a lot of synchronization overhead.

In the next chapter, we will look at another exciting feature of the parallel library called **PLINQ**.

Implementing Data Parallelism

Questions

1. Which of these is not the correct method to provide a `for` loop in TPL?
   1. `Parallel.Invoke`
   2. `Parallel.While`
   3. `Parallel.For`
   4. `Parallel.ForEach`
2. Which is not a default partitioning strategy?
   1. Bulk partitioning
   2. Range partitioning
   3. Chunk partitioning
3. What is the default value for the degree of parallelism?
   1. 1
   2. 64
4. `Parallel.Break` guarantees immediate returns as soon as it is executed.
   1. True
   2. False
5. Can one thread see another thread's thread local or partition local value?
   1. Yes
   2. No

4
Using PLINQ

PLINQ is a parallel implementation of the **Language Integrate Query** (**LINQ**). PLINQ was first introduced in .NET Framework 4.0 and since then has been made feature-rich. Before LINQ, it was difficult for developers to fetch data from various data sources such as XML or databases as each source required different skills. LINQ is a language syntax that relies on .NET delegates and built-in methods to query or modify data without having to worry about learning low-level tasks.

In this chapter, we will start by understanding the LINQ providers in .NET. With PLINQ being the preferred choice for programmers, we will cover its various programming aspects, along with some disadvantages associated with it. Finally, we will understand the factors that affect the performance of PLINQ.

We will cover the following topics:

- LINQ providers in .NET
- Writing PLINQ queries
- Preserving order in PLINQ
- Merge options in PLINQ
- Handling exceptions in PLINQ
- Combining parallel and sequential queries
- PLINQ disadvantages
- Speedups in PLINQ

Technical requirements

To complete this chapter, you should have a good understanding of TPL and C#. The source code for this chapter is available on GitHub at `https://github.com/PacktPublishing/Hands-On-Parallel-Programming-with-C-8-and-.NET-Core-3/tree/master/Chapter04`.

LINQ providers in .NET

LINQ is a set of APIs that help us work with XML, objects, and databases more easily. LINQ has many providers, including the following, all of which are commonly used:

- LINQ to objects: LINQ to objects allows developers to query in-memory objects such as arrays, collections, generic types, and so on. It returns an `IEnumerable` and supports features such as sorting, filtering, grouping, ordering, and aggregate functions. Its functionality is defined in the `System.Linq` namespace.
- LINQ to XML: LINQ to XML, or XLINQ, allows developers to query or modify XML data sources. It's defined in the `System.Xml.Linq` namespace.
- LINQ to ADO.NET: LINQ to ADO.NET is not one but a group of technologies that allows developers to query or modify relational data sources such as the SQL Server, MySQL, or Oracle.
- LINQ to SQL: This is also known as DLINQ. DLINQ uses **Object Relational Mapping (ORM)** and is a legacy technology that is supported but not enhanced by Microsoft. It works only with the SQL Server and allows users to map database tables to .NET classes. It also has an adapter that works like a developer interface to a database.
- LINQ to datasets: This allows developers to query or modify datasets in memory. It works with any database that ADO.NET has a provider for.
- LINQ to entities: This is the most advanced and sought-after technology. It allows developers to work with any relational database, including SQL Server, Oracle, IBM Db2, and MySQL. LINQ to entities also supports ORM.
- PLINQ: This is also known as PLINQ. PLINQ is a parallel implementation of LINQ for objects. LINQ queries execute sequentially and can be really slow for heavy computing operations. PLINQ supports the parallel execution of queries by having a task scheduled to be run on multiple threads and optionally on multiple cores as well.

.NET supports the seamless conversion of LINQ to PLINQ using the `AsParallel()` method. PLINQ is a very good choice for computing heavy operations. It works by portioning the source data into chunks, which are, in turn, executed by different threads running on multiple cores. PLINQ also supports XLINQ and LINQ to objects.

Writing PLINQ queries

To understand PLINQ queries, we need to understand the `ParallelEnumerable` class first. Once we have an understanding of the `ParallelEnumerable` class, we will learn how to write parallel queries.

Introducing the ParallelEnumerable class

The `ParallelEnumerable` class is available in the `System.Linq` namespace and the `System.Core` assembly.

Apart from supporting most of the standard query operators defined by LINQ, the `ParallelEnumerable` class supports a lot of extra methods that support parallel execution:

- `AsParallel()`: This is the seed method that's required for parallelization.
- `AsSequential()`: Enables sequential execution of a parallel query by changing the parallel behavior.
- `AsOrdered()`: By default, PLINQ doesn't preserve the order in which tasks are executed and results are returned. We can preserve this ordering by calling the `AsOrdered()` method.
- `AsUnordered()`: This is the default behavior of `ParallelQuery`, which can be overridden by the `AsOrdered()` method. We can change the behavior from ordered to unordered by calling this method.
- `ForAll()`: Enables query execution to be performed in parallel.
- `Aggregate()`: This method can be used to aggregate results from various thread-local partitions in a parallel query.
- `WithDegreesOfParallelism()`: Using this method, we can specify the maximum number of processors that are used to parallelize query executions.
- `WithParallelOption()`: Using this method, we can buffer the results that are produced by a parallel query.
- `WithExecutionMode()`: Using this method, we can force the parallel execution of a query or let PLINQ decide whether the query needs to be executed as sequential or parallel.

Using PLINQ

We will learn more about these methods later in this chapter through the use of code examples. There is a very handy tool called LINQPad that's worth mentioning here. LINQPad helps us learn about LINQ/PLINQ queries since it has more than 500 available samples and the ability to connect to a variety of data sources. You can download it from `https://www.linqpad.net/`.

Our first PLINQ query

Let's say that we want to find all the numbers that are divisible by three.

First, we define a range of 100,000 numbers:

```
var range = Enumerable.Range(1, 100000);
```

To find all the numbers that are divisible by three sequentially, use the following LINQ query:

```
var resultList = range.Where(i => i % 3 == 0).ToList();
```

The following is a parallel version of the same query using the `AsParallel` method but using the method syntax:

```
var resultList = range.AsParallel().Where(i => i % 3 == 0).ToList();
```

Here is the same version using the query syntax option in LINQ:

```
var resultList = (from i in range.AsParallel()
                  where i % 3 == 0
                  select i).ToList();
```

Here is the complete code:

```
var range = Enumerable.Range(1, 100000);
//Here is sequential version
var resultList = range.Where(i => i % 3 == 0).ToList();
Console.WriteLine($"Sequential: Total items are {resultList.Count}");
//Here is Parallel Version using .AsParallel method
resultList = range.AsParallel().Where(i => i % 3 == 0).ToList();
resultList = (from i in range.AsParallel()
 where i % 3 == 0
 select i).ToList();
 Console.WriteLine($"Parallel: Total items are {resultList.Count}" );
Console.WriteLine($"Parallel: Total items are {resultList.Count}");
```

The output of this will be as follows:

```
C:\Program Files\dotnet\dotnet.exe
Sequential: Total items are 33333
Parallel: Total items are 33333
```

Preserving order in PLINQ while doing parallel executions

PLINQ executes work items in parallel and, by default, doesn't care about preserving the order of items to improve the performance of parallel queries. However, it is sometimes important that items are executed in the same order as they exist in the source collection. For example, imagine you are sending multiple requests to the server to download files in chunks and later on merging those chunks to recreate the file on the client side. Since the file is downloaded in parts, every part needs to be downloaded and merged in the correct order. Preserving the order while executing items in parallel has a direct impact on performance as we need to preserve the original ordering throughout the partitions and ensure that the ordering is consistent when merging items.

We can override the default behavior and turn on order preservation by using the `AsOrdered()` method on the source collection. If, at any point, we want to turn off the order preservation, we can call the `AsUnOrdered()` method.

Let's look at an example:

```
var range = Enumerable.Range(1, 10);
Console.WriteLine("Sequential Ordered");
range.ToList().ForEach(i => Console.Write(i + "-"));
```

This code is sequential, so when we run it, we get the following output:

```
C:\Program Files\dotnet\dotnet.exe
Sequential Ordered
1-2-3-4-5-6-7-8-9-10-
```

We can make a parallel version using the `AsParallel()` method:

```
Console.WriteLine("Parallel Unordered");
var unordered = range.AsParallel().Select(i => i).ToList();
unordered.ForEach(i => Console.WriteLine(i));
```

[97]

Using PLINQ

The preceding code executes in parallel, but the ordering is all messed up:

```
Parallel UnOrdered
4-8-7-2-3-1-6-9-10-5-
```

To get the best of both worlds, that is, parallel execution with ordering, we can modify the code as follows:

```
var range = Enumerable.Range(1, 10);
Console.WriteLine("Parallel Ordered");
var ordered = range.AsParallel().AsOrdered().Select(i => i).ToList();
ordered.ForEach(i => Console.WriteLine(i));
```

Here is the output:

```
Parallel Ordered
1-2-3-4-5-6-7-8-9-10-
```

As you can see, when we call the `AsOrdered()` method, it executes all the work items in parallel while preserving the original order, whereas, in the default one, the order was not preserved. The performance implications of using the `AsOrdered()` method are huge since the order is restored at every step of the execution.

Sequential execution using the AsUnOrdered() method

Once we have called `AsOrdered` on PLINQ, the query will execute sequentially. There may be situations in which we want to execute a query as ordered for a certain period but change to unordered after that to gain performance.

Let's say we want to generate the squares of the first 100 numbers from a range of numbers. One way to do this in parallel is as follows:

```
var range = Enumerable.Range(100, 10000);
var ordered = range.AsParallel().AsOrdered().Take(100).Select(i => i * i);
```

We need `AsOrdered()` to get the first 100 numbers. The problem is that the `Select` query will also perform as ordered. We can improve performance by combining `AsOrdered()` and `AsUnOrdered()`:

```
var range = Enumerable.Range(100, 10000);
var ordered =
range.AsParallel().AsOrdered().Take(100).AsUnordered().Select(i => i *
i).ToList();
```

Now, the first 100 items will be retrieved in parallel and in order. After that, the query will execute without any order preservation.

Merge options in PLINQ

As we mentioned previously, when we create a parallel query, the source collection is partitioned so that multiple tasks can work on sections concurrently. Once the query completes, the results need to be merged so that they can be made available to the consuming thread. There are various ways to merge the results, depending on the query operators. We can specify how we want to merge the results explicitly using the `ParallelMergeOperation` enumeration and the `WithMergeOption()` extension method.

Let's take a look at the various merge options that are available to us.

Using the NotBuffered merge option

The results of concurrent tasks are not buffered. As soon as any of the tasks finish, they return the result to the consuming thread:

```
var range = ParallelEnumerable.Range(1, 100);
Stopwatch watch = null;
ParallelQuery<int> notBufferedQuery =
range.WithMergeOptions(ParallelMergeOptions.NotBuffered)
                                .Where(i => i % 10 == 0)
                                .Select(x => {
                                        Thread.SpinWait(1000);
                                        return x;
                                        });
watch = Stopwatch.StartNew();
foreach (var item in notBufferedQuery)
{
    Console.WriteLine( $"{item}:{watch.ElapsedMilliseconds}");
```

Using PLINQ

```
}
Console.WriteLine($"\nNotBuffered Full Result returned in
{watch.ElapsedMilliseconds} ms");
```

The output of this is as follows:

```
10:397
20:402
30:402
40:402
60:402
70:403
80:403
90:404
50:405
100:406

NotBuffered Full Result returned in 407 ms
```

Using the AutoBuffered merge option

The results from concurrent tasks are buffered and the buffer is made available to consuming threads in periodic intervals. Depending on the size of the collection, multiple buffers might be returned. Using this option, the consuming thread needs to wait longer to get the first result. This is also the default option.

Consider the following code:

```
var range = ParallelEnumerable.Range(1, 100);
Stopwatch watch = null;
ParallelQuery<int> query =
range.WithMergeOptions(ParallelMergeOptions.AutoBuffered)
                    .Where(i => i % 10 == 0)
                    .Select(x => {
                                    Thread.SpinWait(1000);
                                    return x;
                                 });
watch = Stopwatch.StartNew();
foreach (var item in query)
{
    Console.WriteLine($"{item}:{watch.ElapsedMilliseconds}");
}
Console.WriteLine($"\nAutoBuffered Full Result returned in
{watch.ElapsedMilliseconds} ms");
watch.Stop();
```

The output is as follows:

```
C:\Program Files\dotnet\dotnet.exe
70:440
80:446
90:446
10:447
20:447
30:447
40:448
60:448
100:449
50:449

AutoBuffered Full Result returned in 450 ms
```

Using the FullyBuffered merge option

The results from concurrent tasks are fully buffered before they are made available in one go to the consuming thread. This improves the overall performance, though the time it takes to get the first result will be longer:

```
var range = ParallelEnumerable.Range(1, 100);
Stopwatch watch = null;
ParallelQuery<int> fullyBufferedQuery =
range.WithMergeOptions(ParallelMergeOptions.FullyBuffered)
                        .Where(i => i % 10 == 0)
                        .Select(x => {
                                        Thread.SpinWait(1000);
                                        return x;
                                        });
watch = Stopwatch.StartNew();
foreach (var item in fullyBufferedQuery)
{
    Console.WriteLine($"{item}:{watch.ElapsedMilliseconds}");
}
Console.WriteLine($"\nFullyBuffered Full Result returned in {watch.ElapsedMilliseconds} ms");
watch.Stop();
```

Using PLINQ

The output will be as follows:

```
90:424
10:431
20:431
30:432
40:432
60:432
70:432
80:432
100:432
50:433

FullyBuffered Full Result returned in 434 ms
```

Not all query operators support all merge modes. The following is a list of operators, along with their restrictions:

Operator	Restrictions
AsEnumerable	None
Cast	None
Concat	Non-ordered queries that have an Array or List source only.
DefaultIfEmpty	None
OfType	None
Reverse	Non-ordered queries that have an Array or List source only.
Select	None
SelectMany	None
Skip	None
Take	None
Where	None

> This information can be found at http://msdn.microsoft.com/en-us/library/dd997424(v=vs.110).aspx.

Apart from the preceding operators, `ForAll()` is always `NotBuffered` and `OrderBy` is always `FullyBuffered`. If any custom merge options are specified on these operators, they are just ignored.

Throwing and handling exceptions with PLINQ

Just like other parallel primitives, PLINQ throws a `System.AggregateException` whenever it encounters an exception. Exception handling largely depends on your design. You may want the program to fail as soon as possible or you may want all the exceptions to be returned to the caller.

In the following example, we will wrap a parallel query inside a `try-catch` block. When the query throws an exception, it will propagate back to the caller, wrapped in `System.AggregateException`:

```
var range = ParallelEnumerable.Range(1, 20);
ParallelQuery<int> query= range.Select(i => i / (i -
10)).WithDegreeOfParallelism(2);
try
{
    query.ForAll(i => Console.WriteLine(i));
}
catch (AggregateException aggregateException)
{
    foreach (var ex in aggregateException.InnerExceptions)
    {
        Console.WriteLine(ex.Message);
        if (ex is DivideByZeroException)
            Console.WriteLine("Attempt to divide by zero. Query
              stopped.");
    }
}
```

Using PLINQ

The output will be as follows:

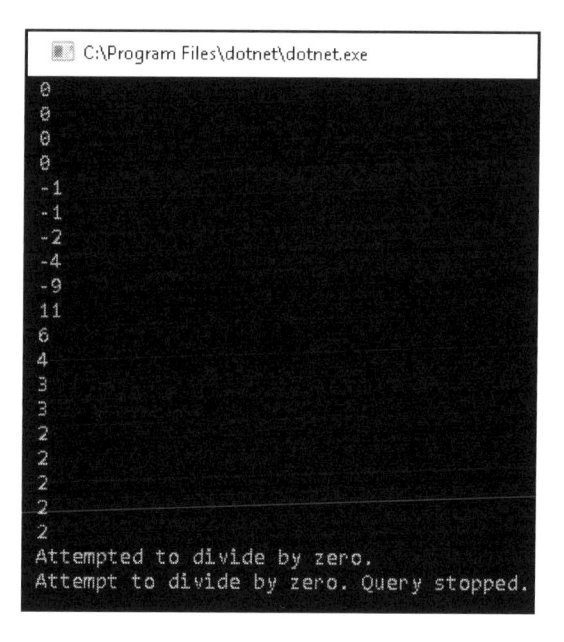

```
0
0
0
0
-1
-1
-2
-4
-9
11
6
4
3
3
2
2
2
2
2
Attempted to divide by zero.
Attempt to divide by zero. Query stopped.
```

We can also specify a `try-catch` block within a delegate, which would alert us about error conditions as soon as possible. It can also be used in a scenario in which we just want to log an exception and continue the query's execution by providing a default value as the query result in the case of an exception:

```
var range = ParallelEnumerable.Range(1, 20);
Func<int, int> selectDivision = (i) =>
{
    try
    {
        return i / (i - 10);
    }
    catch (DivideByZeroException ex)
    {
        Console.WriteLine($"Divide by zero exception for {i}");
        return -1;
    }
};
ParallelQuery<int> query = range.Select(i =>
selectDivision(i)).WithDegreeOfParallelism(2);
try
{
    query.ForAll(i => Console.WriteLine(i));
}
```

```
catch (AggregateException aggregateException)
{
    foreach (var ex in aggregateException.InnerExceptions)
    {
        Console.WriteLine(ex.Message);
        if (ex is DivideByZeroException)
            Console.WriteLine("Attempt to divide by zero. Query stopped.");
    }
}
```

The output is as follows:

```
11
6
4
3
3
2
2
2
2
2
0
0
0
0
-1
-1
-2
-4
-9
Divide by zero exception for 10
-1
```

Exception handling is very important for maintaining the correct flow in the application, as well as to notify the user of applications with error conditions. With proper exception handling and logging, we can troubleshoot application errors in production environments as well. In the next section, we will discuss how to merge parallel and sequential queries.

Combining parallel and sequential LINQ queries

We have already discussed the use of `AsParallel()` to create parallel queries. Sometimes, we may want to execute operators sequentially. We can force PLINQ to operate sequentially using the `AsSequential()` method. Once this method is applied to any parallel query, the following operators execute in a sequence. Consider the following code:

```
var range = Enumerable.Range(1, 1000);
range.AsParallel().Where(i => i % 2 == 0).AsSequential().Where(i => i % 8
== 0).AsParallel().OrderBy(i => i);
```

Here, the first `Where` class, `Where(i => i % 2 == 0)`, will execute in parallel. The second `Where` class, `Where(i => i % 8 == 0)`, however, will execute sequentially. `OrderBy` will also be switched to parallel execution mode.

This is shown in the following diagram:

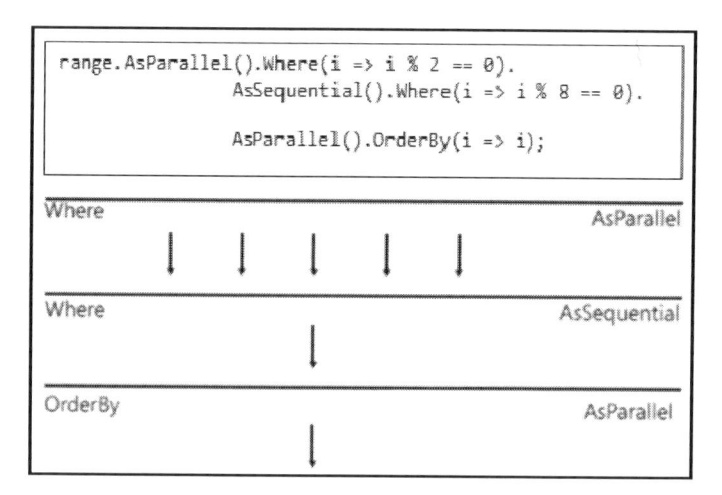

```
range.AsParallel().Where(i => i % 2 == 0).
                AsSequential().Where(i => i % 8 == 0).
        AsParallel().OrderBy(i => i);
```

Where						AsParallel
	↓	↓	↓	↓	↓	
Where						AsSequential
			↓			
OrderBy						AsParallel
			↓			

Now, we should have a good idea about how to merge synchronous and parallel LINQ queries. In the next section, we will learn how to cancel PLINQ queries to save CPU resources.

Canceling PLINQ queries

We can cancel a PLINQ query using the `CancellationTokenSource` and `CancellationToken` classes. The cancellation token is passed to the PLINQ query using the `WithCancellation` clause and then we can call `CancellationToken.Cancel` to cancel the query operation. When a query is canceled, it throws `OperationCancelledException`.

This is done as follows:

1. Create a cancellation token source:

    ```
    CancellationTokenSource cs = new CancellationTokenSource();
    Create a task that starts immediately and cancel the token after 4
    seconds
        Task cancellationTask = Task.Factory.StartNew(() =>
            {
                Thread.Sleep(4000);
                cs.Cancel();
            });
    ```

2. Wrap the PLINQ query inside a `try` block:

    ```
    try
        {
            var result = range.AsParallel()
                .WithCancellation(cs.Token)
                .Select(number => number)
                .ToList();
        }
    ```

3. Add two `catch` blocks; one to catch `OperationCanceledException` and the other to capture `AggregateException`:

    ```
    catch (OperationCanceledException ex)
        {
            Console.WriteLine(ex.Message);
        }
        catch (AggregateException ex)
        {
            foreach (var inner in ex.InnerExceptions)
            {
                Console.WriteLine(inner.Message);
            }
        }
    ```

Using PLINQ

4. Take the range as a very large value that takes more than four seconds to execute:

   ```
   var range = Enumerable.Range(1,1000000);
   ```

5. Run the code. After four seconds, we will see the following output:

   ```
   Select C:\Program Files\dotnet\dotnet.exe
   The query has been canceled via the token supplied to WithCancellation.
   ```

Parallel programming comes with its own caveats. In the next section, we will introduce the disadvantages of writing parallel code with PLINQ.

Disadvantages of parallel programming with PLINQ

In most cases, PLINQ performs much faster than its non-parallel counterpart LINQ. However, there is some performance overhead, which is related to partitioning and merging while parallelizing the LINQ. The following are some of the things we need to consider while using PLINQ:

1. **Parallel is not always faster**: Parallelization is an overhead. Unless your source collection is huge or it has compute-bound operations, it makes more sense to execute the operations in sequence. Always measure the performance of sequential and parallel queries to make an informed decision.
2. **Avoid I/O operations that involve atomicity**: All I/O operations that involve writing to a filesystem, database, network, or shared memory location should be avoided inside PLINQ. This is because these methods are not thread-safe, so using them may lead to exceptions. A solution would be to use synchronization primitives, but this would also reduce performance drastically.
3. **Your queries may not always be running in parallel**: Parallelization in PLINQ is a decision that's taken by CLR. Even if we called the `AsParallel()` method in the query, it isn't guaranteed to take a parallel path and may run sequentially instead.

Understanding the factors that affect the performance of PLINQ (speedups)

The primary purpose of PLINQ is to speed up query execution by splitting the task and executing it in parallel. However, there are a lot of factors that can impact the performance of PLINQ. These include synchronization overheads to do with chunking and partitioning, as well as scheduling and collecting results from threads. PLINQ performs best in *delightfully parallel* scenarios, where threads don't have to share a state and don't have to worry about the order of execution. Being *delightfully parallel* is ideal but not always achievable due to the nature of work. Let's try to understand the factors that can impact the performance of PLINQ.

Degree of parallelism

With a greater number of cores at our disposal, we can achieve significant performance gains since TPL makes sure multiple tasks can execute concurrently on multiple cores. This improvement in performance may not be exponential and, while tuning the performance, we should try to run on different systems with multiple cores and compare results.

Merge option

We can significantly improve the user experience in scenarios where results change often and the user wants to see results as soon as possible without waiting. The default option with PLINQ is to buffer results and later merge them and return them to the user. We can modify this behavior by choosing an appropriate merge option.

Partitioning type

We should always check whether our work items are balanced or unbalanced. For unbalanced work item scenarios, custom partitioners may be introduced to improve performance.

Deciding when to stay sequential with PLINQ

We should always work out the computational cost of each work item and the entire operation as a whole so that we can decide whether we want to stay sequential or move to parallelism. Parallel queries may not always be fast due to the additional overhead of partitioning, scheduling, and so on:

*Computational Cost = Cost to execute 1 work item * total number of work items*

Parallel queries can provide significant performance gains with increasing computational cost per item. However, if the performance gain is very low, it makes sense to execute the query sequentially.

Whether PLINQ decides to execute sequentially or in parallel depends on the combination of operators in the query. Simply put, if the query has any of the following operators, PLINQ may decide to run a query as sequential:

- Take, TakeWhile, Skip, SkipWhile, First, Last, Concat, Zip, or ElementAt
- Indexed Where and Select, which are overloads of Where and Select, respectively

The following code demonstrates using indexed Where and Select:

```
IEnumerable<int> query =
    numbers.AsQueryable()
    .Where((number, index) => number <= index * 10);
IEnumerable<bool> query =
    range.AsQueryable()
    .Select((number, index) => number <= index * 10);
```

Order of operation

PLINQ provides better performance with unordered collections as there are performance costs associated with making collections execute as ordered. This performance cost includes partitioning, scheduling, and gathering results, as well as calling GroupJoin and filters. As a developer, you should consider when you want to use AsOrdered().

ForAll versus calling ToArray() or ToList()

When we call `ToList()` or `ToArray()` or enumerate a result in a loop, we force PLINQ to merge results from all the parallel threads into a single data structure. This is a performance overhead. If we just want to perform some actions on a set of items, it is better to use the `ForAll()` method.

Forcing parallelism

PLINQ is not guaranteed to carry out parallel execution every time. It may decide to run sequential executions, depending on the type of query. We can control this using the `WithExecutionMode` method. `WithExecutionMode` is an extension method that works on objects of the `ParallelQuery` type. It takes `ParallelExecutionMode` as a parameter, which is an `enum`. The default value of `ParallelExecutionMode` lets PLINQ decide on the best execution mode. We can force the execution mode to be parallel using the `ForceParallelism` option:

```
var range = Enumerable.Range(1, 10);
var squares = range.AsParallel().WithExecutionMode
(ParallelExecutionMode.ForceParallelism).Select(i => i * i);
squares.ToList().ForEach(i => Console.Write(i + "-"));
```

Generating sequences

Throughout this book, we used the `Enumerable.Range()` method to generate a sequence of numbers. We can generate numbers in parallel as well using the `ParallelEnumerable` class. Let's do a simple test comparison between `Enumerable` and the `ParallelEnumerable` class:

```
Stopwatch watch = Stopwatch.StartNew();
IEnumerable<int> parallelRange = ParallelEnumerable.Range(0, 5000).Select(i
=> i);
watch.Stop();
Console.WriteLine($"Time elapsed {watch.ElapsedMilliseconds}");
Stopwatch watch2 = Stopwatch.StartNew();
IEnumerable<int> range = Enumerable.Range(0, 5000);
watch2.Stop();
Console.WriteLine($"Time elapsed {watch2.ElapsedMilliseconds}");
Console.ReadLine();
```

Using PLINQ

The output is as follows:

```
Time elapsed using ParallelEnumerable : 3
Time elapsed using Enumerable : 16
```

As you can see, `ParallelEnumerable` works much faster than `Enumerable` for creating a range.

In a similar scenario, we may want to generate a number a certain amount of times. We can use the `ParallelEnumerable.Repeat()` method for this scenario, as follows:

```
IEnumerable<int> rangeRepeat = ParallelEnumerable.Repeat(1, 5000);
```

Now that we've understood the factors that affect the performance of PLINQ, we have come to the end of this chapter. Now, let's summarize what we've learned.

Summary

In this chapter, we discussed the basics of LINQ before moving on to understand how we can write parallel queries using PLINQ. We learned that PLINQ can work well to improve the performance of the application as a whole, but it is important to bear its disadvantages in mind. As a programmer, it is always a good idea to weigh up your options by writing both LINQ and PLINQ queries and comparing their performance.

In the next chapter, we will learn about using synchronization primitives to preserve the consistency and state of data when data is shared across multiple threads.

Questions

1. Which of these LINQ providers has better support for relational objects?
    1. LINQ to SQL
    2. LINQ to entities
2. We can easily convert LINQ into parallel LINQ by using `AsParallel()`.
    1. True
    2. False

3. It's not possible to switch between ordered and unordered execution in PLINQ.
    1. True
    2. False
4. Which of these allows the results for concurrent tasks to be buffered and made available to consuming threads at periodic intervals?
    1. `FullyBuffered`
    2. `AutoBuffered`
    3. `NotBuffered`
5. Which exception will be thrown if the following code is executed inside a task?

```
int i=5;
i = i/i -5;
```

1. `AggregateException`
2. `DivideByZeroException`

Section 2: Data Structures that Support Parallelism in .NET Core

In this section, you will delve more deeply into language and framework constructs that support parallelism, concurrency, and synchronization.

This section comprises the following chapters:

- Chapter 5, *Synchronization Primitives*
- Chapter 6, *Using Concurrent Collections*
- Chapter 7, *Improving Performance with Lazy Initialization*

5
Synchronization Primitives

In the previous chapter, we discussed the potential pitfalls of parallel programming. One of these was synchronization overheads. As we break down work into tasks to be processed by multiple work items, there arises a need to synchronize the results from each thread. We discussed the concept of thread-local-storage and partition-local-storage, which can be used to work around this synchronization issue to a certain extent. However, it is still necessary to synchronize threads so that we can write data to a shared memory location and so that we can perform I/O operations.

In this chapter, we will discuss the synchronization primitives that are provided by the .NET Framework and the TPL.

In this chapter, we will cover the following topics:

- Synchronization primitives
- Interlocked operations
- Locking primitives
- Signaling primitives
- Lightweight synchronization primitives
- Barriers and countdown events

By the end of this chapter, you will have a good understanding of the various locking and signaling primitives that are provided by .NET Framework, including some lightweight synchronization primitives that should be used as much as possible wherever there are synchronization needs.

Technical requirements

To complete this chapter, you should have a good understanding of TPL, primarily parallel loops. The source code for this chapter is available on GitHub at `https://github.com/PacktPublishing/Hands-On-Parallel-Programming-with-C-8-and-.NET-Core-3/tree/master/Chapter05`.

What are synchronization primitives?

Before understanding synchronization primitives, we need to understand critical section. Critical section is part of the execution path of a thread that must be protected from concurrent access in order to maintain some invariants. Critical section is not a synchronization primitive in itself but relies on synchronization primitives.

Synchronization primitives are simple software mechanisms that are provided by the underlying platform (the OS). They help in multithreading the kernel. Synchronization primitives internally use low-level atomic operations, as well as memory barriers. This means that users of synchronization primitives don't have to worry about implementing locks and memory barriers themselves. Some common examples of synchronization primitives are locks, mutexes, conditional variables, and semaphores. The monitor is a higher-level synchronization tool that makes use of other synchronization primitives internally.

The .NET Framework provides a range of synchronization primitives to deal with the interaction among threads, as well as to avoid potential race conditions. Synchronization primitives can be broadly divided into five categories:

- Interlocked operations
- Locking
- Signaling
- Lightweight synchronization types
- `SpinWait`

In the following sections, we will discuss each category and their respective low-level primitives.

Interlocked operations

The interlocked class encapsulates synchronization primitives and is used to provide atomic operations to variables that are shared across threads. It provides methods such as `Increment`, `Decrement`, `Add`, `Exchange`, and `CompareExchange`.

Consider the following code, which tries to increment a counter inside a parallel loop:

```
Parallel.For(1, 1000, i =>
    {
        Thread.Sleep(100);
        _counter++;
    });
Console.WriteLine($"Value for counter should be 999 and
  is {_counter}");
```

If we run this code, we will see the following output:

```
C:\Program Files\dotnet\dotnet.exe
Value for counter should be 999 and is 971
```

As you can see, the expected value and the actual value do not match. This is because of the race condition among the threads, which has arisen because the thread wants to read a value from a variable to which the value has been written but not yet committed.

We can modify the preceding code using the `Interlocked` class to make it thread-safe, as follows:

```
Parallel.For(1, 1000, i =>
    {
        Thread.Sleep(100);
        Interlocked.Increment(ref _counter);
    });
Console.WriteLine($"Value for counter should be 999 and
  is {_counter}");
```

The expected output is as follows:

```
C:\Program Files\dotnet\dotnet.exe
Value for counter should be 999 and is 999
```

Synchronization Primitives

Similarly, we can use `Interlocked.Decrement(ref _counter)` to decrement the value in a thread-safe manner.

The following code shows the complete list of operations:

```
  //_counter becomes 1
Interlocked.Increment(ref _counter);
// _counter becomes 0
Interlocked.Decrement(ref _counter);
// Add: _counter becomes 2
Interlocked.Add(ref _counter, 2);
//Subtract: _counter becomes 0
Interlocked.Add(ref _counter, -2);
// Reads 64 bit field
Console.WriteLine(Interlocked.Read(ref _counter));
// Swaps _counter value with 10
Console.WriteLine(Interlocked.Exchange(ref _counter, 10));
//Checks if _counter is 10 and if yes replace with 100
Console.WriteLine(Interlocked.CompareExchange(ref _counter, 100, 10));
// _counter becomes 100
```

Apart from the preceding methods, two new methods were added in .NET Framework 4.5: `Interlocked.MemoryBarrier()` and `Interlocked.MemoryBarrierProcessWide()`.

In the next section, we will learn more about memory barriers in .NET.

Memory barriers in .NET

Threading models work differently on single-core versus multicore processors. On single-core processors, only one thread gets a CPU slice while other threads wait for their turn. This ensures that whenever a thread accesses the memory (for loading and storing), it is in the right order. This model is also known as a **sequential consistency model**. In the case of multicore processor systems, multiple threads run concurrently. Sequential consistency is not guaranteed in these systems since either the hardware or the **Just in Time (JIT)** compiler might reorder the memory instructions to improve performance. The memory instructions may also be reordered for performance purposes for caching, load speculations, or delaying store operations.

An example of a load speculation is as follows:

```
a=b;
```

An example of a store operation is as follows:

```
c=1;
```

Load and store statements, when encountered by the compiler, are not always executed in the same order as they are written. Compilers do some reordering for performance benefits. Let's try to understand more about reordering.

What is reordering?

For a given sequence of code statements, the compiler can choose to either execute them in the same order as they are received or reorder them to gain performance if multiple threads are working on the same code. For example, take a look at the following code:

```
a = b;
c = 1;
```

The preceding code can be reordered and executed in the following order for another thread:

```
c = 1;
a = b;
```

Code reordering is a problem for multicore processors with weak memory models, such as Intel Itanium processors. It has no impact on single-core processors, however, due to the sequential consistency model. The code is restructured so that another thread can take advantage or store an instruction that is already in the memory. Code reordering can be done either by hardware or by a JIT compiler. To guarantee code reordering, we need some sort of **memory barrier**.

Types of memory barriers

Memory barriers ensure that any code statements above or below the barrier will not cross the barrier, thereby enforcing the order of the code. There are three types of memory barrier:

- **Store (write) memory barrier:** A store memory barrier ensures that no store operations are allowed to move across the barrier. It has no effect on load operations; these can still be reordered. The equivalent CPU instruction to achieve this effect is **SFENCE**:

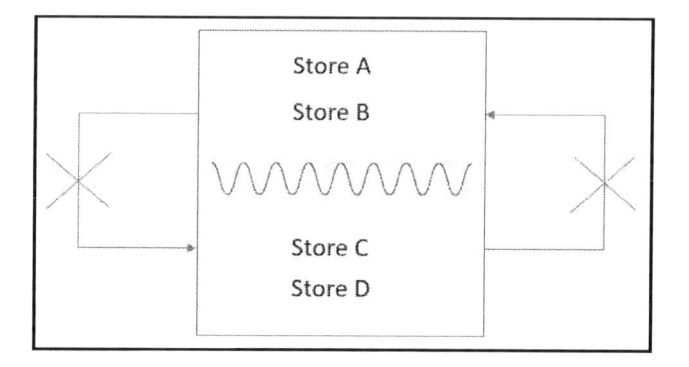

- **Load (read) memory barrier:** A load barrier ensures that no load operations are allowed to move across the barrier but places no such enforcement on store operations. The equivalent CPU instruction to achieve this effect is **LFENCE**:

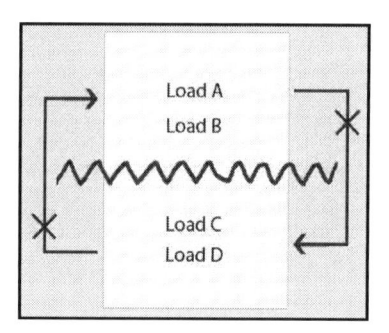

- **Full memory barrier:** A full memory barrier ensures ordering by not allowing store or load operations to move across the memory barrier. The equivalent CPU instruction to achieve this effect is **MFENCE**. The behavior of the full memory barrier is often implemented by .NET synchronization constructs such as the following:
  - `Task.Start`, `Task.Wait`, and `Task.Continuation`
  - `Thread.Sleep`, `Thread.Join`, `Thread.SpinWait`, `Thread.VolatileRead`, and `Thread.VolatileWrite`
  - `Thread.MemoryBarrier`
  - `Lock`, `Monitor.Enter`, and `Monitor.Exit`
  - `Interlocked` class operations

Half barriers are provided by the `Volatile` keyword and the `Volatile` class methods. The .NET Framework provides some built-in patterns using volatile fields in classes such as `Lazy<T>` and `LazyInitializer`. We will discuss these further in Chapter 7, *Improving Performance with Lazy Initialization*.

Avoiding code reordering using constructs

We can avoid reordering using `Thread.MemoryBarrier`, as shown in the following code:

```
static int a = 1, b = 2, c = 0;
private static void BarrierUsingTheadBarrier()
{
    b = c;
    Thread.MemoryBarrier();
    a = 1;
}
```

`Thread.MemoryBarrier` creates a full barrier that doesn't allow load or store operations to pass. It has been wrapped inside `Interlocked.MemoryBarrier`, so the same code can be written as follows:

```
private static void BarrierUsingInterlockedBarrier()
    {
        b = c;
        Interlocked.MemoryBarrier();
        a = 1;
    }
```

[123]

If we want to create a process- and system-wide barrier, we can make use of `Interlocked.MemoryBarrierProcessWide`, which was introduced in .NET Core 2.0. This is a wrapper over the `FlushProcessWriteBuffer` Windows API or `sys_membarrier` on a Linux kernel:

```
private static void BarrierUsingInterlockedProcessWideBarrier()
{
    b = c;
    Interlocked.MemoryBarrierProcessWide();
    a = 1;
}
```

The preceding example shows us how we can create a process-wide barrier. Now, let's look at what locking primitives are.

Introduction to locking primitives

Locks can be used to limit access to a protected resource to only a single thread or group of threads. To be able to implement locking efficiently, we need to identify appropriate critical sections that can be protected via locking primitives.

How locking works

When we apply a lock to a shared resource, the following steps are performed:

1. A thread or group of threads access a shared resource by acquiring a lock.
2. Other threads that cannot get access to a lock go into a wait state.
3. As soon as the lock is freed by one of the threads, it is acquired by another thread, which starts its execution.

To understand locking primitives, we need to understand various thread states, as well as concepts such as blocking and spinning.

Thread state

At any point during the thread's life cycle, we can query a thread state using the `ThreadState` property of the thread. A thread can be in any one of the following states:

- `Unstarted`: The thread has been created by CLR but the `System.Threading.Thread.Start` method hasn't been invoked on the thread yet.
- `Running`: The thread has been started via a call to `Thread.Start`. It is not waiting for any pending operations.
- `WaitSleepJoin`: The thread is in a blocked state as a result of invoking the `Wait()`, `Sleep()`, or `Join()` methods by calling the thread.
- `StopRequested`: The thread has been requested to stop.
- `Stopped`: The thread has stopped executing.
- `AbortRequested`: The `Abort()` method has been called on the thread, but the thread hasn't been aborted yet as it is waiting for `ThreadAbortException`, which will try to terminate it.
- `Aborted`: The thread has been aborted.
- `SuspendRequested`: The thread is requested to suspend as a result of calling the `Suspend` method.
- `Suspended`: The thread has been suspended.
- `Background`: The thread is being executed in the background.

Let's try to explore the journey of a thread from its initial state, `UnStarted`, to its final state, `Stopped`:

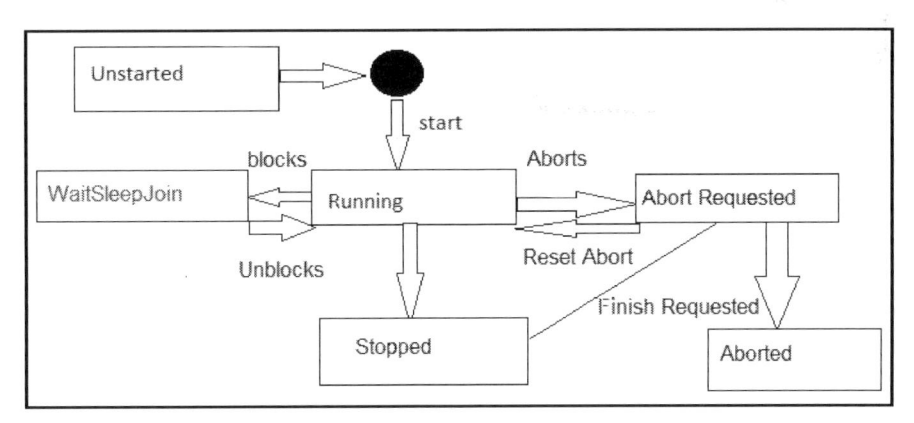

Synchronization Primitives

When a thread is created by CLR, it is in an `Unstarted` state. It makes a transition from `Unstarted` to `Running` when the external thread calls the `Thread.Start()` method on it. From the `Running` state, a thread can transition to the following states:

- `WaitSleepJoin`
- `AbortRequested`
- `Stopped`

A thread is said to be blocked when it is in the `WaitSleepJoin` state. The execution of a blocked thread is paused since it is waiting for some external conditions to be met, which may be the result of some CPU-bound I/O operation or some other thread. Once blocked, the thread immediately yields the CPU time slice and doesn't use the processor slice until the blocked condition is satisfied. At this point, the thread is unblocked. Blocking and unblocking constitutes a performance overhead as this requires the CPU to carry out context switching.

A thread can be unblocked in any of the following events:

- If the blocking condition is satisfied
- By calling `Thread.Interrupt` on the blocked thread
- By aborting a thread using `Thread.Abort`
- When the specified timeout is reached

Blocking versus spinning

A blocked thread relinquishes the processor slice for a specified amount of time. This improves performance by making it available for other threads but incurs the overhead of context switching. It is good in a scenario where the thread has to be blocked for a considerable amount of time. If the waiting time is less, it makes sense to go for spinning without relinquishing the processor slice. For example, the following code simply loops infinitely:

```
while(!done);
```

This is just an empty `while` loop that checks for a Boolean variable. When the wait is over, the variable will be set to false and the loop can break. Although this is a waste of processor time, it can significantly improve performance if the wait isn't very long. The .NET Framework provides some special constructs, which we will discuss later in this chapter, such as `SpinWait` and `SpinLock`.

Let's try to understand some locking primitives with code examples.

Lock, mutex, and semaphore

Lock and mutex are locking constructs that allow only one thread to access a protected resource. Lock is a shortcut implementation that uses another higher-level synchronization class called `Monitor`.

Semaphore is a locking construct that allows a specified number of threads to access a protected resource. Lock can only synchronize access inside a process, but if we need to access a system-level resource or shared memory, we need to actually synchronize access across multiple processes. A mutex allows us to synchronize access to resources across processes by providing a kernel-level lock.

The following table provides a comparison of the capabilities of these constructs:

Synchronization Primitive	Allotted No. of Threads	Cross Process
Lock	1	✗
Mutex	1	✓
Semaphore	Many	✓
SemaphoreSlim	Many	✗

As we can see, **Lock** and **Mutex** only allow single-thread access to shared resources, whereas **Semaphore** and **SemaphoreSlim** can be used to allow access to resources that have been shared by multiple threads. Also, where **Lock** and **SemaphoreSlim** only work inside a process, **Mutex** and **Semaphore** have a process-wide lock.

Lock

Let's consider the following code, which tries to write a number to a text file:

```
var range = Enumerable.Range(1, 1000);
Stopwatch watch = Stopwatch.StartNew();
    for (int i = 0; i < range.Count(); i++)
    {
        Thread.Sleep(10);
        File.AppendAllText("test.txt", i.ToString());
    }
```

Synchronization Primitives

```
watch.Stop();
Console.WriteLine($"Total time to write file is
    {watch.ElapsedMilliseconds}");
```

The output when we run the preceding code is as follows:

```
C:\Program Files\dotnet\dotnet.exe
Total time to write file is 11949
```

As you can see, the task is composed of 1,000 work items and each work item takes approximately 10 milliseconds to execute. The time that's taken by the task is 1,000 multiplied by 10, which is 10,000 milliseconds. We also have to take into consideration the time taken to perform I/O, so the total time turns out to be 11,949.

Let's try to parallelize this task using the `AsParallel()` and `AsOrdered()` clauses, as follows:

```
range.AsParallel().AsOrdered().ForAll(i =>
{
    Thread.Sleep(10);
    File.AppendAllText ("test.txt", i.ToString());
});
```

When we try to run this code, we get the following `System.IO.IOException: 'The process cannot access the file ...\test.txt' because it is being used by another process.'`.

What actually happened here is that the file is a shared resource with a critical section and therefore only allows atomic operations. With the parallel code, we have a situation where multiple threads are actually trying to write to the file and causing an exception. We need to make sure that the code runs in parallel as fast as possible but also maintains atomicity while writing to the file. We need to modify the preceding code using a lock statement.

First, declare a `static` reference type variable. In our case, we take a variable of the `object` type. We need a reference type variable since the lock can only be applied on the heap memory:

```
static object _locker = new object ();
```

Next, we modify the code inside the `ForAll()` method to include a `lock`:

```
range.AsParallel().AsOrdered().ForAll(i =>
    {
        lock (_locker)
        {
            Thread.Sleep(10);
            File.WriteAllText("test.txt", i.ToString());
        }
    });
```

Now, when we run this code, we won't get any exceptions, but the time that the task took was actually more than the sequential execution:

```
C:\Program Files\dotnet\dotnet.exe
Total time to write file is 12464
```

What went wrong here? Lock ensures atomicity by making sure that only one thread is allowed to access the vulnerable code, but this comes with the overhead of blocking the thread that is waiting for the lock to be freed. We call this a dumb lock. We can modify the program slightly to only lock the critical section to improve performance while maintaining atomicity, as follows:

```
range.AsParallel().AsOrdered().ForAll(i =>
    {
        Thread.Sleep(10);
        lock (_locker)
        {
            File.WriteAllText("test.txt", i.ToString());
        }
    });
```

Following is the output of the preceding code:

```
Select C:\Program Files\dotnet\dotnet.exe
Total time to write file is 2065
```

As you can see, we achieved significant gains by mixing synchronization along with parallelization. We can achieve similar results using another locking primitive, that is, the `Monitor` class.

Synchronization Primitives

Lock is actually a shorthand syntax for achieving
`Monitor.Enter()` and `Monitor.Exit()` wrapped inside a `try-catch` block. The same code can, therefore, be written as follows:

```
range.AsParallel().AsOrdered().ForAll(i =>
{
    Thread.Sleep(10);
    Monitor.Enter(_locker);
    try
    {
        File.WriteAllText("test.txt", i.ToString());
    }
    finally
    {
        Monitor.Exit(_locker);
    }
});
```

The output of this code is as follows:

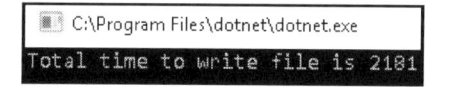

```
C:\Program Files\dotnet\dotnet.exe
Total time to write file is 2101
```

Mutex

The preceding code works well for a single instance application since tasks run inside a process and the lock actually locks a memory barrier inside the process. If we run multiple instances of the application, both applications will have their own copy of the static data members and will, therefore, lock their own memory barriers. This will allow one thread per process to actually enter the critical section and try to write the file. This causes the following `System.IO.IOException: 'The process cannot access the file ...\test.txt' because it is being used by another process.'`.

To be able to apply locks to shared resources, we can apply a lock at the kernel level using the `mutex` class. Like lock, mutex allows only one thread to access a protected resource but can work across processes as well, thereby allowing only one thread per system to access a protected resource, irrespective of the number of processes that are executing.

A mutex can be named or unnamed. An unnamed mutex works like a lock and cannot work across processes.

First, we'll create an unnamed `Mutex`:

```
private static Mutex mutex = new Mutex();
```

Then, we'll modify the preceding parallel code so that we can use `Mutex` like a lock:

```
range.AsParallel().AsOrdered().ForAll(i =>
{
    Thread.Sleep(10);
    mutex.WaitOne();
    File.AppendAllText("test.txt", i.ToString());
    mutex.ReleaseMutex();
});
```

The output of the preceding code is as follows:

```
C:\Program Files\dotnet\dotnet.exe
Total time to write file is 2425
```

With a `Mutex` class, we can call the `WaitHandle.WaitOne()` method to lock the critical section and `ReleaseMutex()` to unlock the critical sections. Closing or disposing of a mutex automatically releases it.

The preceding program works well, but if we try to run it on multiple instances, it will throw an `IOException`. For this, we can create a `namedMutex`, as follows:

```
private static Mutex namedMutex = new Mutex(false,"ShaktiSinghTanwar");
```

Optionally, we can specify a timeout while calling `WaitOne()` on the mutex so that it waits for a signal for a specified amount of time before unblocking itself. This is shown in the following example:

```
namedMutex.WaitOne(3000);
```

The preceding mutex will wait for three seconds before unblocking itself if it doesn't receive a signal.

> **TIP** Lock and mutex can only be released from the thread that obtained them.

Semaphore

Lock, mutex, and monitor allow only one thread to access a protected resource. Sometimes, however, we need to allow multiple threads to be able to access a shared resource. Examples of these include resource pooling scenarios and throttling scenarios. A semaphore, unlike lock or mutex, is thread-agnostic, which means that any thread can call a release of semaphore. Just like a mutex, it works across processes as well.

A typical semaphore constructor is as follows:

```
Semaphore semaphore = new Semaphore()
```
▲ 1 of 3 ▼ Semaphore(int **initialCount**, int maximumCount)
Initializes a new instance of the Semaphore class, specifying the initial number of entries and the maximum number of concurrent entries.
initialCount: *The initial number of requests for the semaphore that can be granted concurrently.*

As you can see, it accepts two parameters: the initialCount, which specifies how many threads are initially allowed to enter, and maximumCount, which specifies the total number of threads that can enter.

Let's say we have a remote service that only allows three concurrent connections per client and takes one second to process a request, as follows:

```
private static void DummyService(int i)
    {
        Thread.Sleep(1000);
    }
```

We have a method that has 1,000 work items that need to call the service with parameters. We need to process a task in parallel but also make sure that there are no more than three calls to the service at any time. We can achieve this by creating a semaphore with a max count of 3:

```
Semaphore semaphore = new Semaphore(3,3);
```

Now, we can write some code that can simulate making 1,000 requests in parallel, but only three at a time, using the following semaphore:

```
range.AsParallel().AsOrdered().ForAll(i =>
        {
            semaphore.WaitOne();
            Console.WriteLine($"Index {i} making service call using
             Task {Task.CurrentId}" );
            //Simulate Http call
            CallService(i);
            Console.WriteLine($"Index {i} releasing semaphore using
```

```
        Task {Task.CurrentId}");
        semaphore.Release();
});
```

The output of this is as follows:

```
Index 2 making service call using Task 4
Index 1 making service call using Task 5
Index 5 making service call using Task 6
Index 1 releasing semaphore using Task 5
Index 5 releasing semaphore using Task 6
Index 2 releasing semaphore using Task 4
Index 3 making service call using Task 9
Index 4 making service call using Task 2
Index 6 making service call using Task 3
Index 4 releasing semaphore using Task 2
Index 3 releasing semaphore using Task 9
Index 11 making service call using Task 4
Index 6 releasing semaphore using Task 3
Index 9 making service call using Task 5
Index 10 making service call using Task 6
Index 11 releasing semaphore using Task 4
Index 12 making service call using Task 2
Index 9 releasing semaphore using Task 5
Index 7 making service call using Task 7
Index 10 releasing semaphore using Task 6
Index 8 making service call using Task 8
Index 12 releasing semaphore using Task 2
Index 7 releasing semaphore using Task 7
Index 8 releasing semaphore using Task 8
```

As you can see, three threads enter and call the service while other threads wait for the lock to be released. As soon as a thread releases the lock, another thread enters but only if three threads are inside the critical section at any one time.

There are two types of semaphores: local and global. We will discuss these next.

Local semaphore

A local `semaphore` is local to the application where it's used. Any `semaphore` that is created without a name will be created as a local `semaphore`, as follows:

```
Semaphore semaphore = new Semaphore(1,10);
```

Global semaphore

A global `semaphore` is global to the operating system as it applies kernel- or system-level locking primitives. Any `semaphore` that is created with a name will be created as a global `semaphore`, as follows:

```
Semaphore semaphore = new Semaphore(1,10,"Globalsemaphore");
```

> **TIP:** If we create a `semaphore` with only one thread, it will act like a lock.

ReaderWriterLock

The `ReaderWriterLock` class defines a lock that supports multiple readers and a single writer at a time. This is handy in scenarios where a shared resource is read frequently by many threads but updated infrequently. There are two reader-writer lock classes that are provided by the .NET Framework: `ReaderWriterLock` and `ReaderWriterLockSlim`. `ReaderWriterLock` is almost outdated now since it can incur potential deadlocks, reduced performance, complex recursion rules, and upgrading or downgrading of locks. We will discuss `ReaderWriterLockSlim` in more detail later in this chapter.

Introduction to signaling primitives

An important aspect of parallel programming is task coordination. While creating tasks, you may come across a producer/consumer scenario where a thread (the consumer) is waiting for a shared resource to be updated by another thread (the producer). Since the consumer doesn't know when the producer is going to update the shared resource, it keeps on polling the shared resource, which can lead to race conditions. Polling is highly inefficient in dealing with these scenarios. It is better to use the signaling primitives that are provided by the .NET Framework. With signaling primitives, the consumer thread is paused until it receives a signal from the producer thread. Let's discuss some common signaling primitives, such as `Thread.Join`, `WaitHandles`, and `EventWaitHandlers`.

Thread.Join

This is the simplest way in which we can make a thread wait for a signal from another thread. `Thread.Join` is blocking in nature, which means that the caller thread is blocked until the joined thread is complete. Optionally, we can specify a timeout that allows the blocked thread to come out of its blocking state once the timeout has been reached.

In the following code, we will create a child thread that simulates a long-running task. Once complete, it will update the output in the local variable, which is called `result`. The program is supposed to print the result `10` to the console. Let's try to run the code:

```
int result = 0;
Thread childThread = new Thread(() =>
{
    Thread.Sleep(5000);
    result = 10;
});
childThread.Start();
Console.WriteLine($"Result is {result}");
```

The output of the preceding code is as follows:

```
Result is 0
```

We expected the result to be `10`, but it has come out as `0`. This happened because the main thread that was supposed to write the value runs before the child thread has finished execution. We can achieve the desired behavior by blocking the main thread until the child thread completes. This can be done by calling `Join()` on the child thread, as follows:

```
int result = 0;
Thread childThread = new Thread(() =>
{
    Thread.Sleep(5000);
    result = 10;
});
childThread.Start();
childThread.Join();
Console.WriteLine($"Result is {result}");
```

If we run the code again now, we will see the desired output after a wait of five seconds, during which the main thread is blocked:

```
C:\Program Files\dotnet\dotnet.exe
Result is 10
```

EventWaitHandle

The `System.Threading.EventWaitHandle` class represents a synchronization event for a thread. It serves as a base class for the `AutoResetEvent` and `ManualResetEvent` classes. We can signal an `EventWaitHandle` by calling `Set()` or `SignalAndWait()`. The `EventWaitHandle` class doesn't have any thread affinity, so it can be signaled by any thread. Let's learn more about `AutoResetEvent` and `ManualResetEvent`.

AutoResetEvent

This refers to `WaitHandle` classes that are automatically reset. Once they are reset, they allow one thread to pass through the barrier that is created. As soon as the thread is passed, they are set again, thereby blocking threads until the next signal.

In the following example, we are trying to find out the sum of 10 numbers in a thread-safe manner, without using locks.

First, create an `AutoResetEvent` with the initial state as non-signaled, or `false`. This means that all the threads should wait until a signal is received. If we set the initial state to signaled, or `true`, the first thread will go through while the others wait for a signal:

```
AutoResetEvent autoResetEvent = new AutoResetEvent(false);
```

Next, create a signaling task that fires a signal 10 times per second using the `autoResetEvent.Set()` method:

```
Task signallingTask = Task.Factory.StartNew(() => {
    for (int i = 0; i < 10; i++)
    {
        Thread.Sleep(1000);
        autoResetEvent.Set();
    }
});
```

Declare a variable sum and initialize it to 0:

```
int sum = 0;
```

Create a parallel `for` loop that creates 10 tasks. Each task will start immediately and wait for a signal to enter, thereby blocking at the `autoResetEvent.WaitOne()` statement. After every second, a signal will be sent by the signaling task and one thread will enter and update the `sum`:

```
Parallel.For(1, 10, (i) => {
    Console.WriteLine($"Task with id {Task.CurrentId} waiting for 
      signal to enter");
    autoResetEvent.WaitOne();
    Console.WriteLine($"Task with id {Task.CurrentId} received 
      signal to enter");
    sum += i;
});
```

The output is as follows:

```
C:\Program Files\dotnet\dotnet.exe
Task with id 2 waiting for signal to enter
Task with id 3 waiting for signal to enter
Task with id 4 waiting for signal to enter
Task with id 5 waiting for signal to enter
Task with id 6 waiting for signal to enter
Task with id 8 waiting for signal to enter
Task with id 7 waiting for signal to enter
Task with id 9 waiting for signal to enter
Task with id 10 waiting for signal to enter
Task with id 2 received signal to enter
Task with id 3 received signal to enter
Task with id 4 received signal to enter
Task with id 5 received signal to enter
Task with id 6 received signal to enter
Task with id 8 received signal to enter
Task with id 9 received signal to enter
Task with id 7 received signal to enter
Task with id 10 received signal to enter
```

As you can see, all 10 tasks blocked initially and released one per second after receiving the signal.

ManualResetEvent

This refers to wait handles that need to be reset manually. Unlike `AutoResetEvent`, which only allows one thread to pass per signal, `ManualResetEvent` allows threads to keep passing through until it is set again. Let's try to understand this using a simple example.

Synchronization Primitives

In the following example, we need to make 15 service calls in batches of 5 in parallel, with a 2-second delay between each batch. While making the service call, we need to make sure that the system is connected to the network. To simulate the network status, we will create two tasks: one that signals the network off and one that signals the network on.

First, we'll create a manual reset event with the initial state *off*:

```
ManualResetEvent manualResetEvent = new ManualResetEvent(false);
```

Next, we'll create two tasks that simulate the network turning on and off by firing the network *off* event every two seconds (which blocks all the network calls) and the network *on* event every five seconds (which allows all the network calls to go through):

```
Task signalOffTask = Task.Factory.StartNew(() => {
        while (true)
        {
            Thread.Sleep(2000);
            Console.WriteLine("Network is down");
            manualResetEvent.Reset();
        }
    });
    Task signalOnTask = Task.Factory.StartNew(() => {
        while (true)
        {
            Thread.Sleep(5000);
            Console.WriteLine("Network is Up");
            manualResetEvent.Set();
        }
    });
```

As you can see from the preceding code, we have signaled a manual reset event every five seconds using `manualResetEvent.Set()`. We turn it off every two seconds using `manualResetEvent.Reset()`. The following code makes the actual service calls:

```
for (int i = 0; i < 3; i++)
    {
        Parallel.For(0, 5, (j) => {
            Console.WriteLine($"Task with id {Task.CurrentId} waiting
              for network to be up");
            manualResetEvent.WaitOne();
            Console.WriteLine($"Task with id {Task.CurrentId} making
              service call");
            DummyServiceCall();
        });
        Thread.Sleep(2000);
    }
```

As you can see from the preceding code, we have created a `for` loop that creates five tasks in each iteration with a sleep interval of two seconds between iterations.

Before making service calls, we wait for the network to be up by calling `manualResetEvent.WaitOne();`.

If we run the preceding code, we'll receive the following output:

```
C:\Program Files\dotnet\dotnet.exe
Task with id 4 waiting for network to be up
Task with id 3 waiting for network to be up
Task with id 5 waiting for network to be up
Task with id 6 waiting for network to be up
Task with id 7 waiting for network to be up
Network is down
Network is Up
Task with id 7 making service call
Task with id 5 making service call
Task with id 3 making service call
Task with id 4 making service call
Task with id 6 making service call
Network is down
Task with id 14 waiting for network to be up
Task with id 17 waiting for network to be up
Task with id 16 waiting for network to be up
Task with id 15 waiting for network to be up
Task with id 18 waiting for network to be up
Network is down
Network is Up
Task with id 18 making service call
Task with id 15 making service call
Task with id 14 making service call
Task with id 16 making service call
Task with id 17 making service call
Network is down
Task with id 25 waiting for network to be up
Task with id 26 waiting for network to be up
Task with id 27 waiting for network to be up
Task with id 28 waiting for network to be up
Task with id 29 waiting for network to be up
Network is down
Network is Up
Task with id 29 making service call
Task with id 28 making service call
Task with id 25 making service call
Task with id 26 making service call
Task with id 27 making service call
Network is down
Network is Up
Network is down
Network is down
Network is Up
```

As you can see, five tasks are started and blocked immediately to wait for the network to be up. After five seconds, when the network is up, we signal using the `Set()` method and all five threads pass through to make the service call. This is repeated with each iteration of the `for` loop.

Synchronization Primitives

WaitHandles

`System.Threading.WaitHandle` is a class that inherits from the `MarshalByRefObject` class and is used to synchronize threads that are running in an application. Blocking and signaling are used to synchronize threads using wait handles. Threads can be blocked by calling any of the methods of the `WaitHandle` class. They are released, depending on the type of signaling construct that is selected. The methods of the `WaitHandle` class are as follows:

- `WaitOne`: Blocks the calling thread until it receives a signal from the wait handles that it's waiting for.
- `WaitAll`: Blocks the calling thread until it receives a signal from all of the wait handles it's waiting for.

The following is an example that shows us how `WaitAll` works:

```
public static bool WaitAll (System.Threading.WaitHandle[]
waitHandles, TimeSpan timeout, bool exitContext);
```

Here is an example that makes use of two threads to simulate two different service calls. Both threads will execute in parallel but will wait at `WaitHandle.WaitAll(waitHandles)` before printing the sum to the console:

```
static int _dataFromService1 = 0;
static int _dataFromService2 = 0;
private static void WaitAll()
{
    List<WaitHandle> waitHandles = new List<WaitHandle>
        {
            new AutoResetEvent(false),
            new AutoResetEvent(false)
        };
    ThreadPool.QueueUserWorkItem(new WaitCallback
      (FetchDataFromService1), waitHandles.First());
    ThreadPool.QueueUserWorkItem(new WaitCallback
      (FetchDataFromService2), waitHandles.Last());
    //Waits for all the threads (waitHandles) to call the .Set()
    //method
    //i.e. wait for data to be returned from both service
    WaitHandle.WaitAll(waitHandles.ToArray());
    Console.WriteLine($"The Sum is
      {_dataFromService1 + _dataFromService2}");
}
private static void FetchDataFromService1(object state)
{
    Thread.Sleep(1000);
```

```
        _dataFromService1 = 890;
        var autoResetEvent = state as AutoResetEvent;
        autoResetEvent.Set();
}
private static void FetchDataFromService2(object state)
{
        Thread.Sleep(1000);
        _dataFromService2 = 3;
        var autoResetEvent = state as AutoResetEvent;
        autoResetEvent.Set();
}
```

The output of the preceding code is as follows:

```
C:\Program Files\dotnet\dotnet.exe
The Sum is 893
```

- `WaitAny`: Blocks the calling thread until it receives a signal from any of the wait handles it's waiting for.

The following is the signature of the `WaitAny` method:

```
public static int WaitAny (System.Threading.WaitHandle[] waitHandles);
```

Here is an example that makes use of two threads to perform an item search. Both threads will execute in parallel and the program waits for any of the threads to finish execution at the `WaitHandle.WaitAny(waitHandles)` method before printing the item index to the console.

We have two methods, binary search and linear search, that perform a search using binary and linear algorithms. We want to get a result as soon as possible from either of these methods. We can achieve this via signaling using `AutoResetEvent` and store the results in the `findIndex` and `winnerAlgo` global variables:

```
static int findIndex = -1;
static string winnerAlgo = string.Empty;
private static void BinarySearch(object state)
{
    dynamic data = state;
    int[] x = data.Range;
    int valueToFind = data.ItemToFind;
    AutoResetEvent autoResetEvent = data.WaitHandle
      as AutoResetEvent;
```

Synchronization Primitives

```
        //Search for item using .NET framework built in Binary Search
        int foundIndex = Array.BinarySearch(x, valueToFind);
        //store the result globally
        Interlocked.CompareExchange(ref findIndex, foundIndex, -1);
        Interlocked.CompareExchange(ref winnerAlgo, "BinarySearch",
          string.Empty);
        //Signal event
        autoResetEvent.Set();
    }

    public static void LinearSearch( object state)
    {
        dynamic data = state;
        int[] x = data.Range;
        int valueToFind = data.ItemToFind;
        AutoResetEvent autoResetEvent = data.WaitHandle as
    AutoResetEvent;
        int foundIndex = -1;
        //Search for item linearly using for loop
        for (int i = 0; i < x.Length; i++)
        {
            if (valueToFind == x[i])
            {
                foundIndex = i;
            }
        }
        //store the result globally
        Interlocked.CompareExchange(ref findIndex, foundIndex, -1);
        Interlocked.CompareExchange(ref winnerAlgo, "LinearSearch",
          string.Empty);
        //Signal event
        autoResetEvent.Set();
    }
```

The following code calls both algorithms in parallel using `ThreadPool`:

```
    private static void AlgoSolverWaitAny()
    {
        WaitHandle[] waitHandles = new WaitHandle[]
        {
        new AutoResetEvent(false),
        new AutoResetEvent(false)
        };
        var itemToSearch = 15000;
        var range = Enumerable.Range(1, 100000).ToArray();
        ThreadPool.QueueUserWorkItem(new WaitCallback
          (LinearSearch),new {Range = range,ItemToFind =
          itemToSearch, WaitHandle= waitHandles[0] });
```

```
ThreadPool.QueueUserWorkItem(new WaitCallback(BinarySearch),
  new { Range = range, ItemToFind =
  itemToSearch, WaitHandle = waitHandles[1] });
WaitHandle.WaitAny(waitHandles);
Console.WriteLine($"Item found at index {findIndex} and faster
  algo is {winnerAlgo}" );
}
```

- `SignalAndWait`: This method is used to call `Set()` on a wait handle and calls `WaitOne` for another wait handle. In a multithreaded environment, this method can be utilized to release one thread at a time and then resets to wait for the next thread:

```
public static bool SignalAndWait (System.Threading.WaitHandle
  toSignal, System.Threading.WaitHandle toWaitOn);
```

Lightweight synchronization primitives

The .NET Framework also provides lightweight synchronization primitives, which are better in performance than their counterparts. They avoid dependency on kernel objects such as wait handles wherever possible, so they only work inside the process. These primitives should be used when the thread's wait time is short. We can divide them into two categories, both of which we'll look at in this section.

Slim locks

Slim locks are slim implementations of legacy synchronization primitives that can improve performance by reducing overheads.

The following table shows the legacy synchronization primitives and their slim counterparts:

Legacy	Slim
ReaderWriterLock	ReaderWriterLockSlim
Semaphore	SemaphoreSlim
ManualResetEvent	ManualResetEventSlim

Synchronization Primitives

Let's try to learn more about slim locks.

ReaderWriterLockSlim

`ReaderWriterLockSlim` is a lightweight implementation of `ReaderWriterLock`. It represents a lock that can be used to manage protected resources in a way that allows multiple threads to share read access while allowing only one thread write access.

The following example uses `ReaderWriterLockSlim` to protect access on a list that is shared by three reader threads and one writer thread:

```csharp
static ReaderWriterLockSlim _readerWriterLockSlim = new ReaderWriterLockSlim();
static List<int> _list = new List<int>();
private static void ReaderWriteLockSlim()
{
    Task writerTask = Task.Factory.StartNew( WriterTask);
    for (int i = 0; i < 3; i++)
    {
        Task readerTask = Task.Factory.StartNew(ReaderTask);
    }
}
static void WriterTask()
{
    for (int i = 0; i < 4; i++)
    {
        try
            {
            _readerWriterLockSlim.EnterWriteLock();
            Console.WriteLine($"Entered WriteLock on Task {Task.CurrentId}");
            int random = new Random().Next(1, 10);
            _list.Add(random);
            Console.WriteLine($"Added {random} to list on Task {Task.CurrentId}");
            Console.WriteLine($"Exiting WriteLock on Task {Task.CurrentId}");
            }
        finally
            {
            _readerWriterLockSlim.ExitWriteLock();
            }
        Thread.Sleep(1000);
    }
}
static void ReaderTask()
```

```
{
    for (int i = 0; i < 2; i++)
    {
        _readerWriterLockSlim.EnterReadLock();
        Console.WriteLine($"Entered ReadLock on Task {Task.CurrentId}");
        Console.WriteLine($"Items: {_list.Select(j=>j.ToString
()).Aggregate((a, b) =>
            a + "," + b)} on Task {Task.CurrentId}");
        Console.WriteLine($"Exiting ReadLock on Task {Task.CurrentId}");
        _readerWriterLockSlim.ExitReadLock();
        Thread.Sleep(1000);
    }
}
```

The output of this code is as follows:

```
Entered WriteLock on Task 1
Added 9 to list on Task 1
Exiting WriteLock on Task 1
Entered ReadLock on Task 2
Entered ReadLock on Task 4
Entered ReadLock on Task 3
Items: 9 on Task 3
Exiting ReadLock on Task 3
Items: 9 on Task 4
Exiting ReadLock on Task 4
Items: 9 on Task 2
Exiting ReadLock on Task 2
Entered WriteLock on Task 1
Added 3 to list on Task 1
Exiting WriteLock on Task 1
Entered ReadLock on Task 4
Entered ReadLock on Task 3
Items: 9,3 on Task 3
Exiting ReadLock on Task 3
Items: 9,3 on Task 4
Exiting ReadLock on Task 4
Entered ReadLock on Task 2
Items: 9,3 on Task 2
Exiting ReadLock on Task 2
Entered WriteLock on Task 1
Added 9 to list on Task 1
Exiting WriteLock on Task 1
Entered WriteLock on Task 1
Added 5 to list on Task 1
Exiting WriteLock on Task 1
```

Synchronization Primitives

SemaphoreSlim

`SemaphoreSlim` is a lightweight implementation of `semaphore`. It throttles access to a protected resource to a number of threads.

Here is a slim version of the `semaphore` program that we showed earlier in this chapter:

```
private static void ThrottlerUsingSemaphoreSlim()
{
    var range = Enumerable.Range(1, 12);
    SemaphoreSlim semaphore = new SemaphoreSlim(3, 3);
    range.AsParallel().AsOrdered().ForAll(i =>
    {
        try
        {
            semaphore.Wait();
            Console.WriteLine($"Index {i} making service call using Task {Task.CurrentId}");
            //Simulate Http call
            CallService(i);
            Console.WriteLine($"Index {i} releasing semaphore using Task {Task.CurrentId}");
        }
        finally
        {
            semaphore.Release();
        }
    });
}
private static void CallService(int i)
{
    Thread.Sleep(1000);
}
```

The difference we can see here, apart from replacing the `Semaphore` class with `SemaphoreSlim`, is that we now have the `Wait()` method instead of `WaitOne()`. This makes much more sense as we are allowing more than one thread to pass through.

Another important difference is that `SemaphoreSlim` is always created as a local `semaphore`, unlike `semaphore`, which can be created globally as well.

ManualResetEventSlim

`ManualResetEventSlim` is a lightweight implementation of `ManualResetEvent`. It has better performance and less overhead than `ManualResetEvent`.

We can create an object using the following syntax, just like `ManualResetEvent`:

```
ManualResetEventSlim manualResetEvent = new ManualResetEventSlim(false);
```

Just like other slim counterparts, one major difference here is that we have replaced the `WaitOne()` method with `Wait()`.

You can try running some `ManualResetEvent` demonstration code by making the preceding changes and see if it works.

Barrier and countdown events

The .NET Framework has some built-in signaling primitives that help us synchronize multiple threads without us having to write lots of synchronization logic. All the synchronization is handled internally by the provided data structures. In this section, let's discuss two very important signaling primitives: `CountDownEvent` and `Barrier`:

- **CountDownEvent**: The `System.Threading.CountDownEvent` class refers to an event that's signaled when its count becomes 0.

- **Barrier**: The `Barrier` class allows multiple threads to run without having the master thread controlling them. It creates a barrier that participating threads must wait in until all the threads have arrived. `Barrier` works well for cases where work needs to be carried out in parallel and in phases.

A case study using Barrier and CountDownEvent

As an example, let's say we need to fetch data from two services that are dynamically hosted. Before fetching the data from service one, we need to host it. Once the data has been fetched, it needs to be closed down. Only when service one has been closed down can we start service two and fetch data from it. The data needs to be fetched as quickly as possible. Let's create some code to meet the requirements of this scenario.

Create a `Barrier` with 5 participants:

```
static Barrier serviceBarrier = new Barrier(5);
```

Synchronization Primitives

Create two `CountdownEvents` that will trigger the start or close of services when six threads have passed through it. Five worker tasks will participate, along with a task that will manage the start or close of services:

```
static CountdownEvent serviceHost1CountdownEvent = new CountdownEvent(6);
static CountdownEvent serviceHost2CountdownEvent = new CountdownEvent(6);
```

Finally, create another `CountdownEvent` with a count of 5. This refers to the number of threads that can pass through before the event is signaled. `CountdownEvent` will trigger when all the worker tasks finish executing:

```
static CountdownEvent finishCountdownEvent = new CountdownEvent(5);
```

Here is our `serviceManagerTask` implementation:

```
Task serviceManager = Task.Factory.StartNew(() =>
    {
        //Block until service name is set by any of thread
        while (string.IsNullOrEmpty(_serviceName))
            Thread.Sleep(1000);
        string serviceName = _serviceName;
        HostService(serviceName);
        //Now signal other threads to proceed making calls to service1
        serviceHost1CountdownEvent.Signal();
        //Wait for worker tasks to finish service1 calls
        serviceHost1CountdownEvent.Wait();
        //Block until service name is set by any of thread
        while (_serviceName != "Service2")
            Thread.Sleep(1000);
        Console.WriteLine($"All tasks completed for service {serviceName}.");
        //Close current service and start the other service
        CloseService(serviceName);
        HostService(_serviceName);
        //Now signal other threads to proceed making calls to service2
        serviceHost2CountdownEvent.Signal();
        serviceHost2CountdownEvent.Wait();
        //Wait for worker tasks to finish service2 calls
        finishCountdownEvent.Wait();
        CloseService(_serviceName);
        Console.WriteLine($"All tasks completed for service {_serviceName}.");
    });
```

Here is the method that is executed by the worker tasks:

```
            private static void GetDataFromService1And2(int j)
            {
                _serviceName = "Service1";
                serviceHost1CountdownEvent.Signal();
                Console.WriteLine($"Task with id {Task.CurrentId} signalled countdown event and waiting for
                service to start");
                //Waiting for service to start
                serviceHost1CountdownEvent.Wait();
                Console.WriteLine($"Task with id {Task.CurrentId} fetching data from service ");
                serviceBarrier.SignalAndWait();
                //change servicename
                _serviceName = "Service2";
                //Signal Countdown event
                serviceHost2CountdownEvent.Signal();
                Console.WriteLine($"Task with id {Task.CurrentId} signalled countdown event and waiting for
                service to start");
                serviceHost2CountdownEvent.Wait();
                Console.WriteLine($"Task with id {Task.CurrentId} fetching data from service ");
                serviceBarrier.SignalAndWait();
                //Signal Countdown event
                finishCountdownEvent.Signal();
            }
        //Finally make worker tasks
        for (int i = 0; i < 5; ++i)
            {
                int j = i;
                tasks[j] = Task.Factory.StartNew(() =>
                {
                    GetDataFromService1And2(j);
                });
            }
            Task.WaitAll(tasks);
            Console.WriteLine("Fetch completed");
```

Synchronization Primitives

The output of the preceding code is as follows:

```
C:\Program Files\dotnet\dotnet.exe
Task with id 5 signaled countdown event and waiting for service to start
Task with id 6 signaled countdown event and waiting for service to start
Task with id 4 signaled countdown event and waiting for service to start
Task with id 3 signaled countdown event and waiting for service to start
Task with id 2 signaled countdown event and waiting for service to start
Service Service1 hosted
Task with id 2 fetching data from service
Task with id 5 fetching data from service
Task with id 3 fetching data from service
Task with id 6 fetching data from service
Task with id 4 fetching data from service
Task with id 6 signaled countdown event and waiting for service to start
Task with id 5 signaled countdown event and waiting for service to start
Task with id 4 signaled countdown event and waiting for service to start
Task with id 2 signaled countdown event and waiting for service to start
Task with id 3 signaled countdown event and waiting for service to start
All tasks completed for service Service1.
Service Service1 closed
Service Service2 hosted
Task with id 2 fetching data from service
Task with id 3 fetching data from service
Task with id 6 fetching data from service
Task with id 5 fetching data from service
Task with id 4 fetching data from service
Service Service2 closed
All tasks completed for service Service2.
Fetch completed
```

In this section, we have looked at various built-in signaling primitives that help make code synchronization easier without the need to lock ourselves as a developer. Blocking still comes at a performance cost as it involves context switching. In the next section, we will look at some spinning techniques that can help remove that context switching overhead.

SpinWait

At the beginning of this chapter, we mentioned that spinning is much more efficient than blocking for smaller waits. Spinning has fewer kernel overheads related to context switching and transitioning.

We can create a `SpinWait` object as follows:

```
var spin = new SpinWait();
```

Then, wherever we need to make a `spin`, we can just call the following command:

```
spin.SpinOnce();
```

SpinLock

Locks and interlocking primitives can significantly slow down performance if the wait time to get a lock is very low. SpinLock provides a lightweight, low-level alternative to locking. SpinLock is a value type, so if we want to use the same object in multiple places, we need to pass it by a reference. For performance reasons, even when SpinLock hasn't even acquired the lock, it yields the time slice of the thread so that the garbage collector can work efficiently. By default, SpinLock doesn't support thread tracking, which refers to determining which thread has acquired the lock. However, this feature can be turned on. This is only recommended for debugging and not for production as it reduces performance.

Create a SpinLock object as follows:

```
static SpinLock _spinLock = new SpinLock();
```

Create a method that will be called by various threads and update a global static list:

```
static List<int> _itemsList = new List<int>();
    private static void SpinLock(int number)
    {
        bool lockTaken = false;
        try
        {
            Console.WriteLine($"Task {Task.CurrentId} Waiting for lock");
            _spinLock.Enter(ref lockTaken);
            Console.WriteLine($"Task {Task.CurrentId} Updating list");
            _itemsList.Add(number);
        }
        finally
        {
            if (lockTaken)
            {
                Console.WriteLine($"Task {Task.CurrentId} Exiting Update");
                _spinLock.Exit(false);
            }
        }
    }
```

As you can see, the lock is acquired using `_spinLock.Enter(ref lockTaken)` and released via `_spinLock.Exit(false)`. Everything between these two statements will be executed as synchronized between all the threads.

Let's call this method in a parallel loop:

```
Parallel.For(1, 5, (i) => SpinLock(i));
```

Here is the synchronized output if we had used locking primitives:

```
Task 2 Waiting for lock
Task 3 Waiting for lock
Task 4 Waiting for lock
Task 1 Waiting for lock
Task 2 Updting list
Task 2 Exiting Update
Task 4 Updting list
Task 4 Exiting Update
Task 1 Updting list
Task 1 Exiting Update
Task 3 Updting list
Task 3 Exiting Update
```

As a rule of thumb, if we have small tasks, context switching can be completely avoided by using spinning.

Summary

In this chapter, we have learned about the synchronization primitives that are provided by .NET Core. Synchronized primitives are a must if you want to write parallel code and ensure that it is correct, even when multiple threads are working on it. Synchronization primitives come with performance overheads and the use of their slim counterparts is advised wherever possible.

We learned about signaling primitives as well, which can come in very handy when threads need to work on some external events. We also discussed the barrier and countdown events, which help us avoid code synchronization issues without the need to write additional logic. Finally, we introduced some spinning techniques, which take away performance overheads that arise from blocking code, that is, `SpinLock` and `SpinWait`.

In the next chapter, we will learn about the various data structures provided by .NET Core. These are synchronized automatically and are parallel at the same time.

Questions

1. Which of these can be used for cross-process synchronization?
   1. `Lock`
   2. `Interlocked.Increment`
   3. `Interlocked.MemoryBarrierProcessWide`
2. Which of these is not a valid memory barrier?
   1. Read memory barrier
   2. Half memory barrier
   3. Full memory barrier
   4. Read and execute memory barrier
3. From which of the following states can we not resume a thread?
   1. `WaitSleepJoin`
   2. `Suspended`
   3. `Aborted`
4. An unnamed `semaphore` can provide synchronization where?
   1. Within process
   2. Across process
5. Which of these constructs support tracking threads?
   1. `SpinWait`
   2. `SpinLock`

6
Using Concurrent Collections

In the last chapter, we saw some parallel programming implementations in which resources needed to be protected from concurrent access by multiple threads. Synchronization primitives are tricky to implement. Often, a shared resource is a collection that needs to be read and written by multiple threads. Since a collection can be accessed in a variety of ways (such as by using `Enumerate`, `Read`, `Write`, `Sort`, or `Filter`), it becomes tricky to write a custom collection with managed synchronization using primitives. Because of this, there has always been a need for thread-safe collections.

In this chapter, we will learn about various programming constructs available in C# that help in parallel development. The following are the high-level topics that will be covered in this chapter:

- An introduction to concurrent collections
- A multiple producer/consumer scenario

Technical requirements

You should have a good understanding of TPL and C#. The source code for this chapter is available on GitHub at `https://github.com/PacktPublishing/Hands-On-Parallel-Programming-with-C-8-and-.NET-Core-3/tree/master/Chapter06`.

An introduction to concurrent collections

From .NET Framework 4, a lot of thread-safe collections were added to the .NET repertoire. A new namespace, `System.Threading.Concurrent`, was also added. This included constructs like the following:

- `IProducerConsumerCollection<T>`
- `BlockingCollection<T>`
- `ConcurrentDictionary<TKey,TValue>`

When using the preceding structs, there is no need for any additional synchronization and both reading and updating can be done atomically.

Thread safety is not an entirely new concept in the case of collections. Even with older collections such as `ArrayList` and `Hashtable`, the `Synchronized` property was exposed, which made it possible to access these collections in a thread-safe manner. This, however, came with a performance hit, because to make the collection thread-safe, the entire collection was wrapped inside a lock with every read or update operation.

Concurrent collections wrap lightweight, slim synchronization primitives such as `SpinLock`, `SpinWait`, `SemaphoreSlim`, and `CountDownEvent`, hence making them less heavy on cores. As we already know, spinning is much more efficient than blocking for smaller wait times. Also, with built-in algorithms in place, if wait times increase, the lighter locks are converted into kernel locks.

Introducing IProducerConsumerCollection<T>

The producer and consumer collections are the collections that provide efficient lock-free alternatives to their generic counterparts, such as `Stack<T>` and `Queue<T>`. Any producer or consumer collection must allow the user to add items and remove items. .NET Framework provides the `IProducerConsumerCollection<T>` interface that represents thread-safe stacks, queues, and bags. The following are the classes that implement the interface:

- `ConcurrentQueue<T>`
- `ConcurrentStack<T>`
- `ConcurrentBag<T>`

Two important methods are provided by the interface: `TryAdd` and `TryTake`. The syntax of `TryAdd` is as follows:

```
bool TryAdd (T item);
```

The `TryAdd` method adds an item and returns `true`. If there is any problem with adding the item, it will return `false`.

The syntax of `TryTake` is as follows:

```
bool TryTake (out T item);
```

The `TryTake` method removes an item and returns `true`. If there is any problem with removing the item, it will return `false`.

Using ConcurrentQueue<T>

Concurrent queues can be used to solve producer/consumer scenarios in application programming. In the producer/consumer programming pattern, one or more threads produce data and one or more threads consume data. This leads to race conditions among threads. We can solve this problem via the following approaches:

- Using queues
- Using `ConcurrentQueue<T>`

Based on which thread (producer/consumer) has the responsibility to add/consume data, the producer-consumer pattern can be classified into the following:

- **Pure producer-consumer**, where a thread can either only produce data or only consume data but cannot do both
- **Mixed producer-consumer**, where any thread can produce or consume data at the same time

Let's try to solve a producer-consumer problem using queues first.

Using queues to solve a producer-consumer problem

In this example, we will create a producer and consumer scenario using queues that are defined in the `System.Collections` namespace. There will be multiple tasks that will attempt to read or write to a queue and we need to ensure that the reads and writes are atomic:

1. Let's first create `queue` and populate it with some data:

   ```
   Queue<int> queue = new Queue<int>();
   for (int i = 0; i < 500; i++)
   {
       queue.Enqueue(i);
   }
   ```

2. Declare a variable that will hold the final result:

   ```
   int sum = 0;
   ```

3. Next, we will create a parallel loop that will read the item from the queue using multiple tasks and add the sum in a thread-safe manner to the sum variable declared previously:

   ```
   Parallel.For(0, 500, (i) =>
   {
       int localSum = 0;
       int localValue;
       while (queue.TryDequeue(out localValue))
       {
           Thread.Sleep(10);
           localSum += localValue;
       }
       Interlocked.Add(ref sum, localSum);
   });
   Console.WriteLine($"Calculated Sum is {sum} and should be {Enumerable.Range(0, 500).Sum()}");
   ```

If we run the program, you will get the following output. As you can see, it's not the expected output due to the race condition that occurred between the tasks while trying to read concurrently:

```
C:\Program Files\dotnet\dotnet.exe
Calculated Sum is 125599 and should be 124750
```

Chapter 6

To make the preceding program thread-safe, we can lock the critical section by modifying the parallel loop code as follows:

```
Parallel.For(0, 500, (i) =>
{
    int localSum = 0;
    int localValue;
    Monitor.Enter(_locker);
    while (cq.TryDequeue(out localValue))
    {
        Thread.Sleep(10);
        localSum += localValue;
    }
    Monitor.Exit(_locker);
    Interlocked.Add(ref sum, localSum);
});
```

Similarly, we need to synchronize all read/write points to the queue that is exposed to the parallel code in more complex scenarios. The following is the output if we run the preceding code:

```
C:\Program Files\dotnet\dotnet.exe
Calculated Sum is 124750 and should be 124750
```

As you can see, everything works as expected, although there is an additional synchronization overhead that can lead to deadlock in frequent read or write scenarios.

Solving problems using concurrent queues

We can solve the producer-consumer problem by making use of the `System.Collections.Concurrent.ConcurrentQueue` class, which is a thread-safe version of a queue. Let's modify the preceding code by using a concurrent queue, as follows:

```
private static void ProducerConsumerUsingConcurrentQueues()
{
    // Create a Queue.
    ConcurrentQueue<int> cq = new ConcurrentQueue<int>();
    // Populate the queue.
    for (int i = 0; i < 500; i++){
        cq.Enqueue(i);
    }
    int sum = 0;
    Parallel.For(0, 500, (i) =>
    {
```

[159]

Using Concurrent Collections

```
        int localSum = 0;
        int localValue;
        while (cq.TryDequeue(out localValue))
        {
            Thread.Sleep(10);
            localSum += localValue;
        }
        Interlocked.Add(ref sum, localSum);
    });
    Console.WriteLine($"outerSum = {sum}, should be {Enumerable.Range(0, 500).Sum()}");
}
```

As you can see, we have just replaced Queue<int> with ConcurrentQueue<int> in the code we wrote previously, which had synchronization overheads. With ConcurrentQueue, we don't have to worry about other synchronization primitives.

Here is the output if we run the preceding code:

```
C:\Program Files\dotnet\dotnet.exe
Calculated Sum is 124750 and should be 124750
```

Just like Queue<T>, ConcurrentQueue<T> also works in **First In, First Out (FIFO)** mode.

Performance consideration – Queue<T> versus ConcurrentQueue<T>

We should use ConcurrentQueue in the following scenarios, where it has slight or very big performance benefits over queues:

- In a pure producer-consumer scenario, where the processing time for each item is very low
- In a pure producer-consumer scenario, where there is only one dedicated producer thread and only one dedicated consumer thread
- In pure as well as mixed producer-consumer scenarios where the processing time is 500 **FLOPS** (short for **Floating-Point Operations Per Second**) or more

We should use queues over concurrent queues in a mixed producer-consumer scenario where the processing time for each item is lower, to gain performance.

Using ConcurrentStack<T>

`ConcurrentStack<T>` is a concurrent version of `Stack<T>` and implements the `IProducerConsumerCollection<T>` interface. We can push or pop items from the stack, which works in the **Last In, First Out (LIFO)** format. It doesn't involve kernel-level locking, rather it relies on spinning and compare-and-swap operations to remove any contention.

The following are some important methods of the `ConcurrentStack<T>` class:

- `Clear`: Removes all elements from the collection
- `Count`: Returns the number of elements in the collection
- `IsEmpty`: Returns `true` if the collection is empty
- `Push (T item)`: Adds an element to the collection
- `TryPop (out T result)`: Removes an element from the collection, and returns `true` if the item is removed; otherwise, it returns `false`
- `PushRange (T [] items)`: Adds a range of items to the collection; the operation is performed atomically
- `TryPopRange (T [] items)`: Removes a range of items from the collection

Let's see how to create a concurrent stack instance.

Creating a concurrent stack

We can create a concurrent stack instance and add items as follows:

```
ConcurrentStack<int> concurrentStack = new ConcurrentStack<int>();
concurrentStack.Push (1);
concurrentStack.PushRange(new[] { 1,2,3,4,5});
```

We can get items from the stack as follows:

```
int localValue;
concurrentStack.TryPop(out localValue)
concurrentStack.TryPopRange (new[] { 1,2,3,4,5});
```

Here is the complete code that creates a concurrent stack, adds items, and iterates on items in parallel:

```
private static void ProducerConsumerUsingConcurrentStack()
{
    // Create a Queue.
    ConcurrentStack<int> concurrentStack = new ConcurrentStack<int>();
```

Using Concurrent Collections

```
    // Populate the queue.
    for (int i = 0; i < 500; i++){
        concurrentStack.Push(i);
    }
    concurrentStack.PushRange(new[] { 1,2,3,4,5});
    int sum = 0;
    Parallel.For(0, 500, (i) =>
    {
        int localSum = 0;
        int localValue;
        while (concurrentStack.TryPop(out localValue))
        {
            Thread.Sleep(10);
            localSum += localValue;
        }
        Interlocked.Add(ref sum, localSum);
    });
    Console.WriteLine($"outerSum = {sum}, should be 124765");
}
```

The output is as follows:

```
outerSum = 124765, should be 124765
```

Using ConcurrentBag<T>

`ConcurrentBag<T>` is an unordered collection, unlike `ConcurrentStack` and `ConcurrentQueues`, which orders the items while storing and retrieving them. `ConcurrentBag<T>` is optimized for scenarios in which the same threads work as a producer as well as a consumer. `ConcurrentBag` supports the work-stealing algorithm and maintains a local queue for each thread.

The following code creates `ConcurrentBag` and adds or gets items from it:

```
ConcurrentBag<int> concurrentBag = new ConcurrentBag<int>();
//Add item to bag
concurrentBag.Add(10);
int item;
//Getting items from Bag
concurrentBag.TryTake(out item)
```

The complete code is as follows:

```
static ConcurrentBag<int> concurrentBag = new ConcurrentBag<int>();
private static void ConcurrentBackDemo()
{
    ManualResetEventSlim manualResetEvent = new ManualResetEventSlim(false);
    Task producerAndConsumerTask = Task.Factory.StartNew(() =>
    {
        for (int i = 1; i <= 3; ++i)
        {
            concurrentBag.Add(i);
        }
        //Allow second thread to add items
        manualResetEvent.Wait();
        while (concurrentBag.IsEmpty == false)
        {
            int item;
            if (concurrentBag.TryTake(out item))
            {
                Console.WriteLine($"Item is {item}");
            }
        }
    });
    Task producerTask = Task.Factory.StartNew(() =>
    {
        for (int i = 4; i <= 6; ++i)
        {
            concurrentBag.Add(i);
        }
        manualResetEvent.Set();
    });
}
```

The output is as follows:

```
C:\Program Files\dotnet\dotnet.exe
Item is 3
Item is 2
Item is 1
Item is 4
Item is 5
Item is 6
```

As you are aware, every thread has a thread-local queue. Items 1, 2, and 3 are added to the local queue of `producerAndConsumerTask` and items 4, 5, and 6 are added to the local queue of `producerTask`. When `producerAndConsumerTask` has added items, we wait for `producerTask` to finish pushing its items. Once all the items are pushed, `producerAndConsumerTask` starts retrieving items. Since it has pushed 1, 2, and 3, which are in the local queue, it will process those first before moving to the local queue of `producerTask`.

Using BlockingCollection<T>

The `BlockingCollection<T>` class is a thread-safe collection that implements the `IProduceConsumerCollection<T>` interface. We can add or remove items from the collection concurrently without worrying about synchronization, which is handled automatically. There will be two threads: the producer and the consumer. The producer thread will produce data and we can limit the maximum number of items that can be produced by the producer thread before it enters sleep mode and is then blocked. The consumer thread will consume data and will be blocked when the collection is emptied. The producer thread is unblocked and the consumer thread removes some items from the collection. The consumer thread is unblocked when the producer thread adds some data to the collection.

There are two important aspects of blocking collections:

- **Bounding**: This means we can bound the collection to a maximum value after which no new objects can be added and the producer thread enters sleep mode.
- **Blocking**: This means we can block the consumer thread when the collection is empty.

Let's see how to create blocking collections.

Creating BlockingCollection<T>

The following code creates a new `BlockingCollection` that creates up to 10 items after which it goes to the blocked state before items are consumed by consumer threads:

```
BlockingCollection<int> blockingCollection = new
BlockingCollection<int>(10);
```

Items can be added to the collection as follows:

```
blockingCollection.Add(1);
blockingCollection.TryAdd(3, TimeSpan.FromSeconds(1))
```

Items can be removed from the collection as follows:

```
int item = blockingCollection.Take();
blockingCollection.TryTake(out item, TimeSpan.FromSeconds(1))
```

The producer thread calls the `CompleteAdding()` method when there are no more items to add. This method, in turn, sets the `IsAddingComplete` property of the collection to `true`.

The consumer thread uses the `IsCompleted` property when the collection is empty and `IsAddingComplete` is also `true`. This is an indication that all items have been processed and the producer will not add any more items.

The complete code is as follows:

```
BlockingCollection<int> blockingCollection = new
BlockingCollection<int>(10);
Task producerTask = Task.Factory.StartNew(() =>
{
    for (int i = 0; i < 5; ++i)
    {
        blockingCollection.Add(i);
    }
    blockingCollection.CompleteAdding();
});
Task consumerTask = Task.Factory.StartNew(() =>
{
    while (!blockingCollection.IsCompleted)
    {
        int item = blockingCollection.Take();
        Console.WriteLine($"Item retrieved is {item}");
    }
});
Task.WaitAll(producerTask, consumerTask);
```

Using Concurrent Collections

The output is as follows:

```
C:\Program Files\dotnet\dotn
Item retrieved is 0
Item retrieved is 1
Item retrieved is 2
Item retrieved is 3
Item retrieved is 4
```

Now, after introducing the concurrent collections, in the next section, we will try to take the producer-consumer scenario forward and learn about how to deal with multiple producers/consumers.

A multiple producer-consumer scenario

In this section, we will see how blocking collections work when there are multiple producer and consumer threads. For the sake of understanding, we will create two producers and one consumer. The producer threads will produce the items. Once all of the producer threads have called `CompleteAdding`, then the consumer will start reading items from the collection:

1. Let's start by creating a blocking collection with multiple producers:

    ```
    BlockingCollection<int>[] produceCollections = new
    BlockingCollection<int>[2];
    produceCollections[0] = new BlockingCollection<int>(5);
    produceCollections[1] = new BlockingCollection<int>(5);
    ```

2. Next, we will create two producer tasks that will add items to the producers:

    ```
    Task producerTask1 = Task.Factory.StartNew(() =>
    {
        for (int i = 1; i <= 5; ++i)
        {
            produceCollections[0].Add(i);
            Thread.Sleep(100);
        }
        produceCollections[0].CompleteAdding();
    });
    Task producerTask2 = Task.Factory.StartNew(() =>
    {
        for (int i = 6; i <= 10; ++i)
        {
            produceCollections[1].Add(i);
    ```

```
        Thread.Sleep(200);
    }
    produceCollections[1].CompleteAdding();
});
```

3. In the end, we will write consumer logic that will try to consume items from both producer collections as soon as the items are available:

```
while (!produceCollections[0].IsCompleted ||
!produceCollections[1].IsCompleted)
{
 int item;
 BlockingCollection<int>.TryTakeFromAny(produceCollections, out
item, TimeSpan.FromSeconds(1));
 if (item != default(int))
 {
 Console.WriteLine($"Item fetched is {item}");
 }
}
```

As you can see from the preceding code method, `TryTakeFromAny` tries to read the item from multiple producers and return when the item is available.

The output is as follows:

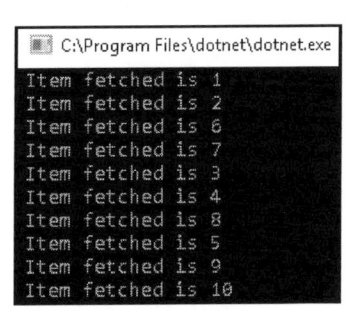

```
C:\Program Files\dotnet\dotnet.exe
Item fetched is 1
Item fetched is 2
Item fetched is 6
Item fetched is 7
Item fetched is 3
Item fetched is 4
Item fetched is 8
Item fetched is 5
Item fetched is 9
Item fetched is 10
```

In programming, we often come across a scenario where we need to store data concurrently as key-value pairs. For that purpose, the `ConcurrentDictionary` collection comes in handy, which we will introduce in the next section.

Using ConcurrentDictionary<TKey,TValue>

`ConcurrentDictionary<TKey, TValue>` represents a thread-safe dictionary. It is used to hold key-value pairs that can be read or written in a thread-safe manner.

Using Concurrent Collections

`ConcurrentDictionary` can be created as follows:

```
ConcurrentDictionary<int, int> concurrentDictionary = new
ConcurrentDictionary<int, int>();
```

Items can be added to the dictionary as follows:

```
concurrentDictionary.TryAdd(i, i * i);
string value = (i * i).ToString();
// Add item if not exist or else update
concurrentDictionary.AddOrUpdate(i, value,(key, val) => (key *
key).ToString());
//Fetches item with key 5 or if not exist than add key 5 with value 25
concurrentDictionary.GetOrAdd(5, "25");
```

Items can be removed from the dictionary as follows:

```
string value;
concurrentDictionary.TryRemove(5, out value);
```

Items in the dictionary can be updated as follows:

```
//If a key with a value of 25 is found, it will be updated to have a value
of 30     concurrentDictionary.TryUpdate(5, "30","25");
```

In the following code, we will create two producer threads that will add items to a dictionary. The producers will create some duplicate items and the dictionary will make sure they are added in a thread-safe manner without throwing duplicate key errors. Once the producer threads finish, the consumer will read all items using the `keys` or `values` property:

```
ConcurrentDictionary<int, string> concurrentDictionary = new
ConcurrentDictionary<int, string>();
Task producerTask1 = Task.Factory.StartNew(() =>
{
    for (int i = 0; i < 20; i++)
    {
        Thread.Sleep(100);
        concurrentDictionary.TryAdd(i, (i * i).ToString());
    }
});
Task producerTask2 = Task.Factory.StartNew(() =>
{
    for (int i = 10; i < 25; i++)
    {
        concurrentDictionary.TryAdd(i, (i * i).ToString());
    }
});
```

```
Task producerTask3 = Task.Factory.StartNew(() =>
{
    for (int i = 15; i < 20; i++)
    {
        Thread.Sleep(100);
        concurrentDictionary.AddOrUpdate(i, (i * i).ToString(),(key, value)
          => (key * key).ToString());
    }
});
Task.WaitAll(producerTask1, producerTask2);
Console.WriteLine("Keys are {0} ", string.Join(",",
concurrentDictionary.Keys.Select(c => c.ToString()).ToArray()));
```

The output is as follows:

```
C:\Program Files\dotnet\dotnet.exe
Keys are 0,1,2,3,4,5,6,7,8,9,10,11,12,13,14,15,16,17,18,19,20,21,22,23,24
```

In this section, we learned how concurrent collections can be very handy in producer-consumer scenarios. With concurrent collections, the onus is on getting code to behave correctly while dealing with multiple tasks without the need for custom synchronization overheads.

Summary

In this chapter, we discussed thread-safe collections that are part of .NET Framework. Concurrent collections are available in the `System.Collection.Concurrent` namespace and there are collections for various use cases in programming. Some common use cases require collections that include dictionaries, lists, bags, and so on.

We also discussed a producer and consumer scenario in which data is produced by some threads and consumed by other threads at the same time. Usually, in these scenarios, there are race conditions, but concurrent collections can deal with them effectively.

In the next chapter, we will learn about improving the performance of parallel code via lazy initialization patterns.

Questions

1. Which of these is not a concurrent collection?
    1. `ConcurrentQueue<T>`
    2. `ConcurrentBag<T>`
    3. `ConcurrentStack<T>`
    4. `ConcurrentList<T>`

2. When a thread can only produce data and another thread can only consume data but not both, what is this arrangement?
    1. Pure producer-consumer
    2. Mixed producer-consumer

3. A queue will perform best when the processing time for items is less in the case of a pure producer-consumer scenario.
    1. True
    2. False

4. Which is not a member of `ConcurrentStack`?
    1. `Push`
    2. `TryPop`
    3. `TryPopRange`
    4. `TryPush`

7
Improving Performance with Lazy Initialization

In the last chapter, we discussed thread-safe concurrent collections in C#. Concurrent collections help to improve the performance of parallel code without having a developer worry about synchronization overheads.

In this chapter, we will discuss some more concepts that help to improve the performance of code, both using custom implementations as well as using built-in constructs. Here are the topics we are going to discuss during this chapter:

- Introduction to lazy initialization concepts
- Introduction to System.Lazy<T>
- How to handle exceptions with the lazy pattern
- Lazy initialization with thread-local storage
- Reducing the overhead with lazy initializations

Let's get started by introducing the lazy initialization pattern.

Technical requirements

Readers should have a good understanding of TPL and C#. The source code for this chapter is available on GitHub at https://github.com/PacktPublishing/-Hands-On-Parallel-Programming-with-C-8-and-.NET-Core-3/tree/master/Chapter07.

Introducing lazy initialization concepts

Lazy loading is a commonly used design pattern in application programming wherein we defer the creation of an object until it is actually required in an application. Proper use of the lazy load pattern can significantly improve the performance of the application.

One of the common usages of this pattern can be seen in cache aside patterns. We use the cache aside pattern for objects whose creation is expensive either in terms of resources or memory. Instead of creating them multiple times, we create objects once and cache them for future use. This pattern is possible when the initialization of an object is moved out of the constructor to the method or properties. The object will only be initialized when the method or property is called for the first time by code. It will then be cached for subsequent calls. Take a look at the following code sample that initializes the underlying data member in the constructor:

```
class _1Eager
{
    //Declare a private variable to hold data
    Data _cachedData;
    public _1Eager()
    {
        //Load data as soon as object is created
        _cachedData = GetDataFromDatabase();
    }
    public Data GetOrCreate()
    {
        return _cachedData;
    }
    //Create a dummy data object every time this method gets called
    private Data GetDataFromDatabase()
    {
        //Dummy Delay
        Thread.Sleep(5000);
        return new Data();
    }
}
```

The problem with the preceding code is that the underlying data is initialized as soon as the object is created, even though the underlying object can only be accessed by calling the `GetOrCreate()` method. The program might not even call the method in some scenarios and so memory gets wasted.

Lazy loading can be implemented entirely using custom code, as shown in the following code sample:

```
class _2SimpleLazy
{
   //Declare a private variable to hold data
    Data _cachedData;

    public _2SimpleLazy()
    {
        //Removed initialization logic from constructor
        Console.WriteLine("Constructor called");
    }
    public Data GetOrCreate()
    {
        //Check is data is null else create and store for later use
        if (_cachedData == null)
        {
            Console.WriteLine("Initializing object");
            _cachedData = GetDataFromDatabase();
        }
        Console.WriteLine("Data returned from cache");
        //Returns cached data
        return _cachedData;
    }

    private Data GetDataFromDatabase()
    {
        //Dummy Delay
        Thread.Sleep(5000);
        return new Data();
    }
}
```

As you can see from the preceding code, we moved the initialization logic out from the constructor to the `GetOrCreate()` method, which checks whether the item is in the cache before returning it to the caller. Data is initialized if it is not present in the cache.

Here is the code calling the preceding method:

```
public static void Main(){
    _2SimpleLazy lazy = new _2SimpleLazy();
     var data = lazy.GetOrCreate();
     data = lazy.GetOrCreate();
}
```

Improving Performance with Lazy Initialization

The output will be as follows:

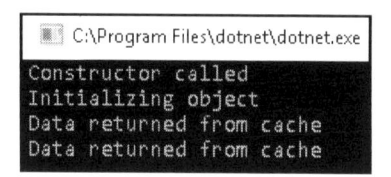

```
C:\Program Files\dotnet\dotnet.exe
Constructor called
Initializing object
Data returned from cache
Data returned from cache
```

The preceding code, although lazy, has the potential problem of multiloading. This means the call to the database might run multiple times if the `GetOrCreate()` method is called by multiple threads at the same time.

This can be improved by introducing locking, as shown in the following code example. For the cache aside pattern, it makes sense to use another pattern, double-checked locking:

```
class _2ThreadSafeSimpleLazy
{
    Data _cachedData;
    static object _locker = new object();

    public Data GetOrCreate()
    {
        //Try to Load cached data
        var data = _cachedData;
        //If data not created yet
        if (data == null)
        {
            //Lock the shared resource
            lock (_locker)
            {
                //Second try to load data from cache as it might have been
                //populate by another thread while current thread was
                // waiting for lock
                data = _cachedData;
                //If Data not cached yet
                if (data == null)
                {
                    //Load data from database and cache for later use
                    data = GetDataFromDatabase();
                    _cachedData = data;
                }
            }
        }
        return _cachedData;
    }
}
```

```
    private Data GetDataFromDatabase()
    {
        //Dummy Delay
        Thread.Sleep(5000);
        return new Data();
    }
    public void ResetCache()
    {
        _cachedData = null;
    }
}
```

The preceding code is self-explanatory. We can see that it is complex to create a lazy pattern from scratch. Fortunately, .NET Framework provides data structures for the lazy pattern.

Introducing System.Lazy<T>

.NET Framework provides a `System.Lazy<T>` class that has all of the benefits of lazy initialization without the need to worry about synchronization overheads. Objects created using `System.Lazy<T>` are deferred until they are accessed for the first time. With the custom lazy code explained in previous sections, we can see that we moved the initialization part from the constructor to the method/property to support lazy initialization. With `Lazy<T>`, we don't need to modify any code.

There are multiple ways to implement lazy initialization patterns in C#. These include the following:

- Construction logic encapsulated inside a constructor
- Construction logic passed as a delegate to `Lazy<T>`

In the subsequent sections, we will try to understand these scenarios in depth.

Construction logic encapsulated inside a constructor

Let's first try to implement the lazy initialization pattern with classes that encapsulate construction logic in the constructor. Let's say we have a `Data` class:

```
class DataWrapper
{
    public DataWrapper()
```

Improving Performance with Lazy Initialization

```
    {
        CachedData = GetDataFromDatabase();
        Console.WriteLine("Object initialized");
    }
    public Data CachedData { get; set; }
    private Data GetDataFromDatabase()
    {
        //Dummy Delay
        Thread.Sleep(5000);
        return new Data();
    }
}
```

As you can see, the initialization happens inside the constructor. If we use this class normally, using the following code, the object is initialized at the moment the `DataWrapper` object is created:

```
DataWrapper dataWrapper = new DataWrapper();
```

The output is as follows:

```
Object initialized
```

The preceding code can be converted using Lazy<T> as follows:

```
Console.WriteLine("Creating Lazy object");
Lazy<DataWrapper> lazyDataWrapper = new Lazy<DataWrapper>();
Console.WriteLine("Lazy Object Created");
Console.WriteLine("Now we want to access data");
var data = lazyDataWrapper.Value.CachedData;
Console.WriteLine("Finishing up");
```

As you can see, rather than creating an object directly, we wrapped it inside the lazy class. The constructor won't be called until we access the Value property of the Lazy object, as you can see from the following output:

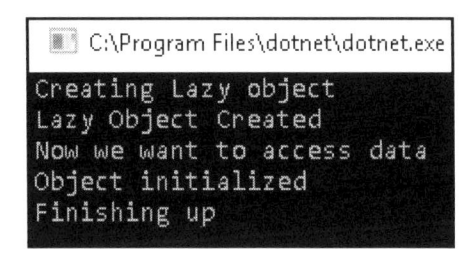

```
Creating Lazy object
Lazy Object Created
Now we want to access data
Object initialized
Finishing up
```

Construction logic passed as a delegate to Lazy<T>

Objects often don't hold construction logic as they are plain data models. We need to fetch data the first time the lazy objects are accessed while also passing the logic to fetch the data. This can be made possible using another overload of `System.Lazy<T>`, as follows:

```csharp
class _5LazyUsingDelegate
{
    public Data CachedData { get; set; }
    static Data GetDataFromDatabase()
    {
        Console.WriteLine("Fetching data");
        //Dummy Delay
        Thread.Sleep(5000);
        return new Data();
    }
}
```

In the following code, we are creating a `Lazy<Data>` object by passing the `Func<Data>` delegate:

```csharp
Console.WriteLine("Creating Lazy object");
Func<Data> dataFetchLogic = new Func<Data>(()=> GetDataFromDatabase());
Lazy<Data> lazyDataWrapper = new Lazy<Data>(dataFetchLogic);
Console.WriteLine("Lazy Object Created");
Console.WriteLine("Now we want to access data");
var data = lazyDataWrapper.Value;
Console.WriteLine("Finishing up");
```

As you can see from the preceding code, we passed `Func<T>` to the `Lazy<T>` constructor. The logic gets called on the first access to the `Value` property of the `Lazy<T>` instance, as shown in the following output:

```
C:\Program Files\dotnet\dotnet.exe
Creating Lazy object
Lazy Object Created
Now we want to access data
Object initialized
Finishing up
```

In addition to having a good idea about how to construct and use lazy objects in .NET, we also need to understand how to handle exceptions with lazy initialization patterns! Let's see the following section.

Handling exceptions with the lazy initialization pattern

Lazy objects are immutable by design. This means that they always return the same instance that they were initialized with. We have seen that we can pass initialization logic to `Lazy<T>` and that we can have initialization logic in the underlying object's constructor. What will happen if the construction/initialization logic is faulty and throws an exception? The behavior of `Lazy<T>` in this scenario depends on the value of the `LazyThreadSafetyMode` enumeration and your choice of `Lazy<T>` constructor. There are many ways to handle exceptions while working with lazy patterns. Some of these are as follows:

- No exceptions occur during initialization
- Random exception while initialization with exception caching
- Not caching exceptions

In the subsequent sections, we will try to understand these scenarios in depth.

No exceptions occur during initialization

The initialization logic runs once and the object is cached to be returned with subsequent access to the `Value` property. We have already seen this behavior while explaining `Lazy<T>` in a previous section.

Random exception while initialization with exception caching

In this case, since the underlying object is not created, the initialization logic will run on every call to the `Value` property. This is helpful in scenarios where the construction logic depends on external factors such as an internet connection while calling the external service. If the internet goes down momentarily, then the initialization call will fail, but subsequent calls can return the data. By default, `Lazy<T>` will cache exceptions for all parameterized constructor implementations, but it will not cache exceptions for the parameter less constructor implementation.

Chapter 7

Let's try to understand what happens when `Lazy<T>` initialization logic throws a random exception:

1. First, we create `Lazy<Data>` with the initialization logic provided by the `GetDataFromDatabase()` function, as follows:

   ```
   Func<Data> dataFetchLogic = new Func<Data>(() =>
   GetDataFromDatabase());
   Lazy<Data> lazyDataWrapper = new Lazy<Data>(dataFetchLogic);
   ```

2. Next, we access the `Value` property of `Lazy<Data>`, which will execute the initialization logic and throw an exception since the value of the counter is 0:

   ```
   try
   {
       data = lazyDataWrapper.Value;
       Console.WriteLine("Data Fetched on Attempt 1");
   }
   catch (Exception)
   {
       Console.WriteLine("Exception 1");
   }
   ```

3. Next, we increment the counter by one and again try to access the `Value` property. According to the logic, this time, it should return the `Data` object, but we see that the code again throws an exception:

   ```
   class _6_1_ExceptionsWithLazyWithCaching
   {
       static int counter = 0;
       public Data CachedData { get; set; }
       static Data GetDataFromDatabase()
       {
           if ( counter == 0)
           {
               Console.WriteLine("Throwing exception");
               throw new Exception("Some Error has occurred");
           }
           else
           {
               return new Data();
           }
       }

       public static void Main()
       {
           Console.WriteLine("Creating Lazy object");
   ```

[179]

Improving Performance with Lazy Initialization

```
            Func<Data> dataFetchLogic = new Func<Data>(() =>
             GetDataFromDatabase());
            Lazy<Data> lazyDataWrapper = new
             Lazy<Data>(dataFetchLogic);
            Console.WriteLine("Lazy Object Created");
            Console.WriteLine("Now we want to access data");
            Data data = null;
            try
            {
                data = lazyDataWrapper.Value;
                Console.WriteLine("Data Fetched on Attempt 1");
            }
            catch (Exception)
            {
                Console.WriteLine("Exception 1");
            }
            try
            {
                counter++;
                data = lazyDataWrapper.Value;
                Console.WriteLine("Data Fetched on Attempt 1");
            }
            catch (Exception)
            {
                Console.WriteLine("Exception 2");
                // throw;
            }
            Console.WriteLine("Finishing up");
            Console.ReadLine();
        }
    }
```

As you can see, the exception is thrown a second time, even though we increased the counter by one. This is because the exception value was cached and returned the next time the `Value` property is accessed. The output is shown as follows:

```
C:\Program Files\dotnet\dotnet.exe
Creating Lazy object
Lazy Object Created
Now we want to access data
Throwing exception
Exception 1
Exception 2
Finishing up
```

The preceding behavior is the same as creating `Lazy<T>` by passing `System.Threading.LazyThreadSafetyMode.None` as a second parameter:

```
Lazy<Data> lazyDataWrapper = new
Lazy<Data>(dataFetchLogic,System.Threading.LazyThreadSafetyMode.None);
```

Not caching exceptions

Let's change the initialization of `Lazy<Data>` in the preceding code to the following:

```
Lazy<Data> lazyDataWrapper = new
Lazy<Data>(dataFetchLogic,System.Threading.LazyThreadSafetyMode.Publication
Only);
```

This will allow the initialization logic to be run multiple times by different threads until one of the threads succeeds in running the initialization without any errors. If any thread throws an error during the initialization process in a multithreaded scenario, then all instances of the underlying object created by the completed threads are discarded and the exception is propagated to the `Value` property. In the case of a single thread, an exception will return when the initialization logic is re-run upon subsequent access of the `Value` property. The exceptions are not cached.

The output is as follows:

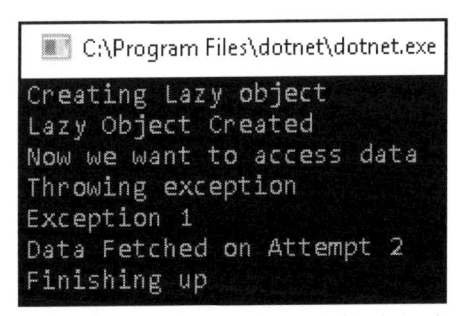

```
C:\Program Files\dotnet\dotnet.exe
Creating Lazy object
Lazy Object Created
Now we want to access data
Throwing exception
Exception 1
Data Fetched on Attempt 2
Finishing up
```

After seeing how to handle exceptions with the lazy initialization pattern, let's now learn about the usage of thread-local storage for lazy initialization.

Lazy initialization with thread-local storage

In multithreaded programming, we often want to create a variable that is local to a thread, which means that each thread will have its own copy of the data. This holds true for all local variables, but global variables are always shared across threads. In old versions of .NET, we used the `ThreadStatic` attribute to make a static variable behave as a thread-local variable. However, this is not foolproof and doesn't work well with initialization. If we are initializing a `ThreadStatic` variable, then only the first thread gets the initialized value, whereas the rest of the threads get the default value of the variable, which is 0 in the case of an integer. This can be demonstrated using the following code:

```
[ThreadStatic]
static int counter = 1;
public static void Main()
{
    for (int i = 0; i < 10; i++)
    {
        Task.Factory.StartNew(() => Console.WriteLine(counter));
    }
    Console.ReadLine();
}
```

In the preceding code, we initialized a static `counter` variable with a value of 1 and made it thread static so that every thread can have its own copy. For demonstration purposes, we created 10 tasks that print the value of the counter. According to the logic, all threads should print **1**, but as you can see from the following output, only one thread prints **1**, and the rest print **0**:

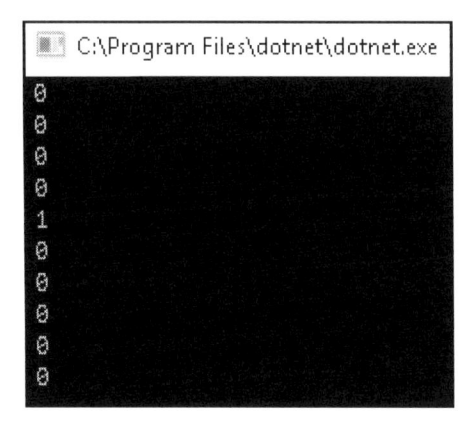

.NET Framework 4 provides `System.Threading.ThreadLocal<T>` as an alternative to `ThreadStatic` and works more like `Lazy<T>`. Using `ThreadLocal<T>`, we can create a thread-local variable that can be initialized by passing an initialization function, as follows:

```
static ThreadLocal<int> counter = new ThreadLocal<int>(() => 1);
public static void Main()
{
    for (int i = 0; i < 10; i++)
    {
        Task.Factory.StartNew(() => Console.WriteLine($"Thread with
            id {Task.CurrentId} has counter value as {counter.Value}"));
    }
    Console.ReadLine();
}
```

The output is as expected:

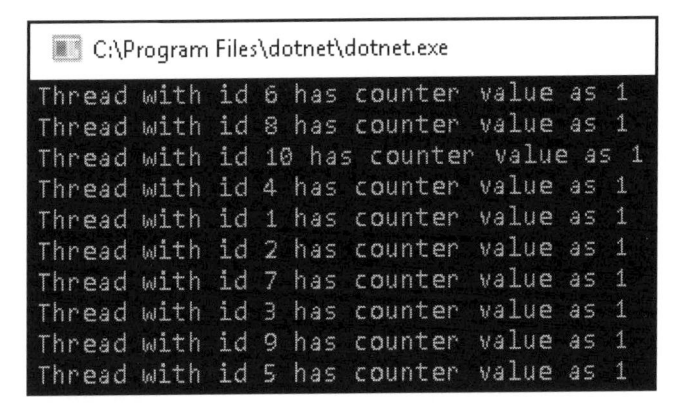

```
C:\Program Files\dotnet\dotnet.exe
Thread with id 6 has counter value as 1
Thread with id 8 has counter value as 1
Thread with id 10 has counter value as 1
Thread with id 4 has counter value as 1
Thread with id 1 has counter value as 1
Thread with id 2 has counter value as 1
Thread with id 7 has counter value as 1
Thread with id 3 has counter value as 1
Thread with id 9 has counter value as 1
Thread with id 5 has counter value as 1
```

The differences between `Lazy<T>` and `ThreadLocal<T>` are as follows:

- Each thread initializes the `ThreadLocal` variable using its own private data whereas, in the case of `Lazy<T>`, the initialization logic only runs once.
- Unlike `Lazy<T>`, the `Value` property in `ThreadLocal<T>` is read/write.
- In the absence of any initialization logic, the default value of `T` will be assigned to the `ThreadLocal` variable.

Reducing the overhead with lazy initializations

`Lazy<T>` uses a level of indirection by wrapping the underlying object. This can cause computational as well as memory issues. To avoid wrapping objects, we can use the static variant of `Lazy<T>` class, which is the `LazyInitializer` class.

We can use `LazyInitializer.EnsureInitialized` to initialize a data member that is passed via a reference as well as an initialization function, like we did with `Lazy<T>`.

The method can be called via multiple threads, but once a value is initialized, it will be used as a result for all of the threads. For the sake of demonstration, I have added a line to the console inside the initialization logic. Though the loop runs 10 times, the initialization will happen only once for single-thread execution:

```
static Data _data;
public static void Main()
{
    for (int i = 0; i < 10; i++)
    {
        Console.WriteLine($"Iteration {i}");
        // Lazily initialize _data
        LazyInitializer.EnsureInitialized(ref _data, () =>
        {
            Console.WriteLine("Initializing data");
            // Returns value that will be assigned in the ref parameter.
            return new Data();
        });
    }
    Console.ReadLine();
}
```

Here is the output:

```
C:\Program Files\dotnet\dotnet.exe
Iteration 0
Initializing data
Iteration 1
Iteration 2
Iteration 3
Iteration 4
Iteration 5
Iteration 6
Iteration 7
Iteration 8
Iteration 9
```

This is good for sequential execution. Let's try to modify the code and run it via multiple threads:

```
static Data _data;
static void Initializer()
{
    LazyInitializer.EnsureInitialized(ref _data, () =>
    {
        Console.WriteLine($"Task with id {Task.CurrentId} is
          Initializing data");
        // Returns value that will be assigned in the ref parameter.
        return new Data();
    });

    public static void Main()
    {
        Parallel.For(0, 10, (i) => Initializer());
        Console.ReadLine();
    }
}
```

Improving Performance with Lazy Initialization

Here is the output:

```
C:\Program Files\dotnet\dotnet.exe
Task with id 1 is Initializing data
Task with id 2 is Initializing data
Task with id 3 is Initializing data
Task with id 4 is Initializing data
Task with id 5 is Initializing data
Task with id 9 is Initializing data
Task with id 6 is Initializing data
Task with id 7 is Initializing data
Task with id 8 is Initializing data
```

As you can see, with multiple threads, there is a race condition and all threads end up initializing the data. We can avoid this race condition by modifying the program as follows:

```
static Data _data;
static bool _initialized;
static object _locker = new object();
static void Initializer()
{
    Console.WriteLine("Task with id {0}", Task.CurrentId);
    LazyInitializer.EnsureInitialized(ref _data, ref _initialized,
     ref _locker, () =>
    {
        Console.WriteLine($"Task with id {Task.CurrentId} is
         Initializing data");
        // Returns value that will be assigned in the ref parameter.
        return new Data();
    });
}
public static void Main()
{
    Parallel.For(0, 10, (i) => Initializer());
    Console.ReadLine();
}
```

As you can see from the preceding code, we have used an overload of the `EnsureInitialized` method and passed a Boolean variable and a `SyncLock` object as a parameter. This will ensure that the initialization logic can be executed only by one thread at a time, as demonstrated in the following output:

```
C:\Program Files\dotnet\dotnet.exe
Task with id 2
Task with id 1
Task with id 4
Task with id 3
Task with id 5
Task with id 6
Task with id 7
Task with id 8
Task with id 9
Task with id 2 is Initializing data
Task with id 2
```

In this section, we discussed how we can work around the overheads associated with `Lazy<T>` by utilizing another built-in static variant of `Lazy<T>` known as the `LazyInitializer` class.

Summary

In this chapter, we discussed various aspects of lazy loading and the data structures provided by .NET Framework to make lazy loading easier to implement.

Lazy loading can significantly improve the performance of applications by reducing memory footprints as well as saving on computing resources by stopping duplicate initialization. We have a choice to either create lazy from scratch using `Lazy<T>` or avoid complexity by using the static `LazyInitializer` class. With optimal usage of thread storages and good exception handling logic, these are certainly great tools for developers.

In the next chapter, we will start discussing asynchronous programming approaches available in C#.

Questions

1. Lazy initialization always involves creation object in the constructor.
    1. True
    2. False
2. In the lazy initialization pattern, object creation is deferred until it's actually needed.
    1. True
    2. False
3. Which of these can be used to create lazy objects that do not cache exceptions?
    1. `LazyThreadSafetyMode.DoNotCacheException`
    2. `LazyThreadSafetyMode.PublicationOnly`
4. Which attribute can be used to create a variable that's local to a thread?
    1. `ThreadLocal`
    2. `ThreadStatic`
    3. Both

Section 3: Asynchronous Programming Using C#

In this section, you will learn about another important aspect of making performant programs (using asynchronous programming techniques) while keeping an eye on how this was done in earlier versions compared to the newer `async` and `await` constructs.

This section comprises the following chapters:

- Chapter 8, *Introduction to Asynchronous Programming*
- Chapter 9, *Async, Await, and Task-Based Asynchronous Programming Basics*

8
Introduction to Asynchronous Programming

In the previous chapters, we have seen how parallel programming works. Parallelism is about creating small tasks called units of work that can be executed simultaneously by one or more application threads. Since threads run inside the application process, they notify the called thread once they finish using delegates.

In this chapter, we will start by introducing the difference between synchronous code and asynchronous code. Then, we'll discuss when to use asynchronous code and when to avoid it. We will also discuss how asynchronous patterns have evolved over time. Finally, we will see how new features in parallel programming help us get around the complexities of asynchronous code.

In this chapter, we'll cover the following topics:

- Synchronous versus asynchronous code
- When to use asynchronous programming
- When to avoid asynchronous programming
- Problems you can solve using asynchronous code
- Asynchronous patterns in early versions of C#

Technical requirements

To complete this chapter, you should have a good understanding of TPL and C#. The source code for this chapter is available on GitHub at `https://github.com/PacktPublishing/Hands-On-Parallel-Programming-with-C-8-and-.NET-Core-3/tree/master/Chapter08`.

Types of program execution

At any point in time, program flow can either be synchronous or asynchronous. Synchronous code is easier to write and maintain but comes with performance overheads and UI responsiveness issues. Asynchronous code improves the performance and responsiveness of an application as a whole but, in turn, is difficult to write, debug, and maintain.

We'll understand the synchronous and asynchronous way of program execution in detail in the following subsections.

Understanding synchronous program execution

In the case of synchronous execution, control never moves out of the calling thread. Code is executed one line at a time, and, when a function is called, the calling thread waits for the function to finish executing before executing the next line of code. Synchronous programming is the most commonly used method of programming and it works well due to the increase in CPU performance we have seen over the past few years. With faster processors, the code completes sooner.

With parallel programming, we have seen that we can create multiple threads that can run concurrently. We can start many threads but also make the main program flow synchronous by calling structures such as `Thread.Join` and `Task.Wait`. Let's take a look at an example of synchronous code:

1. We start the application thread by calling the `M1()` method.
2. At line 3, `M1()` calls `M3()` synchronously.
3. The moment the `M2()` method is called, the control execution transfers to the `M1()` method.
4. Once the called method (`M2`) is finished, the control returns to the main thread, which executes the rest of the code in `M1()`, that is, lines 4 and 5.
5. The same thing happens on line 5 with a call to `M2`. Line 6 executes when `M2` has finished.

Chapter 8

The following is a diagrammatic representation of synchronous code execution:

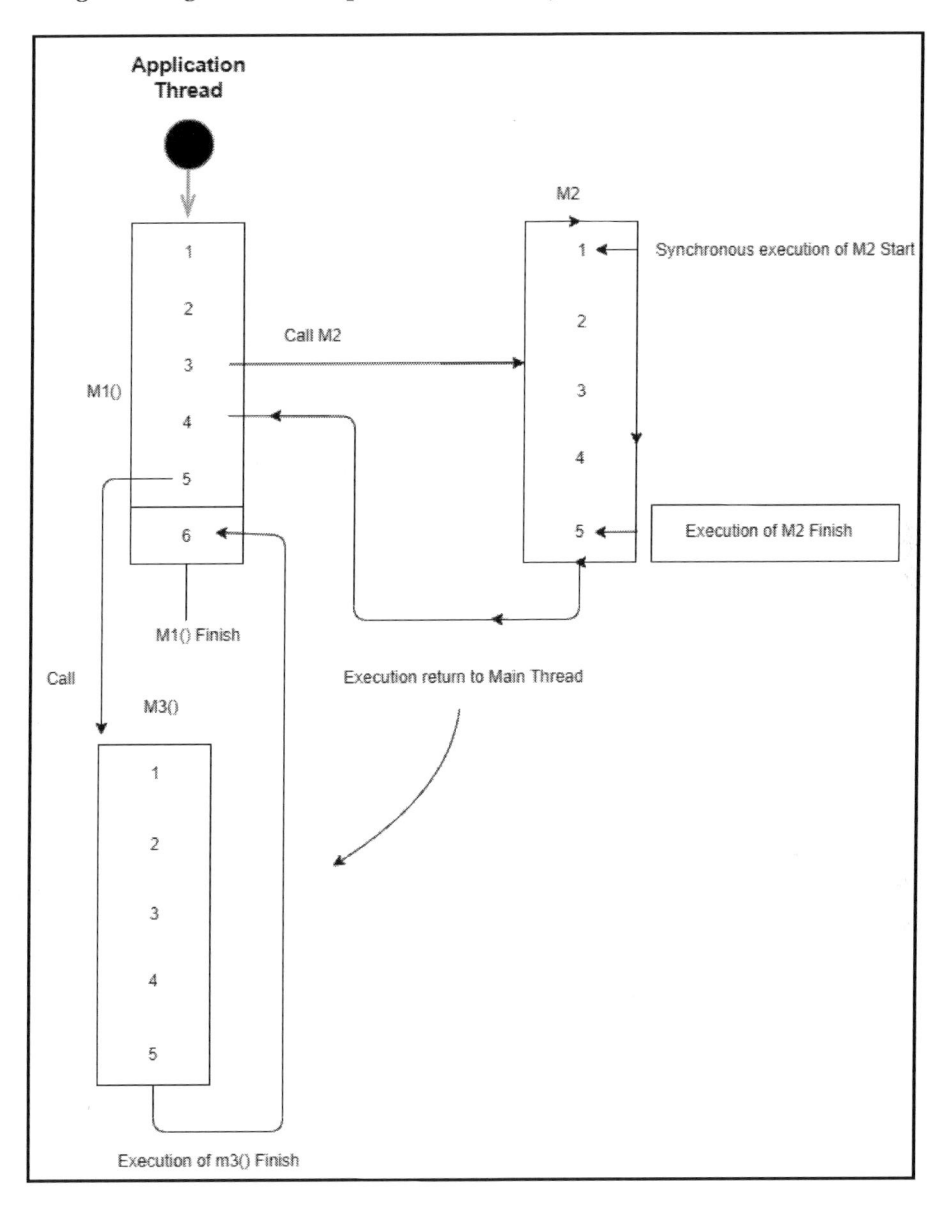

In the next section, we will try to understand more about writing asynchronous code, which will help us compare both program flows.

Understanding asynchronous program execution

The asynchronous model allows us to execute multiple tasks concurrently. If we call a method asynchronously, the method is executed in the background while the thread that is called returns immediately and executes the next line of code. The asynchronous method may or may not create a thread, depending on the type of task we're dealing with. When the asynchronous method finishes, it returns the result to the program via callbacks. An asynchronous method can be void, in which case we don't need to specify callbacks.

The following is a diagram showing a caller thread executing the M1() method, which calls an async method called M2():

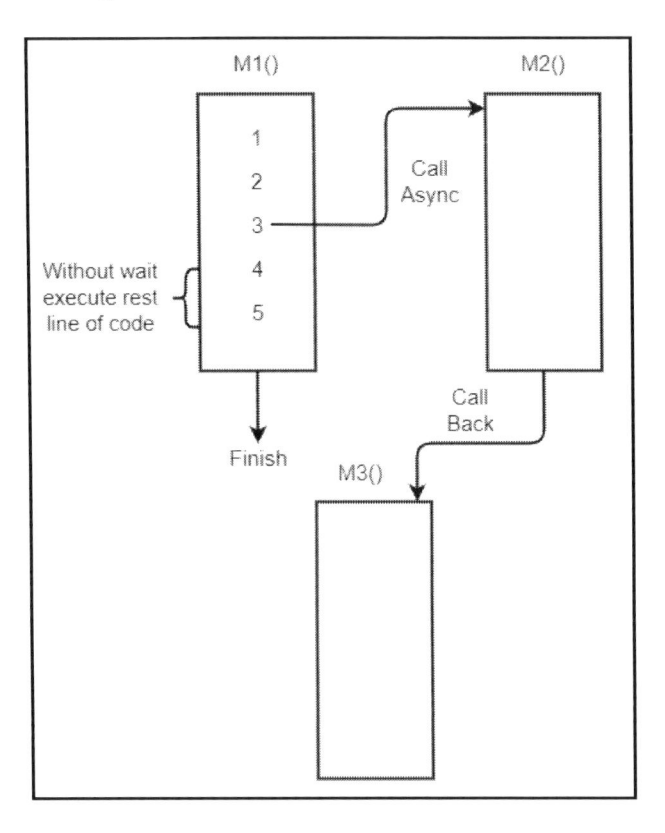

Contrary to the previous approach, here, caller thread doesn't wait for M2() to finish. If there is any output that needs to be utilized from M2(), it needs to be put into some other method, say, M3(), here. This is what happens:

1. While executing M1(), the caller thread makes asynchronous calls to M2().
2. The caller thread provides a callback function, say, M3(), while calling M2().
3. The caller thread doesn't wait for M2() to finish; instead, it finishes the rest of the code in M1() (if there is any to finish).
4. M2() will be executed by the CPU either instantly in a separate thread or at a later date.
5. Once M2() finishes, M3() is called, which receives output from M2() and processes it.

As you can see, it's easy to understand the synchronous program's execution, whereas asynchronous code comes with code branching. We will learn how to mitigate this complexity using the async and await keywords in Chapter 9, *Async, Await, and Task-Based Asynchronous Programming Basics*.

When to use asynchronous programming

There are many situations in which **Direct Memory Access (DMA)** is used to access the host system or I/O operations (such as files, databases, or network access) are used, which is where processing is done by the CPU rather than the application thread. In the preceding scenario, the calling thread makes a call to the I/O API and waits for the task to complete by moving to a blocked state. When the task is completed by the CPU, the thread is unblocked and finishes the rest of the method.

Using asynchronous methods, we can improve the application's performance and responsiveness. We can also execute a method via a different thread.

Writing asynchronous code

Asynchronous programming is not new to C#. We used to write asynchronous code in earlier versions of C# using the BeginInvoke method of the Delegate class, as well as by using the IAsyncResult interface implementations. With the introduction of TPL, we started writing asynchronous code using the Task class. From C# 5.0 onward, the async and await keywords have been the preferred choice for developers writing asynchronous code.

Introduction to Asynchronous Programming

We can write asynchronous code in the following ways:

- Using the `Delegate.BeginInvoke()` method
- Using the `Task` class
- Using the `IAsyncResult` interface
- Using the `async` and `await` keywords

In the subsequent sections, we'll look at each of these in detail with code examples, except for the `async` and `await` keywords – *Chapter 9*, *Async, Await, and Task-Based Asynchronous Programming Basics*, is dedicated to them!

Using the BeginInvoke method of the Delegate class

Using `Delegate.BeginInvoke` is no longer supported in .NET Core, but we will look at it here in terms of backward compatibility with earlier versions of .NET.

We can use the `Delegate.BeginInvoke` method to call any method asynchronously. This can be done to improve the UI's performance if some tasks need to be moved from the UI thread into the background.

Let's look at a `Log` method as an example. The following code works synchronously and writes logs. For the sake of demonstration, the logging code has been removed and replaced with a dummy 5-second delay, after which the `Log` method prints a line to the console:

Here is a dummy `Log` method that takes 5 seconds to finish:

```
private static void Log(string message)
{
    //Simulate long running method
    Thread.Sleep(5000);
    //Log to file or database
    Console.WriteLine("Logging done");
}
```

Here is the call to the `Log` method from the `Main` method:

```
static void Main(string[] args)
{
    Console.WriteLine("Starting program");
    Log("this information need to be logged");
    Console.WriteLine("Press any key to exit");
    Console.ReadLine();
}
```

Clearly, a 5-second delay for writing logs is too long. Since we don't expect any output from the `Log` method (writing to the console is just for demonstration purposes), it makes sense to call it asynchronously and return the response to the caller immediately.

The following is the output of the program as it is currently:

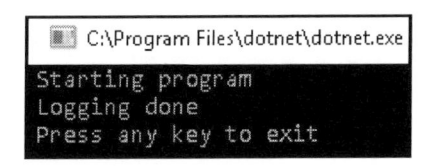

```
C:\Program Files\dotnet\dotnet.exe
Starting program
Logging done
Press any key to exit
```

We can add a `Log` method call to the preceding method. Then, we can wrap the `Log` method call inside a delegate and call the `BeginInvoke` method on the delegate, as follows:

```
//Log("this information need to be logged");
Action logAction = new Action(()=> Log("this information need to be
logged"));               logAction.BeginInvoke(null,null);
```

This time, when we execute the code, we will see asynchronous behavior in older versions of .NET. In .NET Core, however, the code breaks at runtime with the following error message:

`System.PlatformNotSupportedException: 'Operation is not supported on this platform.'`

In .NET Core, wrapping the synchronous methods into async delegates is no longer supported for two main reasons:

- Async delegates use an `IAsyncResult`-based async pattern, which is not supported by .NET Core base class libraries.
- Async delegates are not possible without `System.Runtime.Remoting`, which is also not supported in .NET Core.

Using the Task class

Another way to implement asynchronous programming in .NET Core is to use the `System.Threading.Tasks.Task` class, as we mentioned earlier. The preceding code can be changed to the following:

```
// Log("this information need to be logged");
Task.Factory.StartNew(()=> Log("this information need to be logged"));
```

Introduction to Asynchronous Programming

This will give us the required output without changing too much of the current code flow:

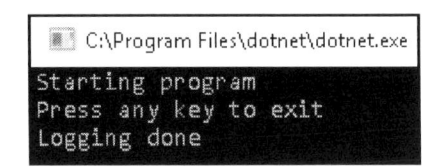

```
C:\Program Files\dotnet\dotnet.exe
Starting program
Press any key to exit
Logging done
```

We discussed `Task` in Chapter 2, *Task Parallelism*. The `Task` class provides us with a very powerful way to implement task-based asynchronous patterns.

Using the IAsyncResult interface

The `IAsyncResult` interface has been used to implement asynchronous programming in older versions of C#. The following is some example code that works well in earlier versions of .NET:

1. First, we create `AsyncCallback` that will be executed when the async method finishes:

    ```
    AsyncCallback callback = new AsyncCallback(MyCallback);
    ```

2. Then, we create a delegate that will execute an `Add` method with the parameters that are passed. Once finished, it will execute the callback method wrapped by `AsyncCallBack`:

    ```
    SumDelegate d = new SumDelegate(Add);
    d.BeginInvoke(100, 200, callback, state);
    ```

3. When the `MyCallBack` method is called, it returns the `IAsyncResult` instance. To get the underlying result, state, and callback, we need to cast the `IAsyncResult` instance to `AsyncResult`:

    ```
    AsyncResult ar = (AsyncResult)result;
    ```

4. Once we have `AsyncResult`, we can call `EndInvoke` to get the values that have been returned by the `Add` method:

    ```
    int i = d.EndInvoke(result);
    ```

Here is the complete code:

```csharp
using System.Runtime.Remoting.Messaging;
public delegate int SumDelegate(int x, int y);

static void Main(string[] args)
{
    AsyncCallback callback = new AsyncCallback(MyCallback);
    int state = 1000;
    SumDelegate d = new SumDelegate(Add);
    d.BeginInvoke(100, 200, callback, state);
    Console.WriteLine("Press any key to exit");
    Console.ReadLine();
}
public static int Add(int a, int b)
{
    return a + b;
}
public static void MyCallback(IAsyncResult result)
{
    AsyncResult ar = (AsyncResult)result;
    SumDelegate d = (SumDelegate)ar.AsyncDelegate;
    int state = (int)ar.AsyncState;
    int i = d.EndInvoke(result);
    Console.WriteLine(i);
    Console.WriteLine(state);
    Console.ReadLine();
}
```

Unfortunately, .NET Core has no support for `System.Runtime.Remoting` and so the preceding code will not work in .NET Core. We can only use task-based asynchronous patterns for all `IAsyncResult` scenarios:

```csharp
FileInfo fi = new FileInfo("test.txt");
            byte[] data = new byte[fi.Length];
            FileStream fs = new FileStream("test.txt", FileMode.Open,
FileAccess.Read, FileShare.Read, data.Length, true);
            // We still pass null for the last parameter because
            // the state variable is visible to the continuation delegate.
            Task<int> task = Task<int>.Factory.FromAsync(
                    fs.BeginRead, fs.EndRead, data, 0, data.Length, null);
            int result = task.Result;
            Console.WriteLine(result);
```

Introduction to Asynchronous Programming

The preceding code reads data from the file using the `FileStream` class. `FileStream` implements `IAsyncResult` and thus supports the `BeginRead` and `EndRead` methods. Then, we used the `Task.Factory.FromAsync` method to wrap `IAsyncResult` and return the data.

When not to use asynchronous programming

Asynchronous programming can be very beneficial when it comes to creating a responsive UI and improving the application's performance. There are, however, scenarios in which asynchronous programming should be avoided as it may reduce performance and increase the complexity of the code. In the following subsections, we'll go through a few situations in which it is best not to use asynchronous programming.

In a single database without connection pooling

In cases where we have a single database server that doesn't have connection pooling enabled, asynchronous programming will have no benefits. With long-running connections and multiple requests, there will be performance bottlenecks, irrespective of whether calls are made synchronously or asynchronously.

When it is important that the code is easy to read and maintain

When using the `IAsyncResult` interface, we have to break down the source method into two methods: `BeginMethodName` and `EndMethodName`. Changing the logic in this way can take a lot of time and effort and make the code hard to read, debug, and maintain.

For simple and short-running operations

We need to consider how much time the code is taking while it's running synchronously. If it isn't taking too long, it makes sense to keep the code synchronous as making code asynchronous comes with a small performance hit that would not be beneficial for small gains.

For applications with lots of shared resources

If your application is using lots of shared resources, such as global variables or system files, it makes sense to keep the code synchronous; otherwise, we will end up reducing the performance benefits. Just like shared resources, we need to apply synchronization primitives that can reduce performance with multiple threads. Sometimes, single-threaded applications can be more performant than their multithreaded counterparts.

Problems you can solve using asynchronous code

Let's go through a few situations where asynchronous programming can be handy to improve the responsiveness of the application and the performance of both the application and the server. Some situations are as follows:

- **Logging and auditing**: Logging and auditing are cross-cutting concerns for applications. If you happen to write your own code for logging and auditing, then calls to the server become slow as they need to write back the logs as well. We can make logging and auditing asynchronous and we should make the implementation stateless wherever possible. This will make sure that callbacks can be returned in a static context so that calls can continue to execute while the response returns to the browser.
- **Service calls**: Web service calls and database calls can be made asynchronous because, once we make a call to the service/database, the control leaves the current application and goes to the CPU, which makes the network call. The caller thread goes into a blocked state. Once the response from the service call comes back, the CPU receives it and raises an event. The calling thread is unblocked and starts further execution. As a pattern, you are likely to have seen that all service proxies return asynchronous methods.
- **Creating responsive UIs**: There may be scenarios in programs where a user clicks a button to save data. Saving data can involve multiple small tasks: reading data from the UI into models, making a connection to a database, and making calls to the database to update the data. This can take a long time and if these calls are made on a UI thread, then the thread is blocked until this completes. This means the user won't be able to do anything on the UI until the call is returned. We can improve the user experience by making asynchronous calls.

- CPU-bound applications: With the advent of new technology and support in .NET, we can now write machine learning, ETL processing, and cryptocurrency mining code in .NET. These tasks are highly CPU-intensive and it makes sense to make these programs asynchronous.

> **Asynchronous patterns in early versions of C#**
>
> In early versions of .NET, two patterns were supported to perform I/O-bound and compute-bound operations:
>
> - **Asynchronous Programming Model (APM)**
> - **Event-Based Asynchronous Pattern (EAP)**
>
> We discussed both of these approaches in detail in `Chapter 2`, *Task Parallelism*. We also learned how to convert these legacy implementations into task-based asynchronous patterns.

Now, let's recall what we've covered in this chapter.

Summary

In this chapter, we discussed what asynchronous programming is and why it makes sense to write asynchronous code. We also discussed scenarios where asynchronous programming can be implemented and where it should be avoided. Finally, we covered various asynchronous patterns that have been implemented in TPL.

Asynchronous programming, if used correctly, can really enhance the performance of server-side applications by efficiently utilizing threads. It also improves the responsiveness of desktop/mobile applications.

In the next chapter, we will discuss the asynchronous programming primitives that are provided by the .NET Framework.

Questions

1. _____ code is easier to write, debug, and maintain.
    1. Synchronous
    2. Asynchronous
2. In what scenario should you use asynchronous programming?
    1. File I/O
    2. Database with connection pooling
    3. Network I/O
    4. Database without connection pooling
3. Which approach can be used to write async code?
    1. `Delegate.BeginInvoke`
    2. `Task`
    3. `IAsyncResult`
4. Which of these cannot be used to write async code in .NET Core?
    1. `IAsyncResult`
    2. `Task`

9
Async, Await, and Task-Based Asynchronous Programming Basics

In the previous chapter, we introduced asynchronous programming practices and solutions available in C#, even prior to .NET Core. We also discussed scenarios where asynchronous programming can be handy, and where it should be avoided.

In this chapter, we will dig more deeply into asynchronous programming, and will introduce two keywords that make writing asynchronous code very easy. We will be covering the following topics in this chapter:

- Introduction to `async` and `await`
- Async delegates and lambda expressions
- The **Task-Based Asynchronous Pattern (TAP)**
- Exception handling in asynchronous code
- Async with PLINQ
- Measuring async code performance
- Guidelines for using async code

Let's start with an introduction to the `async` and `await` keywords, which were first introduced in C# 5.0 and adopted in .NET Core as well.

Technical requirements

Readers should have a good understanding of the **Task Parallel Library** (**TPL**) and C#. The source code for this chapter is available on GitHub at `https://github.com/PacktPublishing/-Hands-On-Parallel-Programming-with-C-8-and-.NET-Core-3/tree/master/Chapter09`.

Introducing async and await

`async` and `await` are two very popular keywords among .NET Core developers writing asynchronous code with the new asynchronous APIs provided by .NET Framework. They are used for marking code when calling asynchronous operations. In the last chapter, we discussed the challenges of converting a synchronous method into an asynchronous one. Previously, we did this by breaking down the method into two methods, `BeginMethodName` and `EndMethodName`, which can be called asynchronously. This approach makes the code clumsy and difficult to write, debug, and maintain. With the `async` and `await` keywords, however, the code can stay how it was in the synchronous implementation, with only small changes required. All the difficult work of breaking down the method, executing the asynchronous method, and getting the response back to the program is done by the compiler.

All new I/O APIs provided by .NET Framework support task-based asynchrony, which we discussed in the previous chapter. Let's now try to understand a few scenarios involving I/O operations, wherein we can take advantage of the `async` and `await` keywords. Let's say we want to download data from a public API that returns data in JSON format. In older versions of C#, we can write synchronous code using the `WebClient` class available in the `System.Net` namespace, as follows.

First, add a reference to the `System.Net` assembly:

```
WebClient client = new WebClient();
string reply = client.DownloadString("http://www.aspnet.com");
Console.WriteLine(reply);
```

Next, create an object of the `WebClient` class and call the `DownloadString` method by passing the URL of the page to download. The method will run synchronously, and the calling thread will be blocked until the download operation is finished. This can hamper the performance of the server (if used in server-side code) and the responsiveness of the application (if used in Windows application code).

To improve performance and responsiveness, we can use the asynchronous version of the `DownloadString` method, which was introduced much later.

Here is a method that creates a download request for a remote resource that is `http://www.aspnet.com` and subscribes to the `DownloadStringCompleted` event, rather than waiting for the download to complete:

```
private static void DownloadAsynchronously()
{
    WebClient client = new WebClient();
    client.DownloadStringCompleted += new
    DownloadStringCompletedEventHandler(DownloadComplete);
    client.DownloadStringAsync(new Uri("http://www.aspnet.com"));
}
```

And here is the `DownloadComplete` event handler, which gets fired when the download is finished:

```
private static void DownloadComplete(object sender,
DownloadStringCompletedEventArgs e)
{
    if (e.Error != null)
    {
        Console.WriteLine("Some error has occurred.");
        return;
    }
    Console.WriteLine(e.Result);
    Console.ReadLine();
}
```

In the preceding code, we have used the **Event-Based Asynchronous Pattern (EAP)**. As you can see, we have subscribed to the `DownloadCompleted` event, which will be raised by the `WebClient` class once the download is finished. Then, we have made a call to the `DownloadStringAsync` method, which will call the code asynchronously and return immediately, avoiding the need to block the thread. When the download finishes in the background, the `DownloadComplete` method will be called, and we can receive either the error, using the `e.Error` property, or the data, using the `e.Result` property of `DownloadStringCompletedEventArgs`.

Async, Await, and Task-Based Asynchronous Programming Basics

If we run the preceding code in a Windows application, the results will be as expected, but the response will always be received by a worker thread (which executes in the background), and not by the main thread. As Windows application developers, we need to be mindful of the fact that we cannot update the UI controls from the `DownloadComplete` method, and that all such calls need to be delegated back to the main UI thread using techniques such as Invoke in classic Windows Forms, or Dispatcher in **Windows Presentation Foundation** (**WPF**). The best thing about using the Invoke/Dispatcher approach is that the main thread is never blocked, and the application is, therefore, more responsive as a whole.

In the code samples accompanying this book, we have included scenarios for Windows Forms as well as for WPF, although .NET Core doesn't yet support Windows applications or WPF. This support is expected to be introduced in the next version of Visual Studio, VS 2019.

Let's try to run the preceding code in a .NET Core console application from the main thread, as follows:

```
public static void Main()
    {
     DownloadAsynchronously();
    }
```

We can modify the `DownloadComplete` method by adding a `Console.WriteLine` statement, as follows:

```
private static void DownloadComplete(object sender,
DownloadStringCompletedEventArgs e)
        {
            ...
            ...
            ...
            Console.ReadLine() ;//Added this line
        }
```

According to the logic, the program should download the page asynchronously, print the output, and wait for the user input before it terminates. When we run the preceding code, we will see that the program terminates without printing anything and without waiting for the user input. Why did this happen?

As already stated, the main thread gets unblocked as soon as it calls the `DownloadStringAsync` method. The main thread doesn't wait for the callback to execute. This is by design, and asynchronous methods are expected to behave in this manner. However, since the main thread has nothing else to do and has already done what it was expected to do, which was calling the method, the application terminates.

As a web application developer, you might face a similar problem if you use the preceding code in a server-side application using Web Forms or ASP.NET MVC. The IIS thread executing your request will return immediately, without waiting for the download to finish, if you have called the method asynchronously. The results will therefore not be as expected. We are not expecting the code to print the output to the console in a web application, and the `Console.WriteLine` statement is simply ignored when run in web application code. Suppose your logic is to return the web page as a response to the client request. We can achieve this using the `WebClient` class synchronously, as shown in the following example, using ASP.NET MVC:

```
public IActionResult Index()
{
    WebClient client = new WebClient();
    string content = client.DownloadString(new
     Uri("http://www.aspnet.com"));
    return Content(content,"text/html");
}
```

The problem here is that the preceding code will block the thread, which can have an impact on the performance of the server and lead to a self-inflicted **Denial-of-Service** (**DoS**) attack, which occurs when a lot of users hit a portion of the application concurrently. As more and more threads are hit and become blocked, there will be a point at which the server won't have any threads free to process client requests, and will start queueing requests. Once the queue limit is reached, the server will start throwing a 503 error: Service Unavailable.

We cannot use the `DownloadStringAsync` method because the moment it is called, the thread will return a response back to the client, without waiting for `DownloadComplete` to finish. We need a way to make the server thread wait without blocking it. `async` and `await` come to our rescue in such a scenario. Apart from helping us to achieve our objective, they also help us to have clean code that is easy to write, debug, and maintain.

To demonstrate `async` and `await`, we can use another important class of .NET Core, `HttpClient`, which is available in the `System.Net.Http` namespace. `HttpClient` should be used instead of `WebClient`, as it has full support for task-based asynchronous operations, has a vastly improved performance, and supports HTTP methods such as GET, POST, PUT, and DELETE.

Here is an async version of the preceding code, using the `HttpClient` class and introducing the `async` and `await` keywords:

```
public async Task<IActionResult> Index()
    {
        HttpClient client = new HttpClient();
```

Async, Await, and Task-Based Asynchronous Programming Basics

```
        HttpResponseMessage response = await
          client.GetAsync("http://www.aspnet.com");
        string content = await response.Content.ReadAsStringAsync();
        return Content(content,"text/html");
}
```

First, we need to change the method signature to include the `async` keyword. This is an instruction to the compiler that this method will execute asynchronously where necessary. Then, we wrap the return type of the method inside `Task<T>`. This is important since .NET Framework supports task-based async operations, and all async methods must return `Task`.

We need to create an instance of the `HttpClient` class and call the `GetAsync()` method, passing the URL of the resource that you want to download. Unlike the EAP pattern, which relies on callbacks, we instead just write the `await` keyword with the call. This makes sure of the following:

- The method executes asynchronously.
- The calling thread gets unblocked so that it can go back to the thread pool and process other client requests, thus making the server responsive.
- When the download is complete, the `ThreadPool` receives an interrupt signal from the processor, and it will take out a free thread from the `ThreadPool`, which can be either the same thread that was operating on the request or a different thread.
- The `ThreadPool` thread receives the response and starts executing the rest of the method.

When the download finishes, we can read the content that is downloaded by using another async operation, called `ReadAsStringAsync()`. This section has shown that it is easy to write async methods that resemble their synchronous counterparts, making their logic straightforward as well.

The return type of async methods

In the preceding example, we changed the return type of the method from `IAsyncResult` to `Task<IAsyncResult>`. There can be three return types from async methods:

- void
- Task
- Task<T>

All async methods must return a `Task` in order to be awaited (using the `await` keyword). This is because, once you call them, they don't return immediately, but rather, they execute a long-running task asynchronously. In doing this, the caller thread may switch in and out of context as well.

`void` can be used with asynchronous methods where the caller thread doesn't want to wait. These methods can be any operation that can happen in the background that's not part of the response being returned to the user. For example, logging and auditing can be made asynchronous. This means that they can be wrapped inside async `void` methods. The caller thread will return immediately on calling the operation, and the logging and auditing operations will take place later on. It's thus highly recommended to return a `Task` instead of `void` from asynchronous methods.

Async delegates and lambda expressions

We can use the `async` keyword to create asynchronous delegates and lambda expressions as well.

Here is a synchronous delegate that returns the square of a number:

```
Func<int, int> square = (x) => {return x * x;};
```

We can make the preceding delegate asynchronous by appending the `async` keyword, as follows:

```
Func<int, Task<int>> square =async (x) => {return x * x;};
```

Similarly, lambda expressions can be converted, as follows:

```
Func<int, Task<int>> square =async (x) => x * x;
```

Asynchronous methods work in a chain. Once you have made any one method asynchronous, then all methods that call that method need to be converted to being asynchronous as well, thus creating a long chain of asynchronous methods.

Task-based asynchronous patterns

In Chapter 2, *Task Parallelism*, we discussed how the TAP can be achieved using the `Task` class. There are two ways to implement this pattern:

- The compiler method, using the `async` keyword
- The manual method

Let's see how these methods operate, in the subsequent sections.

The compiler method, using the async keyword

When we use the `async` keyword to make any method asynchronous, the compiler carries out the required optimization to execute the method asynchronously, using the TAP internally. An async method must return either `System.Threading.Task` or `System.Threading.Task<T>`. The compiler takes care of executing the method asynchronously and returns results or exceptions back to the caller.

Implementing the TAP manually

We have already shown how to implement the TAP manually in the EAP and **Asynchronous Programming Model** (**APM**). Implementing this pattern gives us more control over the overall implementation of the method. We can create a `TaskCompletionSource<TResult>` class and then perform an asynchronous operation. When the asynchronous operation finishes, we can return the result back to the caller by calling the `SetResult`, `SetException`, or `SetCanceled` methods of the `TaskCompletionSource<TResult>` class, as shown in the following code:

```
public static Task<int> ReadFromFileTask(this FileStream stream, byte[] buffer, int offset, int count, object state)
{
    var taskCompletionSource = new TaskCompletionSource<int>();
    stream.BeginRead(buffer, offset, count, ar =>
    {
        try
        {
            taskCompletionSource.SetResult(stream.EndRead(ar));
        }
        catch (Exception exc)
        {
            taskCompletionSource.SetException(exc);
```

```
        }
    }, state);
    return taskCompletionSource.Task;
}
```

In the preceding code, we created a method returning `Task<int>` that can work on any `System.IO.FileStream` object as an extension method. Within the method, we created a `TaskCompletionSource<int>` object, and then called the asynchronous operation provided by the `FileStream` class to read the file into a byte array. If the read operation finishes successfully, we return the results back to the caller using the `SetResult` method; otherwise, we return the exceptions using the `SetException` method. Finally, the method returns the underlying task from the `TaskCompletionSource<int>` object to the caller.

Exception handling with async code

In the case of synchronous code, all exceptions are propagated to the top of the stack until they are handled by a try-catch block or they are thrown as an unhandled exception. When we await on any asynchronous method, the call stack will not be the same, as the thread has made a transition from the method to the thread pool, and is now coming back. C#, however, has made it easier for us to do exception handling by changing the exception behavior for async methods. All async methods return either `Task` or `void`. Let's try to understand both scenarios with examples, and see how the programs will behave.

A method that returns Task and throws an exception

Let's say we have the following method, which is `void`. As a best practice, we return `Task` from it:

```
private static Task DoSomethingFaulty()
{
    Task.Delay(2000);
    throw new Exception("This is custom exception.");
}
```

The method throws an exception after a delay of two seconds.

Async, Await, and Task-Based Asynchronous Programming Basics

We will try to call this method using various methods to try to understand the behavior of how exceptions are handled for async methods. The following scenarios will be discussed in this section:

- Calling the async method from outside the try-catch block without the `await` keyword
- Calling the async method from inside the try-catch block without the `await` keyword
- Calling the async method with the `await` keyword from outside the try-catch block
- Methods returning `void`

We will see these methods in detail in the subsequent sections.

An async method from outside a try-catch block without the await keyword

The following is a sample async method that returns a `Task`. The method, in turn, calls another method, `DoSomethingFaulty()`, which throws an exception.

Here is our `DoSomethingFaulty()` method implementation:

```
private static Task DoSomethingFaulty()
{
    Task.Delay(2000);
    throw new Exception("This is custom exception.");
}
```

And here is the code for the `AsyncReturningTaskExample()` method:

```
private async static Task AsyncReturningTaskExample()
{
    Task<string> task = DoSomethingFaulty();
    Console.WriteLine("This should not execute");
    try
    {
        task.ContinueWith((s) =>
        {
            Console.WriteLine(s);
        });
    }
    catch (Exception ex)
    {
```

[214]

```
            Console.WriteLine(ex.Message);
            Console.WriteLine(ex.StackTrace);
        }
    }
```

Here is a call to this method from the `Main()` method:

```
public static void Main()
{
    Console.WriteLine("Main Method Starts");
    var task = AsyncReturningTaskExample();
    Console.WriteLine("In Main Method After calling method");
    Console.ReadLine();
}
```

> **TIP**
> Async main is a handy addition to C# from version 7.1 onward. It became broken in release 7.2 but was fixed back in .NET Core 3.0.

As you can see, the program calls the async method—that is `AsyncReturningTaskExample()`—without using the `await` keyword. The `AsyncReturningTaskExample()` method further calls the `DoSomethingFaulty()` method, which throws an exception. The following output is produced when we run this code:

```
C:\Program Files\dotnet\dotnet.exe
Main Method Startes
In Main Method After calling method
```

Async, Await, and Task-Based Asynchronous Programming Basics

In the case of synchronous programming, the program would have resulted in an unhandled exception, and it would have crashed. But here, the program continues as if nothing happened. This is due to the way in which `Task` objects are handled by the framework. In this case, the task will return to the caller with a **Status** of **Faulted**, as can be seen in the following screenshot:

```
10      public static void Main()
11      {
12          // AsyncReturningValueExample();
13          Console.WriteLine("Main Method Startes");
14          var task = AsyncReturningTaskExample();
15          Console.WriteLine("In Main Method After calling method");
16          Console.ReadLine();   ≤31ms elapsed
```

Watch 1

Name	Value
▲ task	Id = 2, Status = Faulted, Method = "{null}", Result = "{Not yet computed}"
AsyncState	null
CancellationPending	false
CreationOptions	None
▶ Exception	Count = 1
Id	2
Result	{System.Threading.Tasks.VoidTaskResult}
Status	Faulted
▶ Raw View	

A better code would have been to check the task status and fetch all exceptions if there are any:

```
var task = AsyncReturningTaskExample();
if (task.IsFaulted)
    Console.WriteLine(task.Exception.Flatten().Message.ToString());
```

As we saw in Chapter 2, *Task Parallelism*, this task returns an instance of `AggregateExceptions`. To get all inner exceptions thrown, we can use the `Flatten()` method, as demonstrated in the previous screenshot.

An async method from inside the try-catch block without the await keyword

Let's change the method to move the call to the async method `GetSomethingFaulty()` inside the try-catch block, and call from the `Main()` method.

Here is the `Main` method:

```
public static void Main()
{
    Console.WriteLine("Main Method Started");
    var task = Scenario2CallAsyncWithoutAwaitFromInsideTryCatch();
    if (task.IsFaulted)
        Console.WriteLine(task.Exception.Flatten().Message.ToString());
    Console.WriteLine("In Main Method After calling method");
    Console.ReadLine();
}
```

And here is the `Scenario2CallAsyncWithoutAwaitFromInsideTryCatch()` method:

```
private async static Task
Scenario2CallAsyncWithoutAwaitFromInsideTryCatch()
{
    try
    {
        var task = DoSomethingFaulty();
        Console.WriteLine("This should not execute");
        task.ContinueWith((s) =>
        {
            Console.WriteLine(s);
        });
    }
    catch (Exception ex)
    {
        Console.WriteLine(ex.Message);
        Console.WriteLine(ex.StackTrace);
    }
}
```

This time, we see that the exception will be thrown and received by the catch block, after which time the program will resume as normal.

Async, Await, and Task-Based Asynchronous Programming Basics

It's worth taking a look at the value of the `Task` object inside the `Main` method:

```
29              var task = Scenario2CallAsyncWithoutAwaitFromInsideTryCatch();
30              if (task.IsFaulted)
31                  Console.WriteLine(task.Exception.Flatten().Message.ToString());
32
33              Console.WriteLine("In Main Method After calling method");
34              Console.ReadLine();
35          }
36          private async static Task Scenario3CallAsyncWithAwaitFromOutsideTryCatch()
37          {
38              await DoSomethingFaulty();
39              Console.WriteLine("This should not execute");
40          }
```

Watch 1

Name	Value
▲ ● task	Id = 2, Status = RanToCompletion, Method = "{null}", Result = "System.Threading.Tasks.VoidTaskResult"
AsyncState	null
CancellationPending	false
CreationOptions	None
▶ Exception	null
Id	2
Result	{System.Threading.Tasks.VoidTaskResult}
Status	RanToCompletion
▶ ● Raw View	

> **TIP**
> As you can see, if task creation is not carried out inside the try-catch block, the exceptions will be unobserved. This can cause issues, since the logic may not work as expected. A best practice is to always wrap the task creation inside the try-catch block.

As you can see, since the exceptions were handled, the execution returned normally from the async method. The status of the returned task becomes `RanToCompletion`.

Calling an async method with the await keyword from outside the try-catch block

The following code block shows the code for the method that calls the faulty method, `DoSomethingFaulty()`, and waits for the method to finish, using the `await` keyword:

```
private async static Task Scenario3CallAsyncWithAwaitFromOutsideTryCatch()
{
    await DoSomethingFaulty();
    Console.WriteLine("This should not execute");
}
```

[218]

And here is the call from the `Main` method:

```
public static void Main()
{
    Console.WriteLine("Main Method Starts");
    var task = Scenario3CallAsyncWithAwaitFromOutsideTryCatch();
    if (task.IsFaulted)
        Console.WriteLine(task.Exception.Flatten().Message.ToString());
    Console.WriteLine("In Main Method After calling method");
    Console.ReadLine();
}
```

The behavior of the program, in this case, will be the same as in the first scenario.

Methods returning void

If the methods return `void` instead of `Task`, the program will crash. You can try running the following code.

Here is a method returning `void` instead of `Task`:

```
private async static void
Scenario4CallAsyncWithoutAwaitFromOutsideTryCatch()
{
    Task task = DoSomethingFaulty();
    Console.WriteLine("This should not execute");
}
```

And here is a call from the `Main` method:

```
public static void Main()
{
    Console.WriteLine("Main Method Started");
    Scenario4CallAsyncWithoutAwaitFromOutsideTryCatch();
    Console.WriteLine("In Main Method After calling method");
    Console.ReadLine();
}
```

There will be no output, as the program will crash.

> **TIP** Although it makes sense to never return `void` from async methods, mistakes do happen. We should write code so that it never crashes or only crashes gracefully after logging exceptions.

Async, Await, and Task-Based Asynchronous Programming Basics

We can handle this globally by subscribing to two global event handlers, as follows:

```
AppDomain.CurrentDomain.UnhandledException += (s, e) =>
Console.WriteLine("Program Crashed", "Unhandled Exception Occurred");
TaskScheduler.UnobservedTaskException += (s, e) =>
Console.WriteLine("Program Crashed", "Unhandled Exception Occurred");
```

The preceding code will handle all unhandled exceptions in the program, and accounts for good practices in exception management. The program should not crash randomly, and, if it needs to crash at all, then it should log information and clean up all resources.

Async with PLINQ

PLINQ is a very handy tool for developers, to improve the performance of applications by executing a set of tasks in parallel. Creating a number of tasks can improve performance, but, if tasks are blocking in nature, then the application will end up creating lots of blocking threads and, at some point, will become unresponsive. This is especially true if the task is executing some I/O operations. Here is a method that needs to download 100 pages from the web as quickly as possible:

```
public async static void Main()
    {
        var urls =  Enumerable.Repeat("http://www.dummyurl.com", 100);
        foreach (var url in urls)
        {
            HttpClient client = new HttpClient();
            HttpResponseMessage response = await
             client.GetAsync("http://www.aspnet.com");
            string content = await
               response.Content.ReadAsStringAsync();
            Console.WriteLine();
        }
```

As you can see, the preceding code, being synchronous, has a complexity of $O(n)$. If one request takes one second to finish, the method will take at least 100 seconds (n = 100 here).

To make the download faster (assuming we have a good server configuration that can handle this load multiplied by the number of users your application wants to support), we need to make this method parallel. We can do this using `Parallel.ForEach`, as follows:

```
Parallel.ForEach(urls, url =>
        {
            HttpClient client = new HttpClient();
            HttpResponseMessage response = await
```

```
            client.GetAsync("http://www.aspnet.com");
        string content = await
            response.Content.ReadAsStringAsync();
});
```

Suddenly, the code starts complaining:

The 'await' operator can only be used within an async lambda expression. Consider marking this lambda expression with the 'async' modifier.

This is because we have used a lambda expression, which needs to be made async as well, as shown in the following code:

```
Parallel.ForEach(urls,async url =>
        {
            HttpClient client = new HttpClient();
            HttpResponseMessage response = await
             client.GetAsync("http://www.aspnet.com");
            string content = await
                response.Content.ReadAsStringAsync();
});
```

The code will now compile and work as expected, with much-improved performance. Talking more about performance in the next section, we will dig more deeply into how to measure the performance of asynchronous code.

Measuring the performance of async code

Async code can improve the performance and responsiveness of applications, but there are trade-offs. In the case of GUI-based applications, such as Windows Forms or WPF, if a method is taking a long time, it makes sense to make it async. For server applications, however, you need to measure the trade-off between the extra memory utilized by the blocked threads and the extra processor overhead required to make methods asynchronous.

Consider the following code, which creates three tasks. Each task runs asynchronously, one after another. As one method finishes, it goes on to execute another task asynchronously. The total time taken to finish the method can be calculated using `Stopwatch`:

```
public static void Main(string[] args)
{
    MainAsync(args).GetAwaiter().GetResult();
    Console.ReadLine();
}
```

Async, Await, and Task-Based Asynchronous Programming Basics

```
public static async Task MainAsync(string[] args)
{
    Stopwatch stopwatch = Stopwatch.StartNew();
    var value1 = await Task1();
    var value2 = await Task2();
    var value3 = await Task3();
    stopwatch.Stop();
    Console.WriteLine($"Total time taken is
      {stopwatch.ElapsedMilliseconds}");
}
public static async Task<int> Task1()
{
    await Task.Delay(2000);
    return 100;
}
public static async Task<int> Task2()
{
    await Task.Delay(2000);
    return 200;
}
public static async Task<int> Task3()
{
    await Task.Delay(2000);
    return 300;
}
```

The output of the preceding code is as follows:

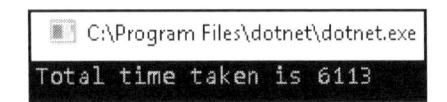

```
C:\Program Files\dotnet\dotnet.exe
Total time taken is 6113
```

This is as good as writing synchronous code. The benefit is that the thread is not blocked, but the overall performance of the application is poor since all code now runs synchronously. We could change the preceding code to improve the performance, as follows:

```
Stopwatch stopwatch = Stopwatch.StartNew();
        await Task.WhenAll(Task1(), Task2(), Task3());
        stopwatch.Stop();
        Console.WriteLine($"Total time taken is
{stopwatch.ElapsedMilliseconds}");
```

As you can see, this is a better use of Parallel and async to get an improved performance:

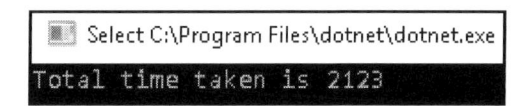

```
Select C:\Program Files\dotnet\dotnet.exe
Total time taken is 2123
```

To understand async better, we also need to understand which thread runs our code. Since new async APIs work with the `Task` class, all the calls are executed by the `ThreadPool` thread. When we make async calls—say, to fetch data from a network—the control gets transferred to the I/O completion port thread, which is managed by the OS. Usually, this is only one thread that is shared across all network requests. When the I/O request completes, the OS fires an interrupt signal that adds a job to the queue of the I/O completion port. In the case of server-side applications, which usually work in **Multi-Threaded Apartment** (**MTA**) mode, any thread can start an async request and any other thread can receive it.

In the case of Windows applications, however, (including both WinForms and WPF), which work in **Single-Threaded Apartment** (**STA**) mode, it becomes important that an async call gets returned to the same thread that started it (normally a UI thread). Every UI thread in a Windows application has a `SynchronizationContext` that makes sure that the code is always executed by the correct thread. This is important due to control ownership. To avoid cross-threading issues, only the owner thread can change the values of the controls. The most important method of the `SynchronizationContext` class is `Post`, which can make a delegate run in the right context, thus avoiding cross-threading issues.

Whenever we await a task, the current `SynchronizationContext` is captured. Then, when the method needs to be resumed, the `await` keyword internally uses the `Post` method to resume the method in the captured `SynchronizationContext`. Calling the `Post` method is very costly, however, but there is a built-in performance optimization provided by the framework. The `Post` method doesn't get called if the captured `SynchronizationContext` is the same as the current `SynchronizationContext` of the returning thread.

If we are writing a class library and we don't really care about which `SynchronizationContext` the call will be returned to, we can completely turn off the `Post` method. We can achieve this by calling the `ConfigureAwait()` method on the returning task, as follows:

```
HttpClient client = new HttpClient();
HttpResponseMessage response = await
client.GetAsync(url).ConfigureAwait(false);
```

So far, we have learned the important aspects of asynchronous programming. We now need to know the guidelines for using async code while programming!

Guidelines for using async code

Some guidelines/best practices while writing with asynchronous code are the following:

- Avoid using async void.
- Async chain all the way.
- Use `ConfigureAwait` wherever possible.

We will learn more about these in the following sections.

Avoid using async void

We have already seen how returning `void` from async methods actually affects the exception handling. Async methods should return `Task` or `Task<T>` so that exceptions can be observed and not become unhandled.

Async chain all the way

Mixing async and blocking methods will have an impact on performance. Once we decide to make a method async, the entire chain of methods that are supposed to be called from that method should be made async as well. Not doing so can sometimes result in a deadlock, as demonstrated in the following code example:

```
private async Task DelayAsync()
{
    await Task.Delay(2000);
}
public void Deadlock()
{
    var task = DelayAsync();
    task.Wait();
}
```

If we call the `Deadlock()` method from any ASP.NET or GUI-based application, it would create a deadlock, although the same code would run fine in a console application. When we call the `DelayAsync()` method, it captures the current `SynchronizationContext`, or the current `TaskScheduler` if the `SynchronizationContext` is null. When the awaited task is complete, it tries to execute the remainder of the method with the captured context. The problem here is that there is already a thread that's waiting synchronously for the async method to finish. In this situation, both threads will be waiting for the other thread to finish, thus causing a deadlock. This problem is raised only in GUI-based or ASP.NET applications because they rely on the `SynchronizationContext` that can only execute one chunk of code at a time. Console applications, on the other hand, utilize `ThreadPool` instead of `SynchronizationContext`. When the await finishes, the pending async method part is scheduled on a `ThreadPool` thread. The method is completed on a separate thread and returns the task back to the caller, so there is no deadlock.

> **TIP**
> Never try to create sample `async/await` code in a console application and copy and paste it in a GUI or ASP.NET application, as they have different models for executing async code.

Using ConfigureAwait wherever possible

We could have avoided deadlock in the preceding code example by completely skipping the use of `SynchronizationContext`:

```
private async Task DelayAsync()
{
await Task.Delay(2000);
}
public void Deadlock()
{
var task = DelayAsync().ConfigureAwait(false);
task.Wait();
}
```

When we use `ConfigureAwait(false)`, the method is awaited. When the await completes, the processor tries to execute the rest of the async method within the thread pool context. The method is able to complete with no issues since there are no blocking contexts. The method completes its returned task, and there's no deadlock.

We have come to the end of this chapter. Let's now see all we have learned!

Summary

In this chapter, we discussed two very important constructs that make writing asynchronous code very easy. All the heavy work is done by the compiler when we use these keywords, and the code looks very similar to its synchronous counterpart. We also discussed which thread the code runs on when we make methods asynchronous, and the performance penalty associated with utilizing `SynchronizationContext`. Finally, we looked at how we can turn off the `SynchronizationContext` completely to improve performance.

In the next chapter, we will introduce parallel debugging techniques using Visual Studio. We will also learn the tools available in Visual Studio to help in parallel code debugging.

Questions

1. What keyword is used to unblock a thread inside async methods?
    1. `async`
    2. `await`
    3. `Thread.Sleep`
    4. `Task`
2. Which of the following are valid return types for async methods?
    1. `void`
    2. `Task`
    3. `Task<T>`
    4. `IAsyncResult`
3. `TaskCompletionSource<T>` can be used to implement a task-based async pattern manually.
    1. True
    2. False

4. Can we write `Main` methods as async?
    1. Yes
    2. No
5. Which property of the `Task` class can be used to check whether an exception has been thrown by an async method?
    1. `IsException`
    2. `IsFaulted`
6. We should always use `void` as a return type for async methods.
    1. True
    2. False

Section 4: Debugging, Diagnostics, and Unit Testing for Async Code

In this section, we will explain debugging techniques and tools that are available for Visual Studio users. The primary focus will be on understanding IDE features such as the parallel Tasks window, the Thread window, the Parallel Stacks window, and Concurrency Visualizer tools. We will also cover how to write unit test cases for code that uses TPL and async programming, how to write mock and stubs for test cases, and some tips and tricks to make sure the test cases the test cases we write for ORM don't fail.

This section comprises the following chapters:

- `Chapter 10`, *Debugging Tasks Using Visual Studio*
- `Chapter 11`, *Writing Unit Test Cases for Parallel and Asynchronous Code*

10 Debugging Tasks Using Visual Studio

Parallel programming can improve the performance and responsiveness of applications, but sometimes the results are not as expected. Common problems related to parallel/asynchronous code are performance and correctness.

With performance, we mean that the results of execution are slow. With correctness, we mean that results are not as expected (this might be due to race conditions). Another big issue when dealing with multiple concurrent tasks is deadlocks. Debugging multithreaded code is always a challenge as threads keep switching while you are debugging. While working on GUI-based applications, it's also important to find out which thread is running our code.

In this chapter, we will explain how to debug threads using tools available in Visual Studio, including the Threads window, the Tasks window, and Concurrency Visualizer.

In this chapter, the following topics will be covered:

- Debugging with VS 2019
- How to debug threads
- Using Parallel Tasks windows
- Debugging using Parallel Stacks windows
- Using Concurrency Visualizer

Technical requirements

A prior understanding of threads, tasks, Visual Studio, and parallel programming is required before you start this chapter.

You can check the accompanying source code at GitHub at the following link: https://github.com/PacktPublishing/-Hands-On-Parallel-Programming-with-C-8-and-.NET-Core-3/tree/master/Chapter10.

Debugging with VS 2019

Visual Studio provides lots of built-in tools to help with the aforementioned debugging and troubleshooting issues. Some of the tools that we are going to discuss in this chapter are as follows:

- The Thread window
- The Parallel Stacks window
- The Parallel Watch window
- The Debug Location toolbar
- Concurrency Visualizer (VS 2017 only as of the time of writing)
- The GPU thread window

In the following sections, we will try to understand all of these tools in depth.

How to debug threads

When working with multiple threads, it becomes important to find out which thread is executing at a particular time. This allows us to troubleshoot cross-threading issues as well as race conditions. Using the `Threads` window, we can check and work with threads while debugging. When you hit a breakpoint while debugging code in Visual Studio IDE, the thread window provides a table with each row containing information about active threads.

Chapter 10

Now, let's explore how to debug threads using Visual Studio:

1. Let's write the following code in Visual Studio:

   ```
   for (int i = 0; i < 10; i++)
   {
       Task task = new TaskFactory().StartNew(() =>
       {
           Console.WriteLine($"Thread with Id
             {Thread.CurrentThread.ManagedThreadId}");
       });
   }
   ```

2. Create a breakpoint by pressing *F9* on the `Console.Writeline` statement.
3. Run the application in debug mode by pressing *F5*. The application will create threads and start executing. When a breakpoint is hit, we will open the **Threads** window from the toolbar's **Debug** | **Windows** | **Threads** window:

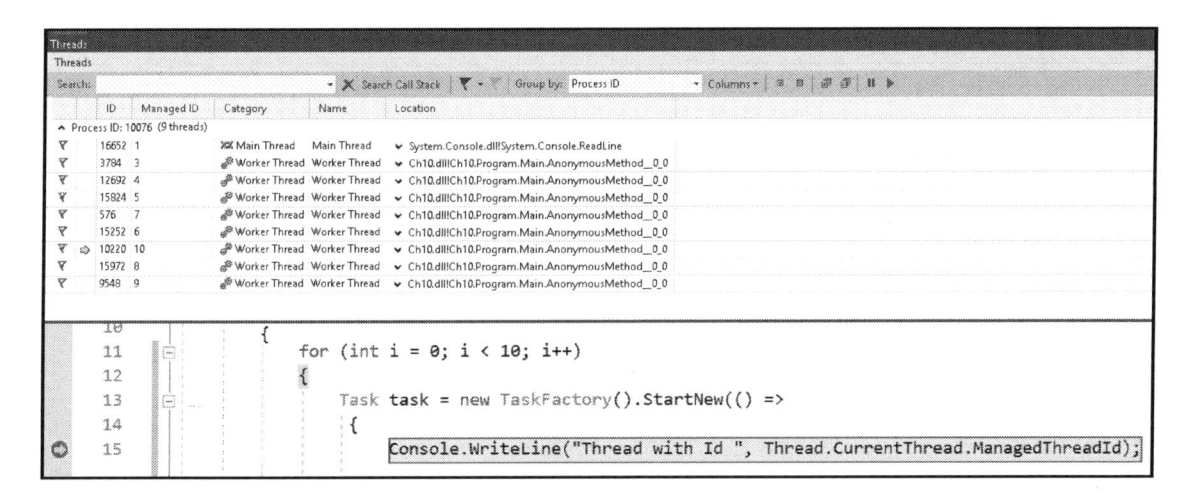

There is a lot of information that is captured by the .NET environment regarding threads that are displayed in columns. A yellow arrow identifies the thread that is currently being executed.

[233]

Debugging Tasks Using Visual Studio

Some of the columns include the following:

- **Flag**: If we want to keep track of a particular thread, we can flag it. This can be done by clicking on the flag icon.
- **ID**: This shows the unique identification number allocated to each thread.
- **Managed ID**: This shows the managed identification number assigned to each thread.
- **Category**: Every thread is assigned a unique category that helps us to identify whether it is a GUI thread (main thread) or a worker thread.
- **Name**: This shows a name for each thread, or is displayed as <No Name>.
- **Location**: This assists in identifying where the thread is executing. We can drill down to see the complete call stack.

We can flag threads that we want to monitor by clicking on the flag icon. To view only flagged threads, we can click on the **Show Flagged Threads Only** option in the **Threads** window:

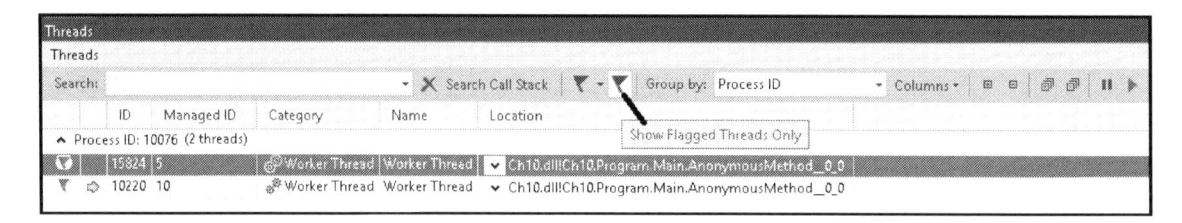

Another cool feature of the **Threads** window is that we can freeze threads that we think might be causing issues during debugging in order to monitor application behavior. The system will not begin execution of frozen threads even if it has sufficient resources available. When frozen, a thread moves to a suspended state:

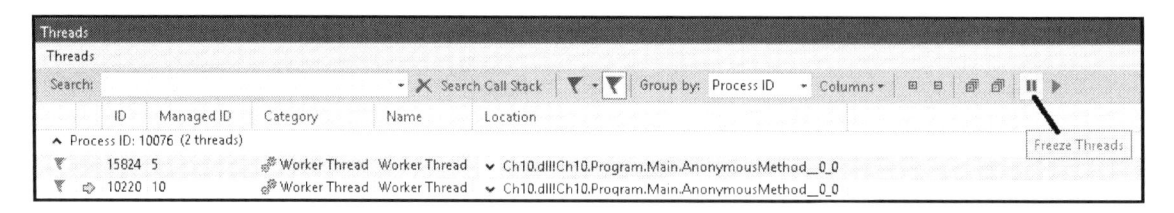

Chapter 10

While debugging, we can also switch execution from one thread to another either by right-clicking the thread in the **Threads** window, or by double-clicking it:

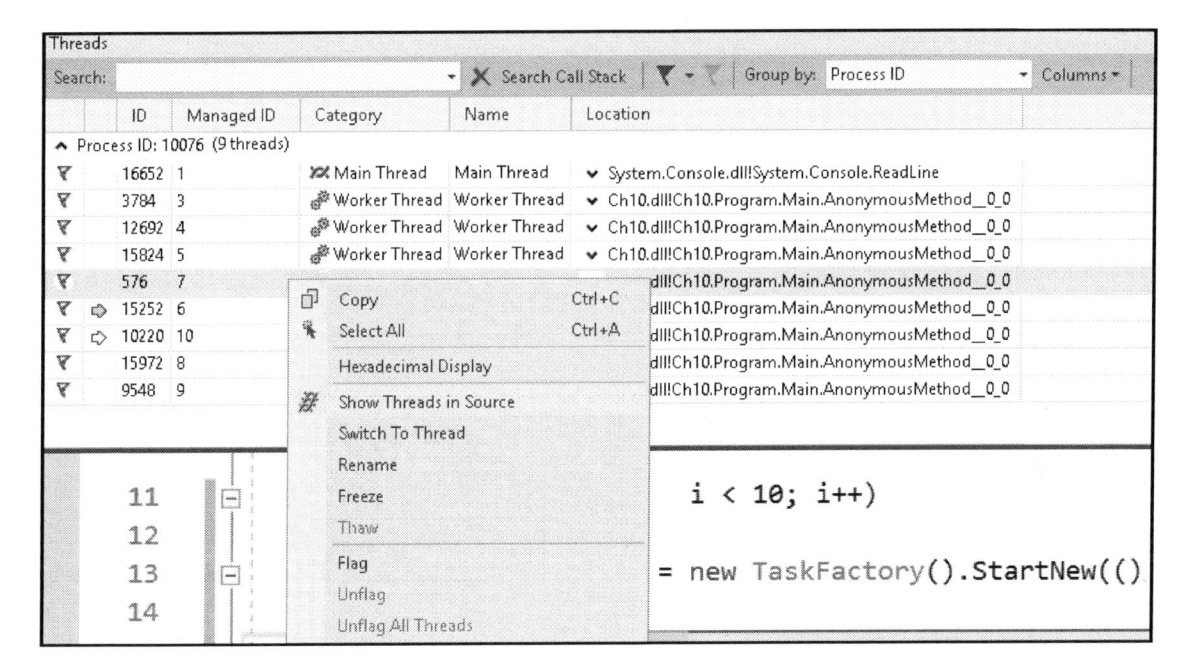

	ID	Managed ID	Category	Name	Location
▲ Process ID: 10076 (9 threads)					
▼	16652	1	Main Thread	Main Thread	System.Console.dll!System.Console.ReadLine
▼	3784	3	Worker Thread	Worker Thread	Ch10.dll!Ch10.Program.Main.AnonymousMethod__0_0
▼	12692	4	Worker Thread	Worker Thread	Ch10.dll!Ch10.Program.Main.AnonymousMethod__0_0
▼	15824	5	Worker Thread	Worker Thread	Ch10.dll!Ch10.Program.Main.AnonymousMethod__0_0
▼	576	7			dll!Ch10.Program.Main.AnonymousMethod__0_0
▼ ⇨	15252	6			dll!Ch10.Program.Main.AnonymousMethod__0_0
▼ ⇨	10220	10			dll!Ch10.Program.Main.AnonymousMethod__0_0
▼	15972	8			dll!Ch10.Program.Main.AnonymousMethod__0_0
▼	9548	9			dll!Ch10.Program.Main.AnonymousMethod__0_0

Context menu:
- Copy   Ctrl+C
- Select All   Ctrl+A
- Hexadecimal Display
- Show Threads in Source
- Switch To Thread
- Rename
- Freeze
- Thaw
- Flag
- Unflag
- Unflag All Threads

```
i < 10; i++)

= new TaskFactory().StartNew(()
```

Visual Studio also supports debugging tasks using Parallel Stacks windows. We will take a look at this in the next section.

Using Parallel Stacks windows

The **Parallel Stacks** window is a very good tool for debugging threads and tasks, and this has been introduced in later versions of Visual Studio. We can open the **Parallel Stacks** window while debugging by navigating to **Debug** | **Windows** | **Parallel Stacks**:

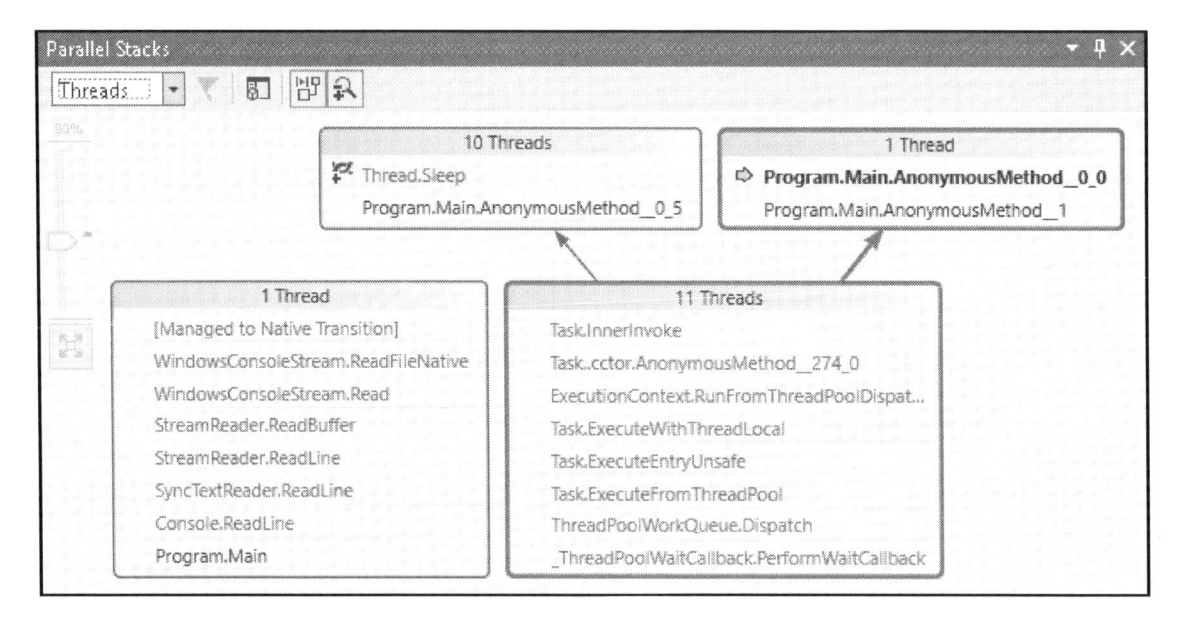

As you can see from the preceding screenshot, there are various views within which we can switch while working on the **Parallel Stacks** window. We will learn about how to debug using **Parallel Stacks** windows and these views in our next topic.

Debugging using Parallel Stacks windows

Parallel Stacks windows have a drop-down menu with two options. We can switch between these options to get several views within the **Parallel Stacks** window. These views are the following:

- **Threads** view
- **Tasks** view

Let's examine these views in detail in the following sections.

Chapter 10

Threads view

The **Threads** view shows call stacks for all threads running while debugging an application:

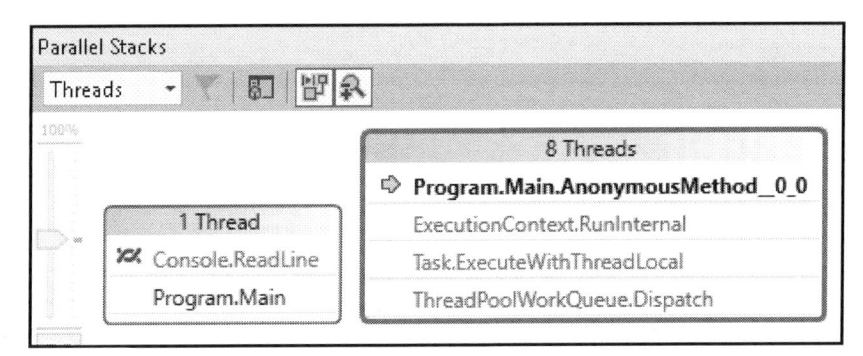

The yellow arrow shows the current location where the code is executing. Hovering over any method from the **Parallel Stacks** window opens up the **Threads** window with information about the thread currently being executed:

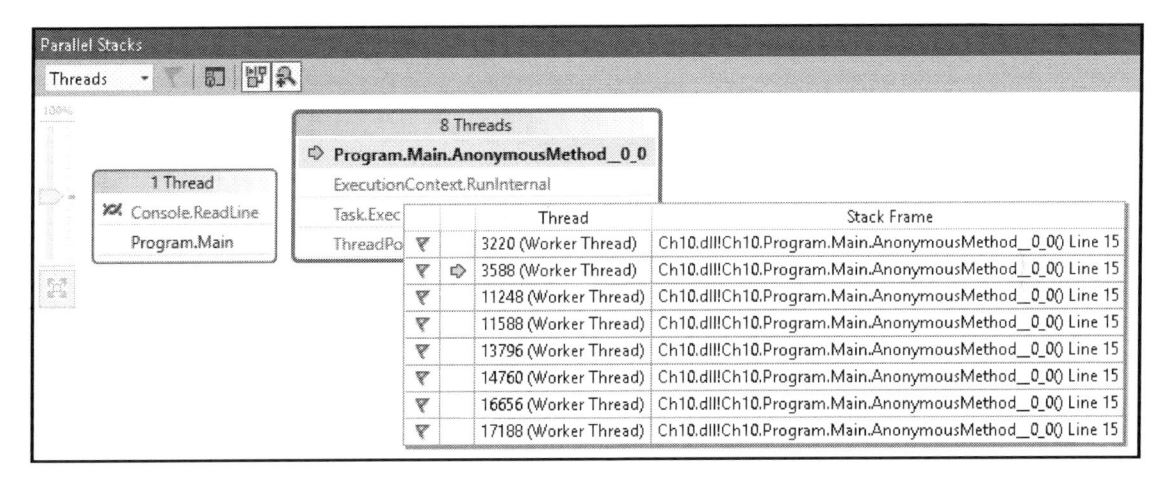

[237]

Debugging Tasks Using Visual Studio

We can switch to any other method by double-clicking on it:

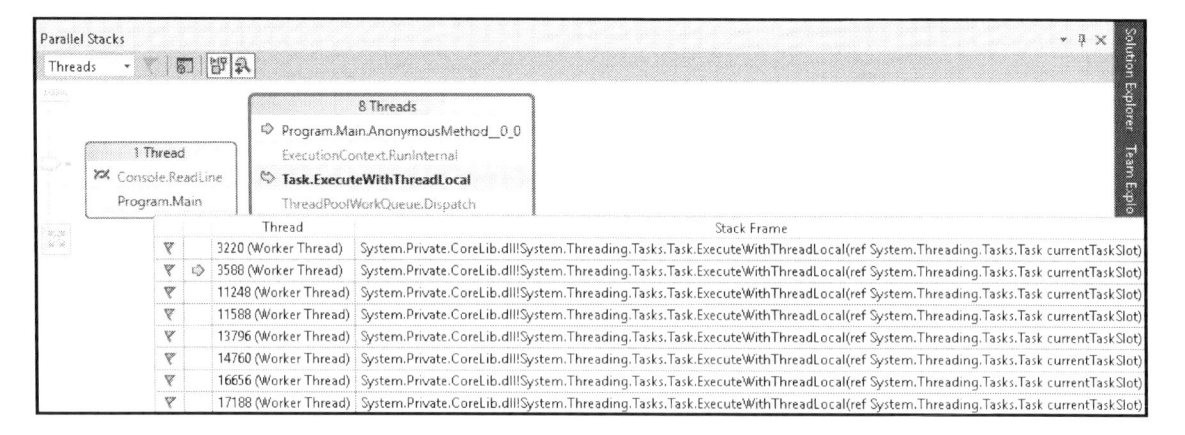

We can also switch to **Method View** to see the complete call stack:

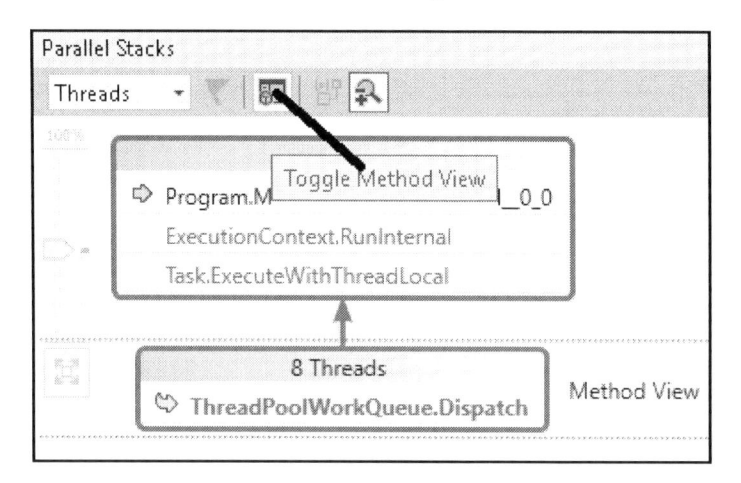

Method View is very handy for debugging a call stack to find out which values were passed to a method at any point in time.

Tasks view

We should use the **Tasks** view if we are using the Task Parallel Library to create `System.Threading.Tasks.Task` objects in our code:

As you can see in the following screenshot, there are currently 10 tasks that are being executed, each shown along with the current line of execution.

The status of all running tasks can be seen by hovering over any method:

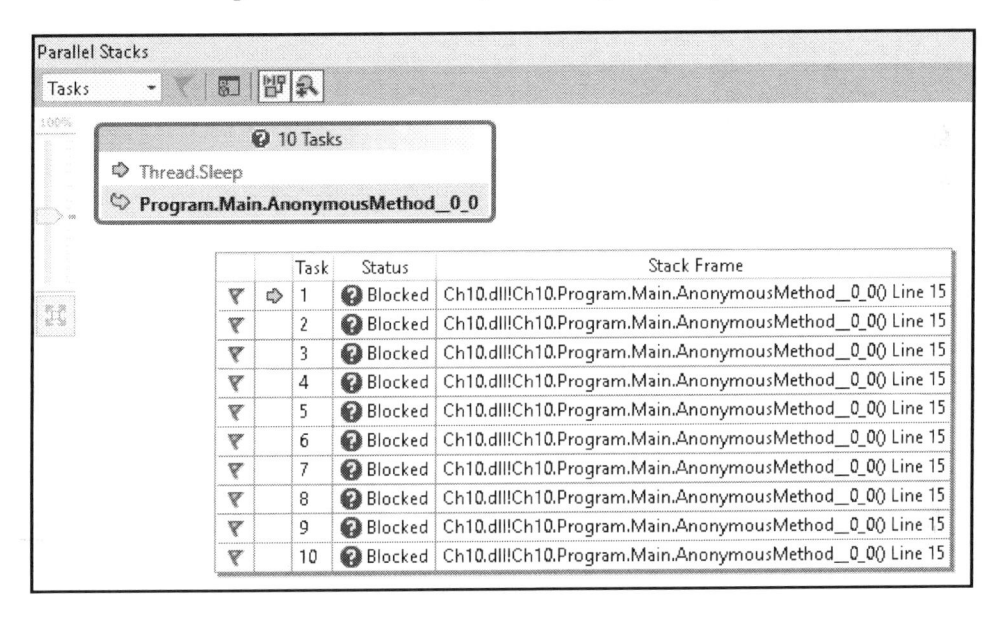

The **Tasks** window helps us in analyzing the performance issues in an application arising from slow method calls or deadlocks.

Debugging using the Parallel Watch window

We can make use of **Parallel Watch** windows when we want to see the value of a variable on different threads. Consider the following code:

```
for (int i = 0; i < 10; i++)
{
    Task task = new Task(() =>
```

Debugging Tasks Using Visual Studio

```
    {
        for (int j = 0; j < 100; j++)
        {
            Thread.Sleep(100);
        }
        Console.WriteLine($"Thread with Id
          {Thread.CurrentThread.ManagedThreadId}");
    });
    task.Start();
}
```

This code creates multiple tasks and every task runs a `for` loop for 100 iterations. In every iteration, the thread goes to sleep for 100 ms. We allow the code to run for some time and then hit a breakpoint. We can see all this in action using the **Parallel Watch** window. We can open **Parallel Watch** windows from **Debug | Windows | Parallel Watch**. We can open four such windows, and each window can monitor only one variable value on different tasks at a time:

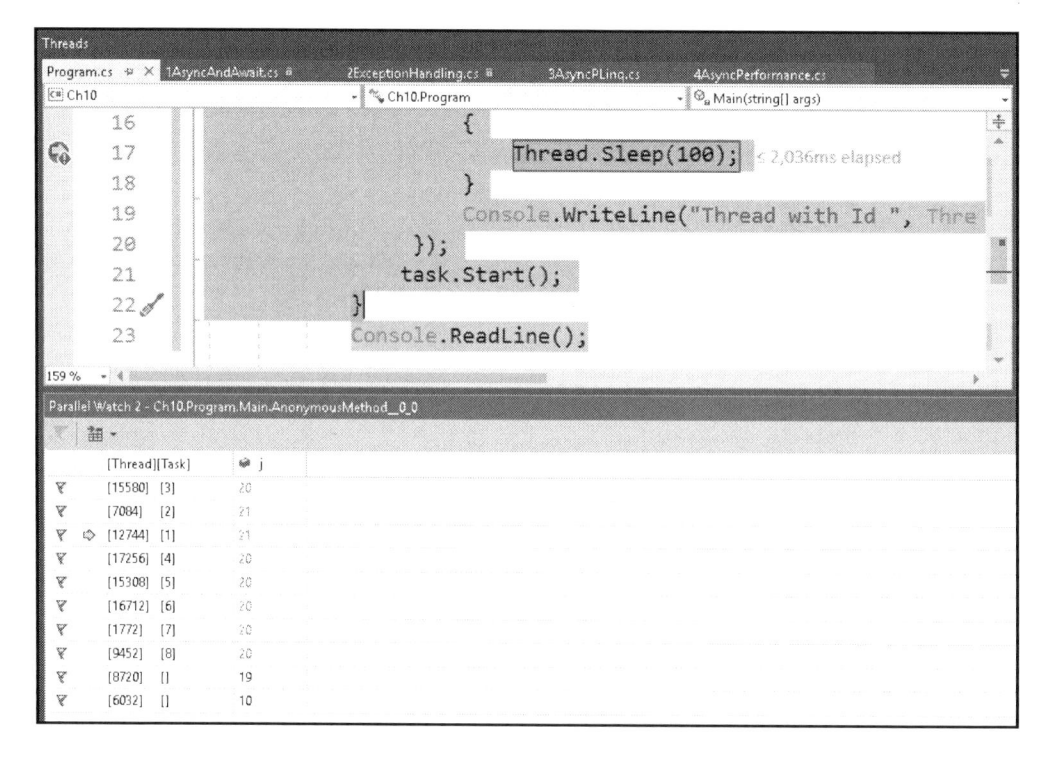

As you can see from the preceding code, we want to monitor the value of **j**. Consequently, we write **j** in the header of the third column and press the *Enter* key. This adds **j** to the watch window shown here and we can see the value of **j** on all threads/tasks.

Using Concurrency Visualizer

Concurrency Visualizer is a very handy addition to the Visual Studio tools collection. It doesn't get shipped by default in Visual Studio, but can be downloaded from the Visual Studio Marketplace here: `https://marketplace.visualstudio.com`.

This is a very advanced tool that can be used to troubleshoot complex threading issues such as performance bottlenecks, thread contention issues, checking CPU utilization, cross-core thread migrations, and areas of overlapped I/O.

Concurrency Visualizer only supports Windows/console projects and is not available for web projects. Let's consider the following code in a console application:

```
Action computeAction = () =>
{
int i = 0;
    while (true)
    {
        i = 1 * 1;
    }
};
Task.Run(() => computeAction());
Task.Run(() => computeAction());
Task.Run(() => computeAction());
Task.Run(() => computeAction());
```

In the preceding code, we created four tasks that run a compute task such as 1*1 indefinitely. We will then put a breakpoint inside the `while` loop and open Concurrency Visualizer.

Now, we will run the preceding code from Visual Studio and, while the code is running, click **Attach to Process...** as shown in the following screenshot:

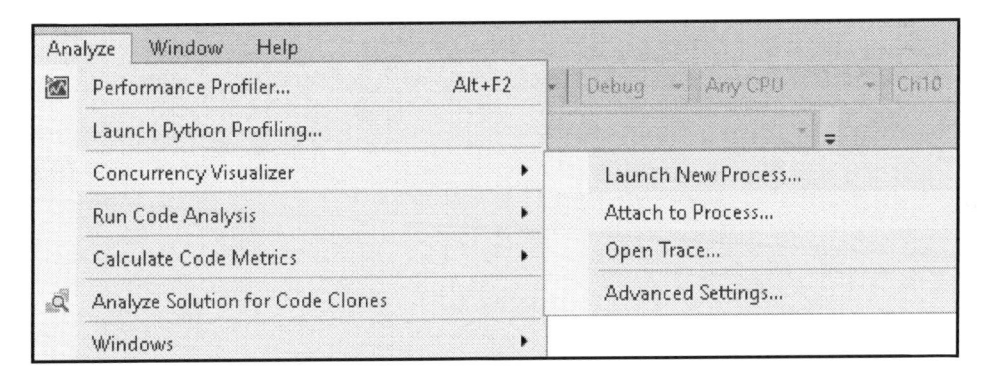

[241]

Debugging Tasks Using Visual Studio

> You first need to install Concurrency Visualizer for your version of Visual Studio. Concurrency Visualizer for Visual Studio 2017 can be found here: `https://marketplace.visualstudio.com/items?itemName=VisualStudioProductTeam.ConcurrencyVisualizer2017#overview`.

Once attached, Concurrency Visualizer will stop profiling. We will let the application run for some time so that it can collect enough data to review and then stop the profiler from generating views.

By default, this opens the **Utilization** view, which is one of the three views present in Concurrency Visualizer. The other two are the **Threads** and **Cores** views. We will explore the **Utilization** view in the following section.

Utilization view

The **Utilization** view shows system activity across all processors. Here is a snapshot of the concurrency profiler once it stops profiling:

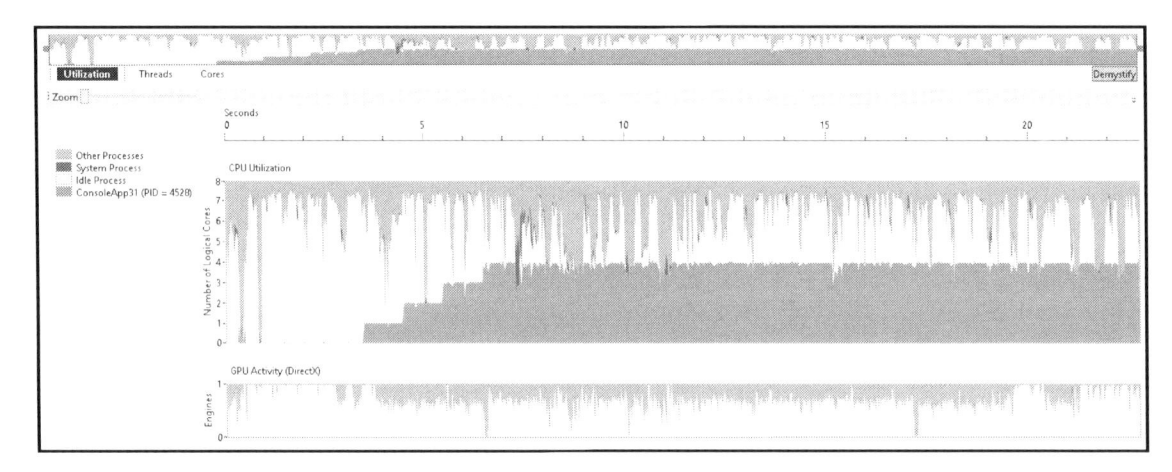

[242]

Chapter 10

As you can see from the preceding screenshot, there are four cores that have 100% CPU load. This is indicated by the green color. This view is typically used to get a high-level overview of concurrency status.

Threads view

The **Threads** view provides a very detailed analysis of the current system state. Through this, we can identity whether threads are executing or blocking on account of issues such as I/O and synchronization:

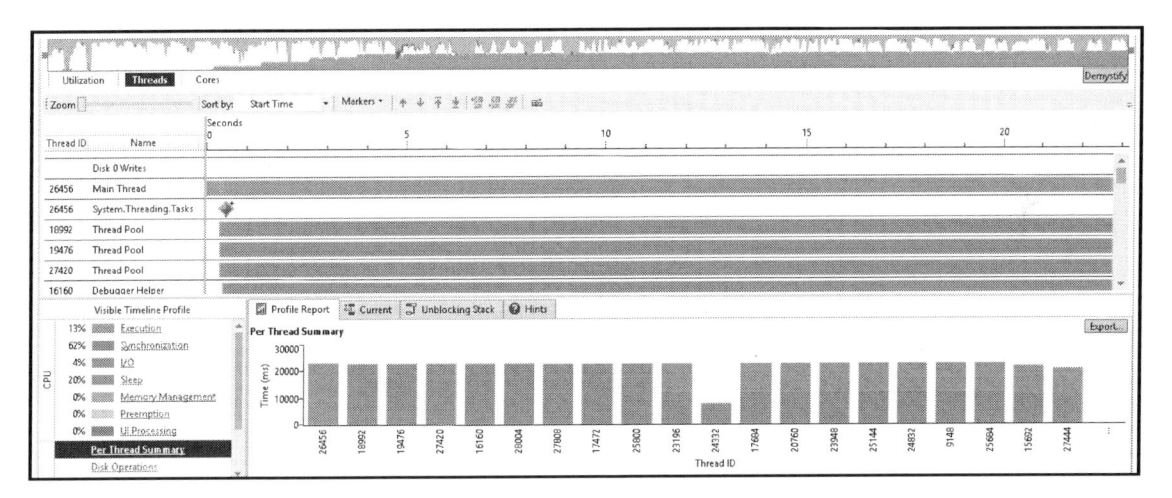

This view becomes very helpful in identifying and fixing performance bottlenecks in a system. We can therefore clearly identify how much time is spent in actual execution and how much time is spent dealing with synchronization issues.

Cores view

The **Cores** view can be used to identify how many times the threads perform a core switch:

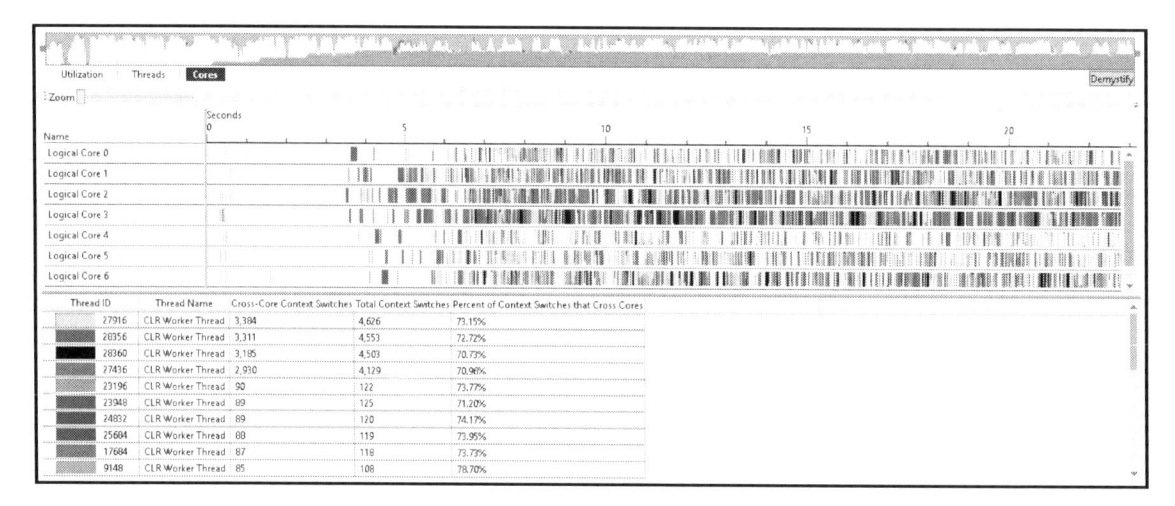

As you can see in the preceding diagram, our four threads with the IDs **12112**, **1604**, **16928**, and **4928** perform context switches across cores almost 60% of the time.

Armed with an understanding of all three views that are present in Concurrency Visualizer, we have come to the end of this chapter. Now, let's summarize what we have learned.

Summary

In this chapter, we discussed how to debug a multithreaded application using **Thread** windows for monitoring innumerable information captured by the .NET environment. We also learned how we can have a better insight into an application by using flag threads, switching among threads, having **Threads** and **Tasks** views in a **Parallel Stacks** window, opening up multiple **Parallel Watch** windows, and observing single-variable values on different tasks at a time.

In addition to this, we explored Concurrency Visualizer, which is an advanced tool used to troubleshoot complex threading issues that support Windows/console projects only.

In the next chapter, we will learn about writing unit test cases for parallel and async code and the problems associated with this. In addition, we'll learn about the challenges involved in setting up mock objects and how we can solve them.

Questions

1. Which of these is not a valid window for debugging threads in Visual Studio?
    1. Parallel Threads
    2. Parallel Stack
    3. GPU Thread
    4. Parallel Watch
2. We can track a particular thread while debugging by flagging it.
    1. True
    2. False
3. Which of these is not a valid view in Parallel Watch windows?
    1. Tasks
    2. Process
    3. Threads
4. How can we check a call stack of threads?
    1. Method view
    2. Task view
5. Which of these is not a valid view for Concurrency Visualizer?
    1. Threads view
    2. Cores view
    3. Process view

Further reading

You can read about parallel programming and debugging techniques at the following links:

- https://www.packtpub.com/application-development/c-multithreaded-and-parallel-programming
- https://www.packtpub.com/application-development/net-45-parallel-extensions-cookbook

11
Writing Unit Test Cases for Parallel and Asynchronous Code

In this chapter, we will introduce how to write unit test cases for parallel and asynchronous code. Writing unit test cases is an important aspect of writing robust code that is easy to maintain when you're working with large teams.

With the new CI/CD platforms, it's easier to make running unit test cases a part of the build process. This helps in finding issues at a very early stage. It also makes sense to write integration tests so that we can evaluate whether different components are working correctly together. Although you will find more features in Visual Studio's Community and Professional editions, only Visual Studio Enterprise edition has support for analyzing code coverage for unit test cases.

In this chapter, we will cover the following topics:

- Understanding the problems with writing unit test cases for async code
- Writing unit test cases for parallel and async code
- Mocking the setup for async code using Moq
- Using testing tools

Writing Unit Test Cases for Parallel and Asynchronous Code

Technical requirements

A basic understanding of unit testing and C# is required for learning how to write unit test cases using frameworks supported by Visual Studio. The source code for this chapter can be found on GitHub at `https://github.com/PacktPublishing/Hands-On-Parallel-Programming-with-C-8-and-.NET-Core-3/tree/master/Chapter11`.

Unit testing with .NET Core

.NET Core supports three frameworks for writing unit tests, that is, **MSTest**, **NUnit**, and **xUnit**, as shown in the following screenshot:

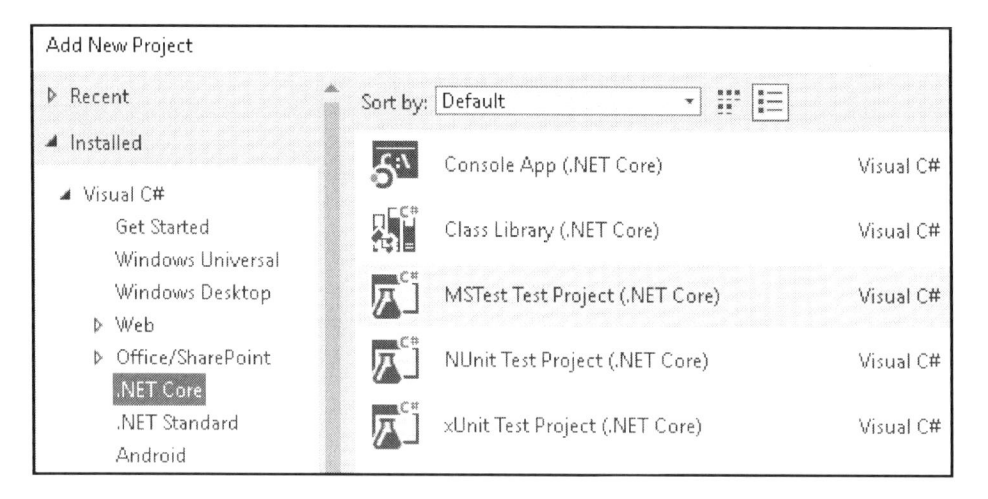

Initially, the preferred framework for writing test cases was **NUnit**. Then, **MSTest** was added to Visual Studio, before **xUnit** was introduced into .NET Core. **xUnit** is a very lean version in comparison to **NUnit** and helps users write clean tests and take advantage of new features. Some of the benefits of **xUnit** are as follows:

- It is lightweight.
- It uses new features.
- It has improved test isolation.
- The xUnit creator is also from Microsoft and is a tool that's used within Microsoft.
- The `Setup` and `TearDown` attributes have been replaced with a constructor and `System.IDisposable`, thereby forcing the developer to write clean code.

A unit test case is just a simple function that returns `void`, which is used to test the function logic and verify the output against a predefined set of inputs. To make the function recognizable as a test case, it must be decorated with the `[Fact]` attribute, as follows:

```
[Fact]
public void SomeFunctionWillReturn5AsWeUseResultToLetItFinish()
{
    var result = SomeFunction().Result;
    Assert.Equal(5, result);
}
```

To run this test case, we need to right-click on the function in the code and click **Run Test(s)** or **Debug Test(s)**:

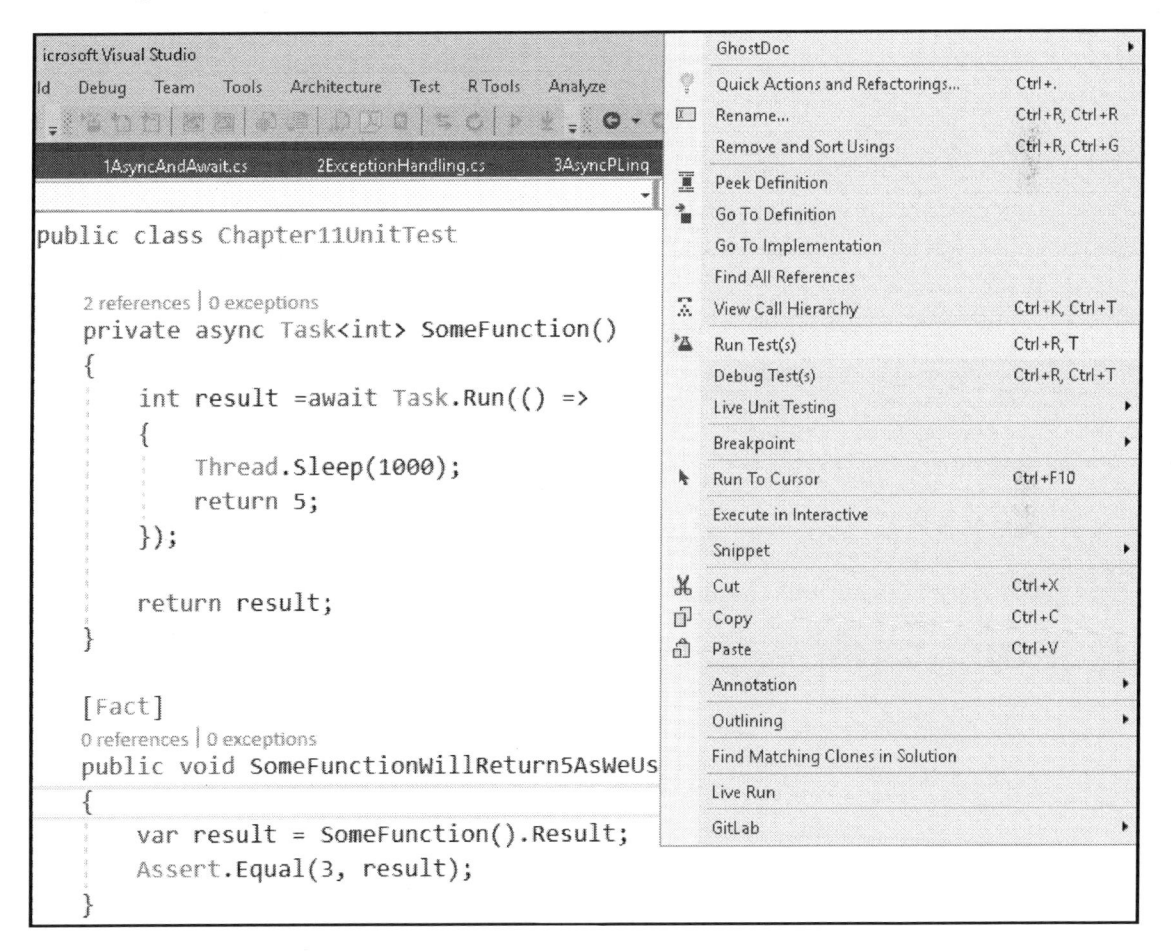

Writing Unit Test Cases for Parallel and Asynchronous Code

The output of the test case's execution can be seen in the **Test Explorer** window:

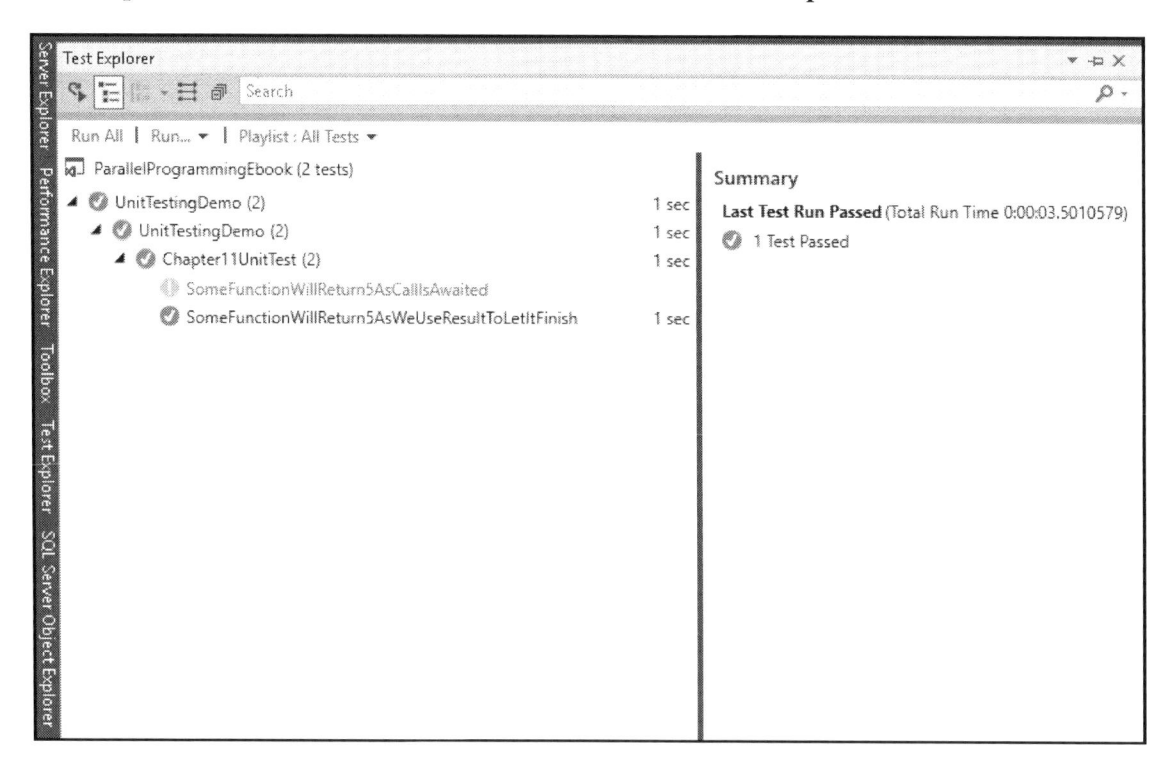

While this is fairly straightforward, writing unit test cases for parallel and asynchronous code is challenging. We'll discuss this in more detail in the next section.

Understanding the problems with writing unit test cases for async code

Async methods return a `Task` that needs to be awaited to get results. If it is not awaited, the method will return immediately, without waiting for the async task to finish. Consider the following method, which we're using to write a unit test case with xUnit:

```
private async Task<int> SomeFunction()
{
    int result =await Task.Run(() =>
    {
        Thread.Sleep(1000);
        return 5;
```

[250]

```
    });
    return result;
}
```

The method returns a constant value of 5 after a delay of 1 second. Since the method used `Task`, we made use of the `async` and `await` keywords to get the expected results. The following is a very simple test case we can use to test this method using MSTest:

```
[TestMethod]
public async void SomeFunctionShouldFailAsExpectedValueShouldBe5AndNot3()
{
    var result = await SomeFunction();
    Assert.AreEqual(3, result);
}
```

As you can see, the method should fail as the expected return value is 3 whereas the method is returning 5. When we run this test, however, it passes:

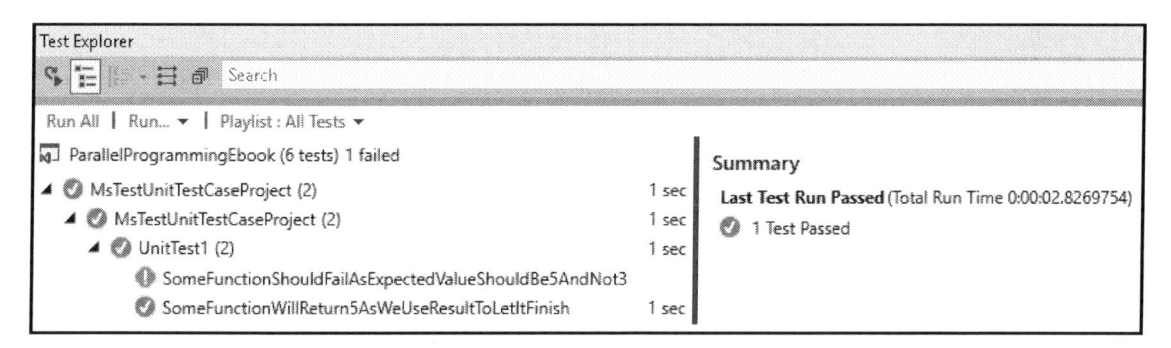

What happened here is that, since the method is marked as async, it returned immediately when it encountered the `await` keyword. When a task is returned, it's deemed to run at a future point in time, but since the test case returned without any failures, it was marked as a pass by the test framework. This is a major cause of concern as this means the tests will pass, even if the task throws an exception.

The preceding test case can be written slightly differently to make it run with MSTest:

```
[TestMethod]
public void SomeFunctionWillReturn5AsWeUseResultToLetItFinish()
{
    var result = SomeFunction().Result;
    Assert.AreEqual(3, result);
}
```

Writing Unit Test Cases for Parallel and Asynchronous Code

The same unit test case can be written in xUnit as follows:

```
[Fact]
public void SomeFunctionWillReturn5AsWeUseResultToLetItFinish()
{
    var result = SomeFunction().Result;
    Assert.Equal(5, result);
}
```

When we run the preceding xUnit test case, it runs successfully. However, the problem with this code is that it's a blocking test case, which can have a significant impact on the performance of our test suite. A better unit test case would be as follows:

```
[Fact]
public async void SomeFunctionWillReturn5AsCallIsAwaited()
{
    var result = await SomeFunction();
    Assert.Equal(5, result);
}
```

Initially, async unit test cases were not supported by every unit testing framework, as we saw in the case of MSTest. However, they are supported by xUnit and NUnit. The preceding test case once again returns as a success.

The preceding unit test case can be written using NUnit as follows:

```
[Test]
public async void SomeFunctionWillReturn5AsCallIsAwaited()
{
    var result = await SomeFunction();
    Assert.AreEqual(3, result);
}
```

There are some differences here compared to the preceding code. The `[Fact]` attribute is replaced by `[Test]`, while `Assert.Equal` is replaced by `Assert.AreEqual`. The main difference, however, which you will see when you try running the preceding test case in Visual Studio, is that it will fail with the following error: `"Message: Async test method must have non-void return type"`. So, for NUnit, the method needs to be changed, as follows:

```
[Test]
public async Task SomeFunctionWillReturn5AsCallIsAwaited()
{
    var result = await SomeFunction();
    Assert.AreEqual(3, result);
}
```

[252]

The only difference here is that `void` is replaced with `Task`.

In this section, we have seen the problems that we may face when we use various frameworks that are provided for unit testing. Now, let's take a look at how to write better unit test cases.

Writing unit test cases for parallel and async code

In the previous section, we learned how to write unit test cases for async code. In this section, we will discuss writing unit test cases for exception scenarios. Consider the following method:

```
private async Task<float> GetDivisionAsync(int number , int divisor)
{
    if (divisor == 0)
    {
        throw new DivideByZeroException();
    }
    int result = await Task.Run(() =>
    {
        Thread.Sleep(1000);
        return number / divisor;
    });
    return result;
}
```

The preceding method returns the result of the division of two numbers asynchronously. If the divisor is 0, then the `DivideByZero` exception is thrown by the method. We need two types of test cases to cover both scenarios:

- Checking for a successful result
- Checking for an exception result when the divisor is 0

Checking for a successful result

The test case will look as follows:

```
[Test]
public async Task GetDivisionAsyncShouldReturnSuccessIfDivisorIsNotZero()
{
    int number = 20;
```

```
        int divisor = 4;
        var result = await GetDivisionAsync(number, divisor);
        Assert.AreEqual(result, 5);
}
```

As you can see, the expected result is 5. When we run the test, it will show up as successful in the **Test Explorer**.

Checking for an exception result when the divisor is 0

We can write a test case for a method that throws an exception using the `Assert.ThrowsAsync<>` method:

```
[Test]
public void GetDivisionAsyncShouldCheckForExceptionIfDivisorIsNotZero()
{
    int number = 20;
    int divisor = 0;
    Assert.ThrowsAsync<DivideByZeroException>(async () =>
      await GetDivisionAsync(number, divisor));
}
```

As you can see, we checked the assertion using `Assert.ThrowsAsync<DivideByZeroException>` while calling the `GetDivisionAsync` method asynchronously. Since we pass the `divisor` as 0, the method will throw an exception and the assertion will hold true.

Mocking the setup for async code using Moq

Mocking objects is a very important aspect of unit testing. As you may be aware, unit testing is about testing one module at a time; any external dependency is assumed to be working fine.

There are many mocking frameworks available for .NET, including the following:

- NSubstitute (not supported in .NET core)
- Rhino Mocks (not supported in .NET core)
- Moq (supported in .NET core)
- NMock3 (not supported in .NET core)

For the sake of demonstration, we will be using Moq to mock our serviced components.

In this section, we will create a simple service containing asynchronous methods. Then, we will try to write unit test cases for the methods that call the service. Let's consider a service interface:

```
public interface IService
{
    Task<string> GetDataAsync();
}
```

As we can see, the interface has a `GetDataAsync()` method, which fetches data in an asynchronous manner. The following snippet shows a controller class that makes use of some dependency injection frameworks to gain access to the service instance:

```
class Controller
{
    public Controller (IService service)
    {
        Service = service;
    }
    public IService Service { get; }
    public async Task DisplayData()
    {
        var data =await Service.GetDataAsync();
        Console.WriteLine(data);
    }
}
```

The preceding `Controller` class also exposes an asynchronous method called `DisplayData()`, which fetches data from a service and writes it to the console. When we try to write a unit test case for the preceding method, the first problem we will encounter is that we have no way of creating the service instance in the absence of any concrete implementation. Even if we do have a concrete implementation, we should avoid calling the actual service method as this would be more appropriate in an integration test case rather than a unit test case. Mocking comes to our rescue here.

Writing Unit Test Cases for Parallel and Asynchronous Code

Let's try to write a unit test case for the preceding method using Moq:

1. We need to install `Moq` as a NuGet package.
2. Add the namespace for it as follows:

   ```
   using Moq;
   ```

3. Create a mock object, as follows:

   ```
   var serviceMock = new Mock<IService>();
   ```

4. Set up a mock object that returns dummy data. This can be achieved using the `Task.FromResult` method, as follows:

   ```
   serviceMock.Setup(s => s.GetDataAsync()).Returns(
              Task.FromResult("Some Dummy Value"));
   ```

5. Next, we need to create a controller object by passing the mocked object we just created:

   ```
   var controller = new Controller(serviceMock.Object);
   ```

The following is a simple test case for the `DisplayData()` method:

```
[Test]
    public async System.Threading.Tasks.Task DisplayDataTestAsync()
    {
        var serviceMock = new Mock<IService>();
        serviceMock.Setup(s => s.GetDataAsync()).Returns(
            Task.FromResult("Some Dummy Value"));
        var controller = new Controller(serviceMock.Object);
        await controller.DisplayData();
    }
```

The preceding code shows how we can set up data for mock objects. Another way to set up data for mock objects is via the `TaskCompletionSource` class, as follows:

```
[Test]
public async Task DisplayDataTestAsyncUsingTaskCompletionSource()
{
    // Create a mock service
    var serviceMock = new Mock<IService>();
    string data = "Some Dummy Value";
    //Create task completion source
    var tcs = new TaskCompletionSource<string>();
    //Setup completion source to return test data
    tcs.SetResult(data);
    //Setup mock service object to return Task underlined by tcs
```

```
        //when GetDataAsync method of service is called
        serviceMock.Setup(s => s.GetDataAsync()).Returns(tcs.Task);
        //Pass mock service instance to Controller
        var controller = new Controller(serviceMock.Object);
        //Call DisplayData method of controller asynchronously
        await controller.DisplayData();
    }
```

Since the number of test cases can really grow in an enterprise project, the need to be able to find and execute test cases arises. In the next section, we will discuss some common testing tools in Visual Studio that can help us manage the test case execution process.

Testing tools

One of the most important tools in Visual Studio to run a test or see the results of test execution is **Test Explorer**. We had a brief look at **Test Explorer** at the start of this chapter. One key feature of **Test Explorer** is its ability to run test cases in parallel. If you have a system with multiple cores, you can easily take advantage of parallelism to run test cases faster. This can be done by clicking on the **Run Tests** in parallel toolbar button in **Test Explorer**:

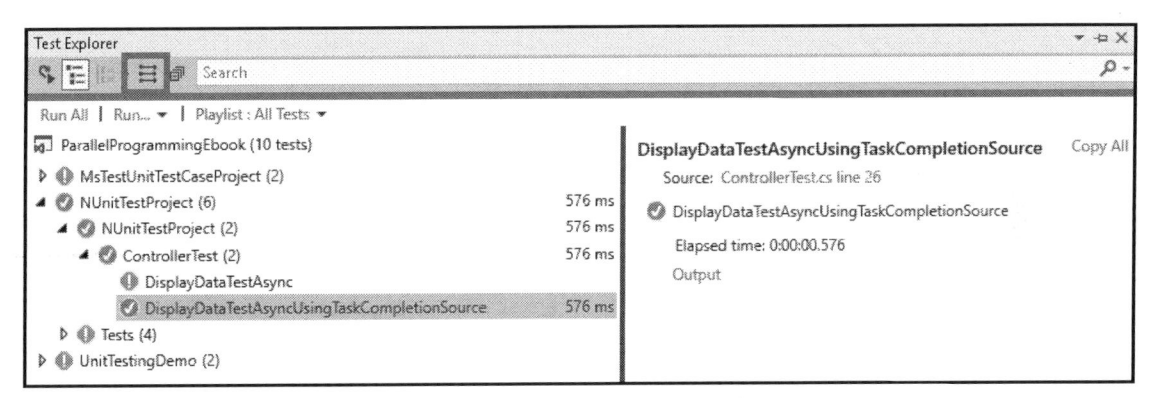

Depending on your version of Visual Studio, some additional support is provided by Microsoft. One useful tool is the option to generate unit test cases automatically using **Intellitest**. Intellitest analyzes your source code and automatically generates test cases, test data, and test suites. Intellitest isn't supported in .NET core yet, though it's available for other versions of the .NET Framework. It's likely to have a future upgrade to Visual Studio.

Summary

In this chapter, we have learned about writing unit test cases for async methods, which helps in achieving robust code, supporting large teams, and adapting to new CI/CD platforms, which helps in finding issues at a very early stage. We started by introducing a few problems that you may come across while writing unit test cases for parallel and async code and how you can mitigate them using correct coding practices. Then, we moved on and looked at mocking, which is a very important aspect of unit testing.

We learned that Moq has support for .NET Core and that .NET Core is evolving very fast; soon, there will be support for all the major mocking frameworks. All the steps for writing test cases were explained as well, including installing Moq as a NuGet package and setting up data for mock objects. Finally, we explored the features of an important testing tool, **Test Explorer**, which we can use to write cleaner test cases, and how to parallelize unit test cases for faster execution.

In the next chapter, we will introduce the concepts and roles of IIS and Kestrel in a .NET Core web application development environment.

Questions

1. Which of these is not a supported unit testing framework in Visual Studio?
    1. JUnit
    2. NUnit
    3. xUnit
    4. MSTest
2. How can we check the output of a unit test case?
    1. By using the **Task Explorer** window
    2. By using the **Test Explorer** window
3. Which attributes can you apply to a test method when the testing framework is xUnit?
    1. Fact
    2. TestMethod
    3. Test

4. How can you verify the success of a test case that throws an exception?
    1. `Assert.AreEqual(ex, typeof(Exception)`
    2. `Assert.IsException`
    3. `Assert.ThrowAsync<T>`

5. Which of these mocking frameworks is supported in .NET Core?
    1. NSubstitute
    2. Moq
    3. Rhino Mocks
    4. NMock

Further reading

You can read about parallel programming and unit testing techniques at the following web pages:

- `https://www.packtpub.com/application-development/c-multithreaded-and-parallel-programming`
- `https://www.packtpub.com/application-development/net-45-parallel-extensions-cookbook`

Section 5: Parallel Programming Feature Additions to .NET Core

In this section, you will become familiar with new breakthroughs in .NET Core that support parallel programming.

This section comprises the following chapters:

- `Chapter 12`, *IIS and Kestrel in ASP.NET Core*
- `Chapter 13`, *Patterns in Parallel Programming*
- `Chapter 14`, *Distributed Memory Management*

12
IIS and Kestrel in ASP.NET Core

In the previous chapter, we discussed writing unit test cases for parallel and asynchronous code. We also discussed three unit testing frameworks that are available in Visual Studio: MSUnit, NUnit, and xUnit.

In this chapter, we will introduce how the threading model works with **Internet Information Services** (**IIS**) and Kestrel. We will also look at various tweaks we can make to take maximum advantage of resources on a server. We will introduce the working model of Kestrel and how we can take advantage of parallel programming techniques while creating microservices.

In this chapter, we will cover the following topics:

- The IIS threading model and internals
- The Kestrel threading model and internals
- Introduction to best practices of threading in microservices
- Introduction to async in ASP.NET MVC Core
- Async streams (new in .NET Core 3.0)

Let's get started.

Technical requirements

A good understanding of how servers work is required so that you can understand this chapter. You should also learn about threading models before you start this chapter. The source code for this chapter is available on GitHub at `https://github.com/PacktPublishing/-Hands-On-Parallel-Programming-with-C-8-and-.NET-Core-3/tree/master/Chapter12`.

IIS threading model and internals

As the name suggests, these are services that are utilized on the Windows system to connect your web applications from other systems via the internet over a set of protocols such as HTTP, TCP, web sockets, and more.

In this section, we will discuss how the **IIS threading model** works. At the core of IIS lies the **CLR thread pool**. It's very important to understand how the CLR thread pool adds and removes threads in order to understand how IIS works to serve user requests.

Every application that gets deployed to IIS is assigned a unique worker process. Each worker process has two thread pools: the **worker thread pool** and the **IOCP** (short for **I/O completion port**) thread pool:

- Whenever we create a new thread pool thread using either legacy `ThreadPool.QueueUserWorkItem` or **TPL**, the ASP.NET runtime makes use of worker threads for processing.
- Whenever we perform any I/O operations, that is, database calls, file read/write, or network calls to another web service, the ASP.NET runtime makes use of IOCP threads.

By default, there is one worker thread and one IOCP thread per processor. So, a dual-core CPU will have two workers and two IOCP threads by default. `ThreadPool` keeps adding and removing threads, depending on load and demand. IIS assigns a thread to each request that it receives. This allows every request to have a different context from other requests hitting the server at the same time. It's the responsibility of the thread to cater to requests, as well as generating and sending a response back to a client.

If the number of available thread pool threads is less than the number of requests that are received by a server at any time, the requests will start to be queued. Later, the thread pool generates threads using one of two important algorithms, known as *Hill Climbing* and *Starvation Avoidance*. The creation of threads is not instant and it usually takes up to 500 ms from the time `ThreadPool` comes to know that there is a shortage of threads. Let's try to understand both algorithms that are used by `ThreadPool` to generate threads.

Starvation Avoidance

In this algorithm, `ThreadPool` keeps monitoring the queue, and if it doesn't progress, then it keeps pumping new threads into the queue.

Hill Climbing

In this algorithm, `ThreadPool` tries to maximize the throughput using as few threads as possible.

Running IIS with the default settings will have a significant impact on performance since, by default, only one worker thread is available per processor. We can increase this setting by modifying the configuration element in the `machine.config` file, as follows:

```
<configuration>
    <system.web>
        <processModel minWorkerThreads="25" minIoThreads="25" />
    </system.web>
</configuration>
```

As you can see, we increased the minimum worker threads and IOCP threads to 25. As more requests come in, additional threads will be created. An important thing to note here is that since every request is assigned one unique thread, we should avoid writing blocking code. With blocking code, there will not be free threads. Once a thread pool is exhausted, the requests will start to queue. IIS can only queue up to 1,000 requests per application pool. We can modify this by changing the `requestQueueLimit` application settings in the `machine.config` file.

To modify the settings for all the application pools, we need to add the `applicationPool` element with the required values:

```
<system.web>
  <applicationPool
    maxConcurrentRequestPerCPU="5000"
    maxConcurrentThreadsPerCPU="0"
    requestQueueLimit="5000" />
</system.web>
```

To modify the settings for a single application pool, we need to navigate to the **Advanced Settings** of a specific application pool in IIS. As shown in the following screenshot, we can change the **Queue Length** property to modify a number of requests that can be queued per application pool:

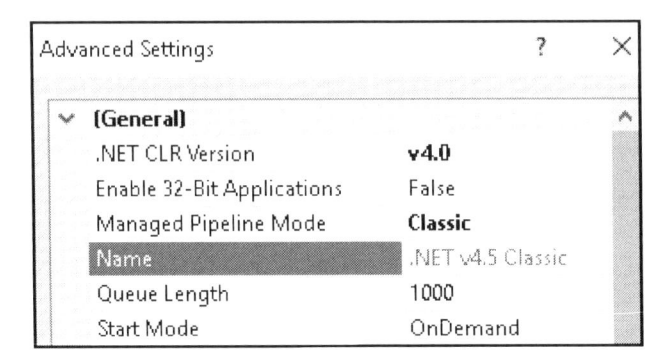

![Advanced Settings dialog showing General section with .NET CLR Version v4.0, Enable 32-Bit Applications False, Managed Pipeline Mode Classic, Name .NET v4.5 Classic, Queue Length 1000, Start Mode OnDemand]

As a good coding practice for developers to reduce contention issues and thus avoid queues on the server, we should try to use the `async/await` keywords for any blocking I/O code. This will reduce contention issues on a server as threads will not be blocked and return to the thread pool to serve other requests.

Kestrel threading model and internals

IIS has been the most popular server for hosting .NET applications, but it's tied to the Windows OS. With more and more cloud providers coming and non-Windows cloud hosting options becoming a lot cheaper, there was a need for a cross-platform hosting server. Microsoft introduced Kestrel as a cross-platform web server for hosting ASP.NET Core applications. If we create and run ASP.NET Core applications, Kestrel is the default web server that runs them. Kestrel is open source and uses an event-driven, asynchronous I/O-based server. Kestrel is not a full-fledged web server and is recommended to be used behind full-featured web servers such as IIS and Nginx.

When it was initially launched, Kestrel was based on the `libuv` library, which is also open source. The use of `libuv` in .NET is not new and dates back to ASP.NET 5. `libuv` has been specifically built for asynchronous I/O operations and uses a single-threaded event looping model. The library also supports cross-platform asynchronous sockets on Windows, macOS, and Linux. You can check its progress and download the source code for `libuv` for custom implementation from GitHub at https://github.com/libuv/libuv.

libuv has been used in Kestrel to only support async I/O. Apart from I/O operations, all the other work that's done in Kestrel is still done by .NET worker threads using managed code. The core idea behind creating Kestrel is improving the performance of servers. The stack is very robust and extensible. libuv in Kestrel is used as a transport layer only and, due to excellent abstraction, it can be replaced by other network implementations as well. Kestrel also supports running multiple event loops, thereby making it a more robust choice than Node.js. The number of event loops that are used depends on the number of logical processors on the machine and on there being one thread running one event loop. We can configure this number via code as well while creating the host.

The following is an excerpt from the Program.cs file, which is present in all ASP.NET Core projects:

```
public class Program
{
    public static void Main(string[] args)
    {
        CreateWebHostBuilder(args).Build().Run();
    }
    public static IWebHostBuilder CreateWebHostBuilder(string[] args) =>
      WebHost.CreateDefaultBuilder(args).UseStartup<Startup>();
}
```

As you will see, the Kestrel server is based on the builder pattern, and functionality can be added using the appropriate packages and extension methods. In the following sections, we will learn how to modify the settings of Kestrel for different versions of .NET Core.

ASP.NET Core 1.x

We can use an extension method called UseLibuv to set the thread count. We can do this by setting the ThreadCount property, as shown in the following code:

```
public static IWebHostBuilder CreateWebHostBuilder(string[] args) =>
        WebHost.CreateDefaultBuilder(args)
        .UseLibuv(opts => opts.ThreadCount = 4)
        .UseStartup<Startup>();
```

> **TIP:** `WebHost` has been replaced by a generic host in .NET Core 3.0. The following is a code snippet for ASP.NET Core 3.0:

```
public static IHostBuilder CreateHostBuilder(string[] args) =>
        Host.CreateDefaultBuilder(args)
            .ConfigureWebHostDefaults(webBuilder =>
            {
                webBuilder.UseStartup<Startup>();
            });
```

ASP.NET Core 2.x

Starting from ASP.NET 2.1, Kestrel has replaced the default transport from `libuv` for managed sockets. So, if you are upgrading your project from ASP.NET Core to ASP.NET 2.x or 3.x and still want to use `libuv`, you need to add the `Microsoft.AspNetCore.Server.Kestrel.Transport.Libuv` NuGet package to make the code work.

Kestrel currently supports the following scenarios:

- HTTPS
- Opaque upgrades, which are used to enable web sockets (https://github.com/aspnet/websockets)
- Unix sockets behind Nginx for high performance
- HTTP/2 (not currently supported on macOS)

Since Kestrel is built on sockets, you can configure the connection limits of them by using the `ConfigureLimits` method on `Host`:

```
Host.CreateDefaultBuilder(args)
.ConfigureKestrel((context, options) =>
{
    options.Limits.MaxConcurrentConnections = 100;
    options.Limits.MaxConcurrentUpgradedConnections = 100;
}
```

The default connection limit is unlimited if we set `MaxConcurrentConnections` to null.

Introducing the best practices of threading in microservices

Microservices are the most popular software design patterns for making very performant and scalable backend services. Rather than building one service for an entire application, multiple loosely coupled services are created, with each being responsible for a single feature. Depending on the load on features, each service can be scaled up or down individually. Consequently, while designing microservices, the choice of the threading model you use becomes very important.

Microservices can be stateless or stateful. The choice between stateless and stateful does have an impact on performance. With stateless services, the requests can be served in any order without regard to what happened before or after the current request, whereas with stateful services, all the requests should be processed in a particular order, like a queue. This can have an impact on performance. Since microservices are asynchronous, we need to write some logic to make sure the request is processed in the correct order and state after each request is communicated to the next message. Microservices can be single-threaded or multithreaded as well, and this choice coupled with the state can really improve or degrade performance and should be well thought out while planning services.

The microservice design approaches can be categorized as follows:

- Single thread-single process microservices
- Single thread-multiple processes microservices
- Multiple threads-single process microservices

We'll look at these design approaches in more detail in the following sections.

Single thread-single process microservices

This is the most basic design for microservices. The microservice runs on a single thread in a single CPU core. With every new request from a client, a new thread is created, which spawns a new process. This takes away the connection pooling caching benefits. While working with a database, every new process will create a new connection pool. Also, since only one process can be created at a time, only one client can be served.

The cons of single thread-single process microservices include the fact that it is a waste of resources and that the throughput of the service doesn't increase when the load is increased.

Single thread-multiple process microservices

The microservice runs on a single thread but can spawn multiple processes, thereby improving their throughput. Since a new process is created for each client, we cannot take advantage of connection pooling while connecting to databases. There are some third-party environments, such as Zend, OpCache, and APC, that provide cross-process opcode caches.

The pros of the single thread-multiple processes microservices approach is that it improves throughput on load, but note that we cannot take advantage of connection pooling.

Multiple threads-single process

Microservice runs on multiple threads and there is a single long-lived process. With the same database, we can take advantage of connection pooling and also limit the number of connections as and when needed. The problem with the single process is that all the threads will use a shared resource and can have resource contention issues.

The pro of the multiple threads-single process approach is that it improves the performance of stateless services, whereas its con is that there can be synchronization issues when sharing a resource.

Asynchronous services

We can avoid performance issues during integration with various application components by decoupling communication between microservices. Microservices must be created asynchronously by design to achieve this decoupling.

Dedicated thread pools

If the application flow requires us to connect to various microservices, then it makes more sense to create a dedicated thread pool for such tasks. With a single thread pool, if a service starts having issues, then all the threads from the pool can become exhausted. This can impact the performance of a microservice. This pattern is also known as the **Bulkheads** pattern. The following diagram shows two microservices with a shared pool. As you can see, both microservices use a shared connection pool:

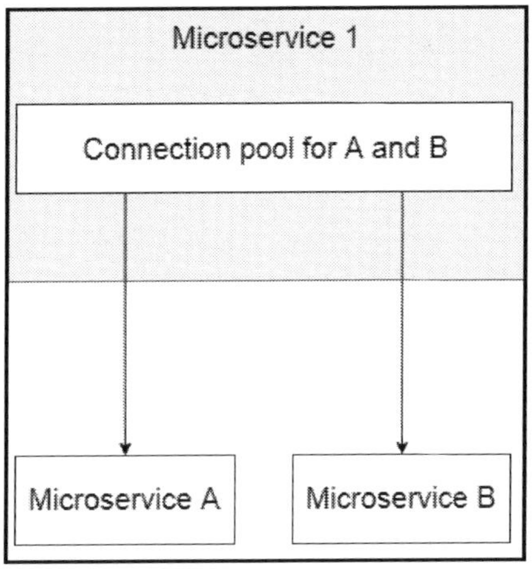
Microservice 1
Connection pool for A and B
Microservice A
Microservice B

The following diagram shows two microservices with dedicated thread pools:

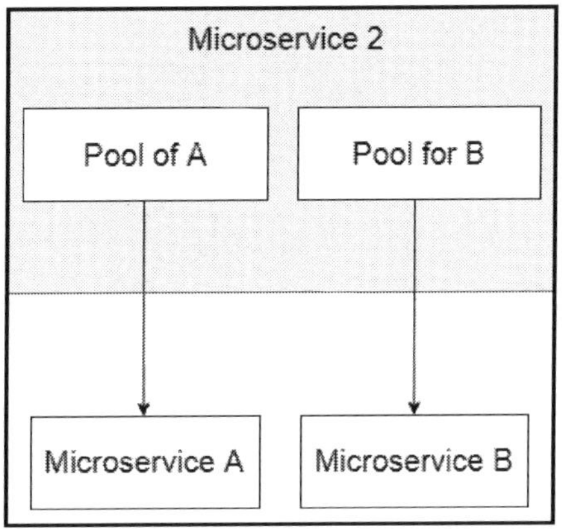
Microservice 2
Pool of A
Pool for B
Microservice A
Microservice B

In the next section, we will introduce how async can be used in ASP.NET MVC core.

Introducing async in ASP.NET MVC core

`async` and `await` are code markers that help us write asynchronous code using TPL. They help maintain the structure of code and make it look synchronous while processing code asynchronously in the background.

IIS and Kestrel in ASP.NET Core

> We introduced `async` and `await` in Chapter 9, *Async, Await, and Task-Based Asynchronous Programming Basics*.

Now, let's create an asynchronous web API with ASP.NET Core 3.0 and VS 2019 preview. The API will read a file from the server:

1. Open Visual Studio 2019 to be presented with the following screen. Create a new **ASP.NET Core Web Application** project in VS 2019, as shown in the following screenshot:

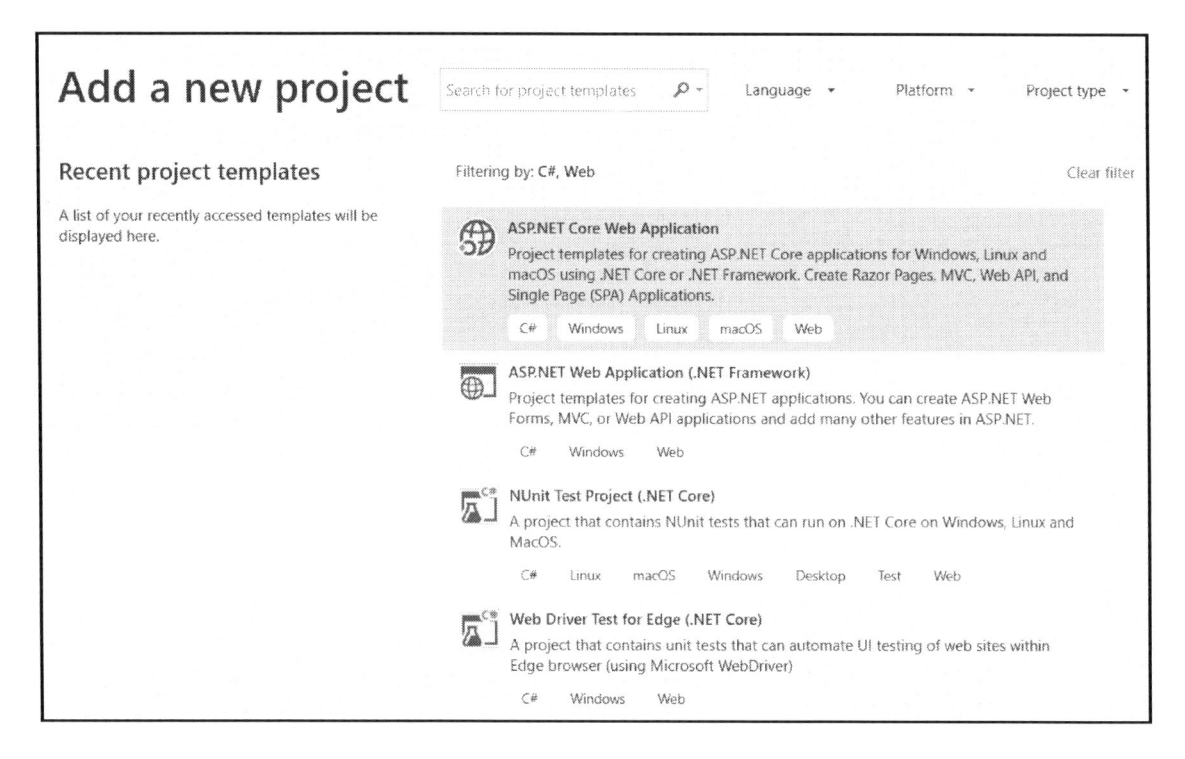

2. Give the project a name and the location where you want it to be created:

Configure your new project

ASP.NET Core Web Application   C#   Windows   Linux   macOS   Web

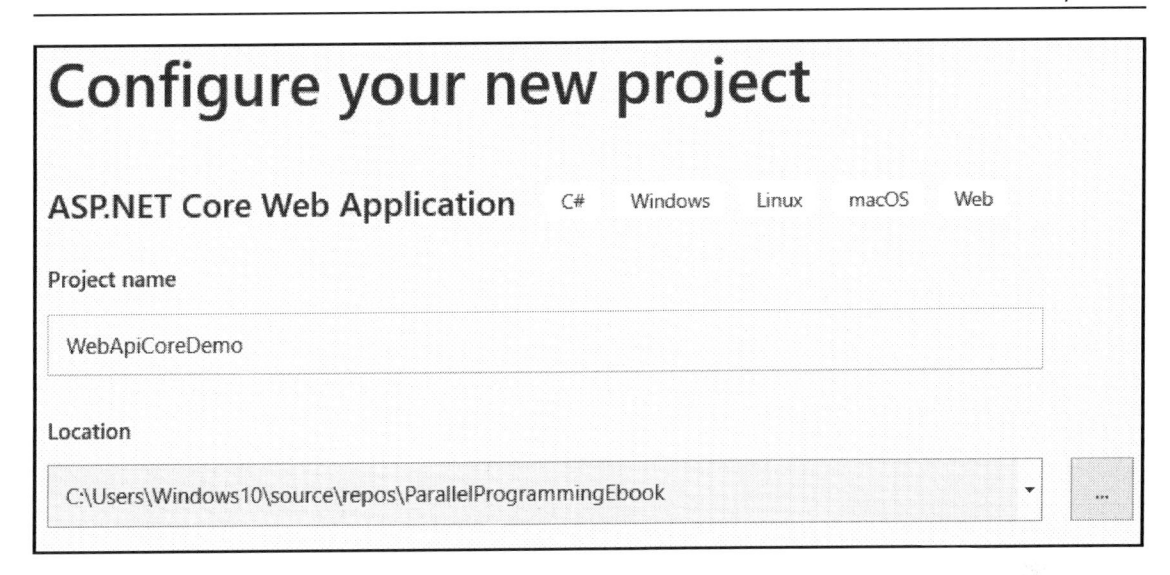

Project name

`WebApiCoreDemo`

Location

`C:\Users\Windows10\source\repos\ParallelProgrammingEbook`

3. Select the project's type, which in our case is **API**, and click **Create**:

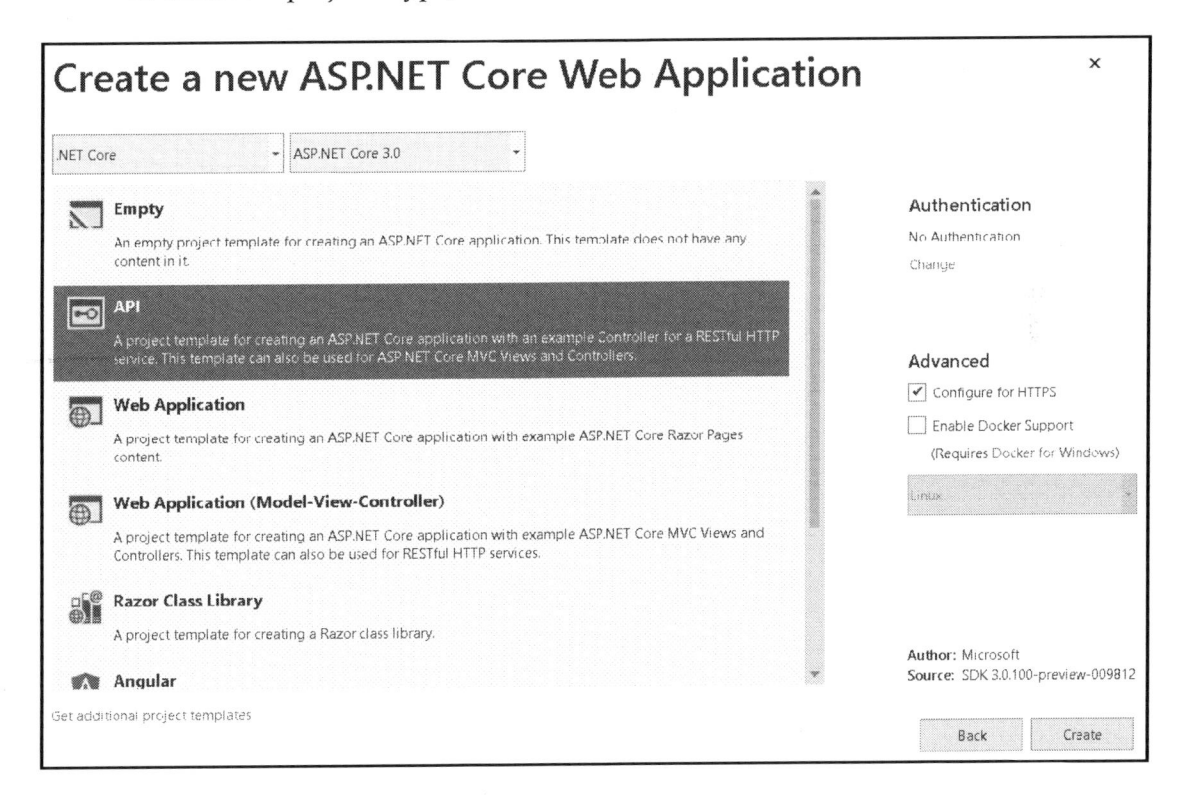

Create a new ASP.NET Core Web Application

.NET Core   ASP.NET Core 3.0

Empty
An empty project template for creating an ASP.NET Core application. This template does not have any content in it.

API
A project template for creating an ASP.NET Core application with an example Controller for a RESTful HTTP service. This template can also be used for ASP.NET Core MVC Views and Controllers.

Web Application
A project template for creating an ASP.NET Core application with example ASP.NET Core Razor Pages content.

Web Application (Model-View-Controller)
A project template for creating an ASP.NET Core application with example ASP.NET Core MVC Views and Controllers. This template can also be used for RESTful HTTP services.

Razor Class Library
A project template for creating a Razor class library.

Angular

Get additional project templates

Authentication
No Authentication
Change

Advanced
☑ Configure for HTTPS
☐ Enable Docker Support
(Requires Docker for Windows)

Linux

Author: Microsoft
Source: SDK 3.0.100-preview-009812

Back   Create

4. Now, create a new folder in our project called `Files` and add a file named `data.txt` that contains the following content:

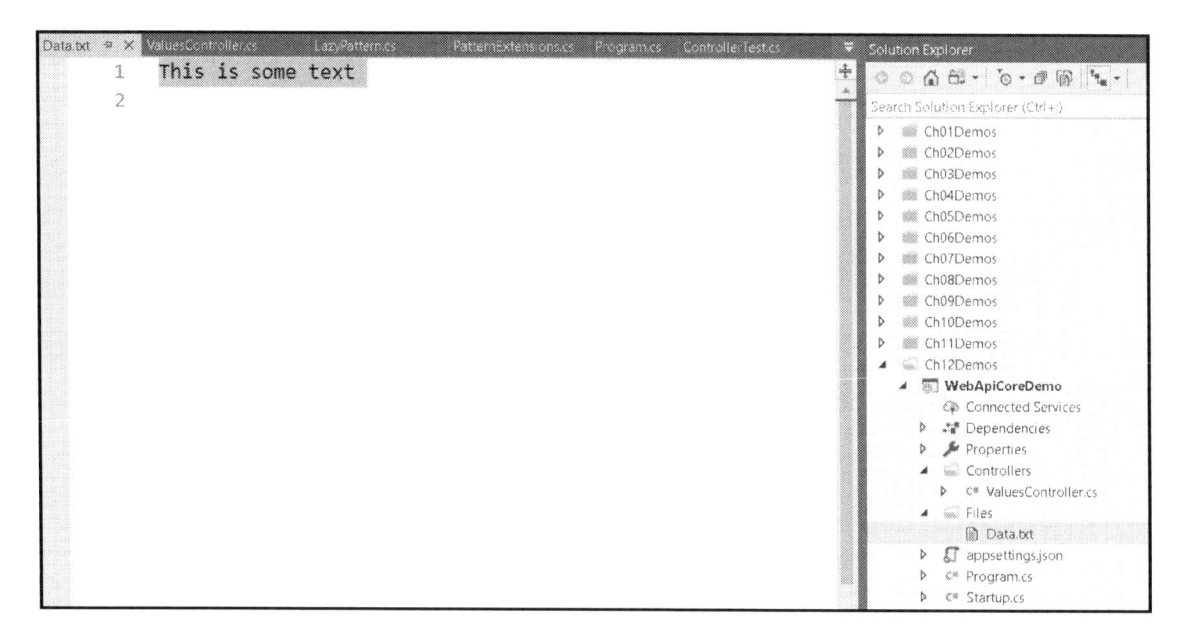

```
1  This is some text
2
```

5. Next, we will modify the `Get` method in `ValuesController.cs`, as follows:

```
[HttpGet]
public ActionResult<IEnumerable<string>> Get()
{
    var filePath = System.IO.Path.Combine(
      HostingEnvironment.ContentRootPath,"Files","data.txt");
    var text = System.IO.File.ReadAllText(filePath);
    return Content(text);
}
```

This is a simple method that reads a file from the server and returns the content as a string to the user. The problem with this code is that, when `File.ReadAllText` is called, the calling thread will be blocked until the file is read completely. As we now know, our server's response will be to make the call asynchronous, as follows:

```
[HttpGet]
public async Task<ActionResult<IEnumerable<string>>> GetAsync()
{
    var filePath = System.IO.Path.Combine(
      HostingEnvironment.ContentRootPath, "Files", "data.txt");
    var text = await System.IO.File.ReadAllTextAsync(filePath);
```

```
    return Content(text);
}
```

The ASP.NET Core web API supports all the new features of parallel programming, including async, as we have seen from the preceding code example.

Async streams

.NET Core 3.0 also introduced asynchronous streams support. `IAsyncEnumerable<T>` is the asynchronous version of `IEnumerable<T>`. This new feature allows developers to await `foreach` loops over `IAsyncEnumerable<T>` to consume elements from the stream and use `yield` to return a stream to produce elements.

This is very important in scenarios where we want to iterate over elements asynchronously and perform some compute operations on iterated elements. With more emphasis being on big data nowadays (which is available as streamed output), it makes more sense to go for *async* streams, which support high volumes of data while making servers responsive by efficiently utilizing threads at the same time.

Two new interfaces have been added to support async streams:

```
public interface IAsyncEnumerable<T>
{
  public IAsyncEnumerator<T> GetEnumerator();
}
public interface IAsyncEnumerator<out T>
{
  public T Current { get; }
  public Task<bool> MoveNextAsync();
}
```

As you can see from the definition of `IAsyncEnumerator`, `MoveNext` has been made asynchronous. This has two benefits:

- It's easy to cache `Task<bool>` over `Task<T>` so that there will be fewer memory allocations
- Existing collections just need to add one extra method to support asynchronous behaviors

Let's try to understand this using some sample code that enumerates numbers at odd indexes asynchronously.

Here is a custom enumerator:

```
class OddIndexEnumerator : IAsyncEnumerator<int>
{
    List<int> _numbers;
    int _currentIndex = 1;
    public OddIndexEnumerator(IEnumerable<int> numbers)
    {
        _numbers = numbers.ToList();
    }
    public int Current
    {
        get
        {
            Task.Delay(2000);
            return _numbers[_currentIndex];
        }
    }
    public ValueTask DisposeAsync()
    {
        return new ValueTask(Task.CompletedTask);
    }
    public ValueTask<bool> MoveNextAsync()
    {
        Task.Delay(2000);
        if (_currentIndex < _numbers.Count() - 2)
        {
            _currentIndex += 2;
            return new ValueTask<bool>(Task.FromResult<bool>(true));
        }
        return new ValueTask<bool>(Task.FromResult<bool>(false));
    }
}
```

As you can see from the `MoveNextAsync()` method we defined in the preceding code, this method starts with an odd index (that is, index 1) and keeps reading items at odd indexes.

The following is our collection, which makes use of the custom enumeration logic we created previously and implements the `GetAsyncEnumerator()` method of the `IAsyncEnumerable<T>` interface to return the `OddIndexEnumerator` enumerator we created:

```
class CustomAsyncIntegerCollection : IAsyncEnumerable<int>
{
    List<int> _numbers;
    public CustomAsyncIntegerCollection(IEnumerable<int> numbers)
    {
```

```
        _numbers = numbers.ToList();
    }
    public IAsyncEnumerator<int> GetAsyncEnumerator(
      CancellationToken cancellationToken = default)
    {
        return new OddIndexEnumerator(_numbers);
    }
}
```

Here is our magic extension method, which will convert our custom collection into an `AsyncEnumerable`. As you can see, it works on any collection that implements `IEnumerable<int>` and wraps the underlying collection with `CustomAsyncIntegerCollection`, which, in turn, implements `IAsyncEnumerable<T>`:

```
public static class CollectionExtensions
{
    public static IAsyncEnumerable<int> AsEnumerable(this
      IEnumerable<int> source) => new CustomAsyncIntegerCollection(source);
}
```

Once all the pieces are in place, we can create a method that returns an asynchronous stream. We can see how items are generated by using the `yield` keyword:

```
static async IAsyncEnumerable<int> GetBigResultsAsync()
{
    var list = Enumerable.Range(1, 20);
    await foreach (var item in list.AsEnumerable())
    {
        yield return item;
    }
}
```

The following code calls the stream. Here, we call the `GetBigResultsAsync()` method, which returns `IAsyncEnumerable<int>` inside a `foreach` loop and then iterates over it asynchronously:

```
async static Task Main(string[] args)
{
    await foreach (var dataPoint in GetBigResultsAsync())
    {
        Console.WriteLine(dataPoint);
    }
    Console.WriteLine("Hello World!");
}
```

The following is the output of the preceding code. As you can see, it generated numbers at the odd indexes in the collection:

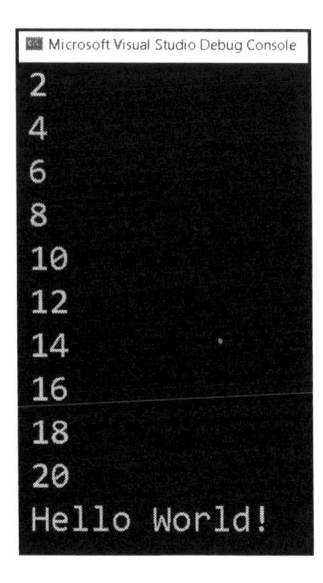

```
2
4
6
8
10
12
14
16
18
20
Hello World!
```

In this section, we introduced async streams, which make it very efficient for us to iterate over a collection in parallel without blocking the caller thread, which is something that's been missing since TPL was introduced.

Now, let's take a look at what we covered in this chapter.

Summary

In this chapter, we discussed IIS threading models and making changes to .NET Core implementations of a server by going from using `libuv` to .NET Core 2.0 in order to manage sockets from .NET Core 2.1 onward. We also discussed ways to improve the performance of IIS, Kestrel, and some thread pool algorithms such as Starvation Avoidance and Hill Climbing. We introduced the concepts of microservices and various threading patterns that are used in microservices, such as single thread-single process microservices, single thread-multiple process microservices, and multiple threads-single process microservices.

We also discussed the process of using async in ASP.NET MVC Core 3.0 and introduced the new concept of async streams in .NET Core 3.0, as well as its usage. Async streams can be very handy in big data scenarios in which the load on servers can be huge due to a rapid influx of data.

In the next chapter, we will learn about some patterns that are commonly used in parallel and asynchronous programming. These patterns will enhance our understanding of parallel programming.

Questions

1. Which of these is used to host web applications?
    1. `IWebHostBuilder`
    2. `IHostBuilder`
2. Which of the following `ThreadPool` algorithms tries to maximize the throughput using as few threads as possible?
    1. Hill Climbing
    2. Starvation Avoidance
3. Which is not a valid microservice design approach?
    1. Single thread-single process
    2. Single thread-multiple processes
    3. Multiple threads-single process
    4. Multiple threads-multiple processes
4. We can await `foreach` loops in new versions of .NET Core.
    1. True
    2. False

13
Patterns in Parallel Programming

In the previous chapter, we introduced threading models in IIS and Kestrel and how they can be optimized to improve performance, as well as some new async feature support in .NET Core 3.0.

In this chapter, we will introduce parallel programming patterns and focus on understanding the parallel code problem scenarios and solving them using parallel programming/async techniques.

Although there are numerous patterns that have been utilized in parallel programming techniques, we will limit ourselves to explaining the most important ones.

In this chapter, we will cover the following topics:

- `MapReduce`
- Aggregation
- Fork/join
- Speculative processing
- Laziness
- Shared state

Technical requirements

Knowledge of C# and parallel programming is required in order to understand this chapter. The source code for this chapter can be found on GitHub at `https://github.com/PacktPublishing/-Hands-On-Parallel-Programming-with-C-8-and-.NET-Core-3/tree/master/Chapter13`.

The MapReduce pattern

The `MapReduce` pattern was introduced in order to handle big data problems such as large-scale computing requirements spanning across a cluster of servers. The pattern can also be used on single-core machines.

A `MapReduce` program is composed of two tasks: **map** and **reduce**. The input for the `MapReduce` program is passed as a set of key-value pairs and the output is also received as such.

To implement this pattern, we need to start by writing a `map` function that takes in data (key/value pair) as a single input value and converts it into another set of intermediate data (key/value pair). The user then writes a `reduce` function that takes the output from the `map` function (key/value pair) as input and combines the data with a smaller dataset containing any number of rows of data.

Let's look at how to implement a basic `MapReduce` pattern using LINQ and convert it into a PLINQ-based implementation.

Implementing MapReduce using LINQ

The following is a typical graphical representation of the `MapReduce` pattern. The input goes through various mapped functions, with each returning a set of mapped values as output. These are then grouped and joined by `Reduce()` functions to create the final output:

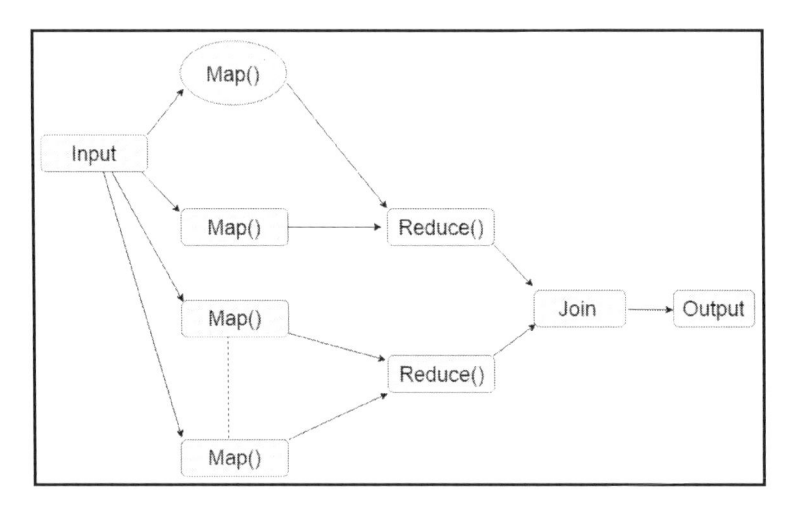

Follow these steps to implement the `MapReduce` pattern using LINQ:

1. First, we need to write a `map` function with a single input value that returns a set of mapped values. We can use LINQ's `SelectMany` function for this.
2. Then, we need to group data according to the intermediate key. We can use LINQ's `GroupBy` method for this.
3. Finally, we need a `reduce` method that will take an intermediate key as input. It will also take a corresponding set of values for that and produce output. We can use `SelectMany` for this.
4. Our final `MapReduce` pattern will now look as follows:

   ```
   public static IEnumerable<TResult> MapReduce<TSource, TMapped,
   TKey, TResult>(
   this IEnumerable<TSource> source,
   Func<TSource, IEnumerable<TMapped>> map,
   Func<TMapped, TKey> keySelector,
   Func<IGrouping<TKey, TMapped>, IEnumerable<TResult>> reduce)
   {
   return source.SelectMany(map)
   .GroupBy(keySelector)
   .SelectMany(reduce);
   }
   ```

5. Now, we can change the input and output so that it works with `ParallelQuery<T>` rather than `IEnumerable<T>`, as follows:

   ```
   public static ParallelQuery<TResult> MapReduce<TSource, TMapped,
   TKey, TResult>(
   this ParallelQuery<TSource> source,
   Func<TSource, IEnumerable<TMapped>> map,
   Func<TMapped, TKey> keySelector,
   Func<IGrouping<TKey, TMapped>, IEnumerable<TResult>> reduce)
   {
   return source.SelectMany(map)
   .GroupBy(keySelector)
   .SelectMany(reduce);
   }
   ```

Patterns in Parallel Programming

The following is an example of using the custom implementation of MapReduce in .NET Core. The program generates some positive and negative random numbers in a range. Then, it applies a map to filter out any positive numbers and group them by number. Finally, it applies the reduce function to return a list of numbers, along with their counts:

```
private static void MapReduceTest()
{
    //Maps only positive number from list
    Func<int, IEnumerable<int>> mapPositiveNumbers = number =>
    {
        IList<int> positiveNumbers = new List<int>();
        if (number > 0)
            positiveNumbers.Add( number);
            return positiveNumbers;
    };
    // Group results together
    Func<int, int> groupNumbers = value => value;
    //Reduce function that counts the occurrence of each number
    Func<IGrouping<int, int>,IEnumerable<KeyValuePair<int, int>>>
     reduceNumbers =  grouping => new[] {
        new KeyValuePair<int, int>( grouping.Key, grouping.Count())
    };
    // Generate a list of random numbers between -10 and 10
    IList<int> sourceData = new List<int>();
    var rand = new Random();
    for (int i = 0; i < 1000; i++)
    {
        sourceData.Add(rand.Next(-10, 10));
    }
    // Use MapReduce function
    var result = sourceData.AsParallel().MapReduce(mapPositiveNumbers,
                                                groupNumbers,
                                                reduceNumbers);
    // process the results
    foreach (var item in result)
    {
        Console.WriteLine($"{item.Key} came {item.Value} times" );
    }
}
```

The following is an excerpt from the output we receive if we run the preceding program code in Visual Studio. As you can see, it iterates the provided list and finds the count of how many times the numbers occurred:

```
1 came 65 times
2 came 36 times
3 came 48 times
4 came 45 times
5 came 57 times
6 came 56 times
7 came 63 times
8 came 55 times
9 came 47 times
```

In the next section, we will discuss another common and important parallel design pattern called aggregation. While the `MapReduce` pattern acts as a filter, aggregation just combines all the data from the input and puts it in another format.

Aggregation

Aggregation is another common design pattern that's used in parallel applications. In parallel programs, the data is divided into units so that it can be processed across cores by a number of threads. At some point, there is a need to combine data from all the relevant sources before it can be presented to the user. This is where aggregation comes into the picture.

Now, let's explore the need for aggregation and what is provided by PLINQ.

A common use case of aggregation is as follows. Here, we are trying to iterate a set of values, perform some operations, and return the result to the caller:

```
var output = new List<int>();
var input = Enumerable.Range(1, 50);
Func<int,int> action = (i) => i * i;
foreach (var item in input)
{
    var result = action(item);
    output.Add(result);
}
```

Patterns in Parallel Programming

The problem with the preceding code is that the output isn't thread-safe. Due to this, to avoid cross-threading issues, we need to make use of synchronization primitives:

```
var output = new List<int>();
var input = Enumerable.Range(1, 50);
Func<int, int> action = (i) => i * i;
Parallel.ForEach(input, item =>
{
    var result = action(item);
    lock (output)
        output.Add(result);
});
```

The preceding code works well if the computation that's done per item is small. However, as the computation that's done per item increases the cost of taking and releasing, the lock will also increase. This results in degraded performance. Concurrent collections, which we discussed in Chapter 6, *Using Concurrent Collections*, comes to the rescue here. With concurrent collections, we don't have to worry about synchronizations. The following code snippet is using concurrent collection:

```
var input = Enumerable.Range(1, 50);
Func<int, int> action = (i) => i * i;
var output = new ConcurrentBag<int>();
Parallel.ForEach(input, item =>
{
    var result = action(item);
    output.Add(result);
});
```

PLINQ also defines methods that help with aggregation and handle synchronization. Some of these methods are ToArray, ToList, ToDictionary, and ToLookup:

```
var input = Enumerable.Range(1, 50);
Func<int, int> action = (i) => i * i;
var output = input.AsParallel()
            .Select(item => action(item))
            .ToList();
```

In the preceding code, the ToList() method takes care of aggregating all the data while also dealing with synchronization. Some implementation patterns are available in TPL and are built into programming languages. One of them is the fork/join pattern, which we will discuss next.

The fork/join pattern

In fork/join patterns, work is *forked* (*split*) into a set of tasks that can be executed asynchronously. Later, the forked work is joined in the same order or a different order, as per the requirements and scope of parallelization. We have already seen some common examples of fork/join patterns in this book when we discussed delightfully parallel loops. Some implementations of fork/join are as follows:

- `Parallel.For`
- `Parallel.ForEach`
- `Parallel.Invoke`
- `System.Threading.CountdownEvent`

Utilizing these framework-provided methods aids in faster development without developers having to worry about synchronization overheads. These patterns result in high throughput. To achieve high throughput and to reduce latency, another pattern, called speculative processing, is widely used.

The speculative processing pattern

The speculative processing pattern is another parallel programming pattern that relies on high throughput to reduce latency. This is very useful in scenarios where there are multiple ways of performing a task but the user doesn't know which way will return the results fastest. This approach creates a task for each possible method, which is then executed across processors. The task that finishes first is used as output, ignoring the others (which may still complete successfully but are slow).

The following is a typical `SpeculativeInvoke` representation. It accepts an array of `Func<T>` as parameters and executes them in parallel until one of them returns:

```
public static T SpeculativeInvoke<T>(params Func<T>[] functions)
{
    return SpeculativeForEach(functions, function => function());
}
```

The following method executes each action that's passed to it in parallel and breaks out of a parallel loop by calling the `ParallelLoopState.Stop()` method as soon as any of the called implementations execute successfully:

```
public static TResult SpeculativeForEach<TSource, TResult>(
                IEnumerable<TSource> source,
```

Patterns in Parallel Programming

```
                        Func<TSource, TResult> body)
{
    object result = null;
    Parallel.ForEach(source, (item, loopState) =>
    {
        result = body(item);
        loopState.Stop();
    });
    return (TResult)result;
}
```

The following code uses two different logics to calculate the square of 5. We will pass both approaches to the `SpeculativeInvoke` method and print the `result` as soon as possible:

```
Func<string> Square = () => {
            Console.WriteLine("Square Called");
            return $"Result From Square is {5 * 5}";
        };
Func<string> Square2 = () =>
        {
            Console.WriteLine("Square2 Called");
            var square = 0;
            for (int j = 0; j < 5; j++)
            {
                square += 5;
            }
            return $"Result From Square2 is {square}";
        };
string result = SpeculativeInvoke(Square, Square2);
Console.WriteLine(result);
```

Here is the output of the preceding code:

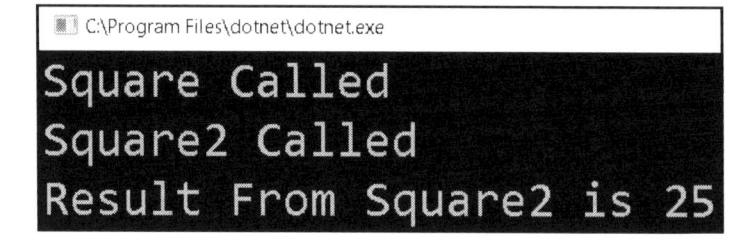

```
C:\Program Files\dotnet\dotnet.exe
Square Called
Square2 Called
Result From Square2 is 25
```

As you will see, both methods finish but only the output of the first finished execution is returned to the caller. Creating too many tasks can have an adverse effect on system memory as more and more variables need to be allocated and kept in memory. Therefore, it becomes very important to allocate objects only when they are actually required. Our next pattern helps us achieve this.

The lazy pattern

Lazy is another programming pattern that is used by application developers to improve application performance. Laziness is about delaying computation until it's actually needed. In a best-case scenario, the computation might not be needed at all, which helps in not wasting compute resources and thus improving the performance of the system as a whole. Lazy evaluation is not new to computing, and LINQ uses *lazy loading* heavily. LINQ follows the deferred execution model in which queries are not executed until we call `MoveNext()` on them using some iterator functions.

The following is an example of a thread-safe lazy singleton pattern that utilizes some heavy compute operations for creation and is thus deferred:

```
public class LazySingleton<T> where T : class
    {
        static object _syncObj = new object();
        static T _value;
        private LazySingleton()
        {
        }
        public static T Value
        {
            get
            {
                if (_value == null)
                {
                    lock (_syncObj)
                    {
                        if (_value == null)
                            _value = SomeHeavyCompute();
                    }
                }
                return _value;
            }
        }
        private static T SomeHeavyCompute() { return default(T); }
    }
```

A lazy object is created by calling the `LazySingleton<T>` class's `Value` property. Laziness guarantees that an object is not created until the `Value` property is called. Once created, the singleton implementation ensures that the same object is returned on subsequent calls. A null check on `_value` avoids creating a lock on subsequent calls, thereby saving some memory I/O operations and improving performance.

We can get around writing so much code by making use of `System.Lazy<T>`, as shown in the following code example:

```
public class MyLazySingleton<T>
{
    //Declare a Lazy<T> instance with initialization
    //function (SomeHeavyCompute)
    static Lazy<T> _value = new Lazy<T>();
    //Value property to return value of Lazy instance when
    //actually required by code
    public T Value { get { return _value.Value; } }
    //Initialization function
    private static T SomeHeavyCompute()
    {
        return default(T);
    }
}
```

While working with asynchronous programming, we can combine the power of `Lazy<T>` with TPL to achieve significant results.

The following is an example of using both `Lazy<T>` and `Task<T>` to implement lazy and asynchronous behavior:

```
var data = new Lazy<Task<T>>(() =>
Task<T>.Factory.StartNew(SomeHeavyCompute));
```

We can access the underlying `Task` through the `data.Value` property. The underlying lazy implementation will ensure that the same task instance is returned every time, no matter how many times you call the `data.Value` property. This is useful in scenarios where you don't want to launch many threads and just want to launch a single thread that may carry out some asynchronous processing.

Consider the following piece of code, which fetches data from a service and saves it to an Excel or CSV file from two different thread implementations:

```
public static string GetDataFromService()
{
    Console.WriteLine("Service called");
    return "Some Dummy Data";
}
```

The following are two example methods that have logic we can save as text or in CSV format:

```
public static void SaveToText(string data)
{
    Console.WriteLine("Save to Text called");
    //Save to Text
}
public static void SaveToCsv(string data)
{
    Console.WriteLine("Save to CSV called");
    //Save to CSV
}
```

The following code shows how we can wrap the service call inside `lazy` and make sure that a service call is made only once while the output can be used asynchronously. As you can see, we have wrapped the lazy initialization method as a task using `Task.Factory.StartNew(GetDataFromService)`:

```
//
Lazy<Task<string>> lazy = new Lazy<Task<string>>(
  Task.Factory.StartNew(GetDataFromService));
lazy.Value.ContinueWith((s)=> SaveToText(s.Result));
lazy.Value.ContinueWith((s) => SaveToCsv(s.Result));
```

The following is the output of the preceding code:

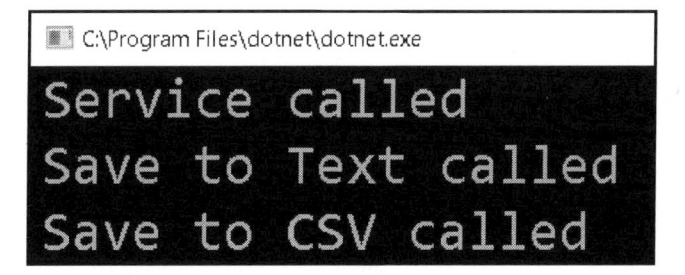

```
C:\Program Files\dotnet\dotnet.exe
Service called
Save to Text called
Save to CSV called
```

As you can see, the service is only called once. Whenever you need to create objects, the lazy pattern is an advisable proposition for developers. When we create multiple tasks, we face problems associated with the synchronization of resources. An understanding of shared state patterns comes in handy in these scenarios.

Shared state pattern

We covered the implementation of these patterns in Chapter 5, *Synchronization Primitives*.

A parallel application has to deal with a shared state problem constantly. The application will have some data members that need to be protected when they're accessed in a multithreaded environment. There are many ways to deal with shared state problems, such as using Synchronization, Isolation, and Immutability. Synchronization can be achieved using the synchronization primitives provided by the .NET Framework and it can also provide mutual exclusion over a shared data member. Immutability guarantees only one state for a data member and never changes. Consequently, the same state can be shared across threads without any issues. Isolation deals with each thread having its own copy of data members.

Now, we'll summarize what we learned in this chapter.

Summary

In this chapter, we introduced various patterns of parallel programming and provided examples of each. Though not an exhaustive list, these patterns can prove to be a good starting point for parallel application programming developers.

In a nutshell, we discussed the MapReduce pattern, the speculative processing pattern, the lazy pattern, and the aggregation pattern. We also introduced some implementation patterns, such as fork/join and the shared state pattern, both are which are used in .NET Framework libraries for parallel programming.

In the next chapter, we will introduce distributed memory management and focus on understanding the shared memory model as well as the distributed memory model. We will also discuss various types of communication networks and their properties with example implementations.

Questions

1. Which of these is not an implementation of the fork/join pattern?
    1. `System.Threading.Barrier`
    2. `System.Threading.Countdown`
    3. `Parallel.For`
    4. `Parallel.ForEach`
2. Which of these is the implementation of the lazy pattern in TPL?
    1. `Lazy<T>`
    2. `LazySingleton`
    3. `LazyInitializer`
3. Which pattern relies on achieving high throughput to reduce latency?
    1. Lazy
    2. Shared state
    3. Speculative processing
4. Which pattern can you use if you need to filter out data from a list and return a single output?
    1. Aggregation
    2. `MapReduce`

14
Distributed Memory Management

In the last two decades, the industry has seen a paradigm shift to big data and machine learning architectures that involve processing terabytes/petabytes of data as quickly as possible. As computing power became cheaper, there was a need to use multiple processors to speed up processing to a larger scale. This has led to distributed computing. Distributed computing refers to an arrangement of computer systems that are connected via some networking/distribution middleware. All the connected systems share resources and coordinate their activities via middleware so that they work in a way that is perceived as a single system by the end user. Distributed computing is needed due to the huge volume and throughput requirements of modern applications. Some typical examples of scenarios where computing demands cannot be fulfilled by a single system and that need to be distributed across a grid of computers are as follows:

- Google performs at least 1.5 trillion searches per year.
- IOT devices send multiple terabytes of data to event hubs.
- Data warehouses receive and compute terabytes of records in minimal time.

In this chapter, we will discuss distributed memory management and the need for distributed computing. We will also learn about how messages are passed across communication networks for distributed systems, as well as various types of communicated networks.

This chapter will cover the following topics:

- Advantages of distributed systems
- Shared memory model versus distributed memory model
- Types of communication network
- Properties of communication networks
- Exploring topologies
- Programming distributed memory machines using message passing
- Collectives

Technical requirements

To complete this chapter, you'll need knowledge of programming in C and C# Windows platform API invocation programming.

Introduction to distributed systems

We have already discussed how distributed computing works in this book. In this section, we will try to understand distributed computing with a small example that works on arrays.

Let's say we have an array of 1,040 elements and we would like to find the sum of all the numbers:

```
a = [1,2,3, 4...., n]
```

If the total time that's taken to add numbers is x (let's say all of the numbers are large) and we want to compute them all as fast as possible, we can take advantage of distributed computing. We would divide the array into multiple arrays (let's say, four arrays), each with 25% of the original number of elements, and send each array to a different processor to calculate the sum, as follows:

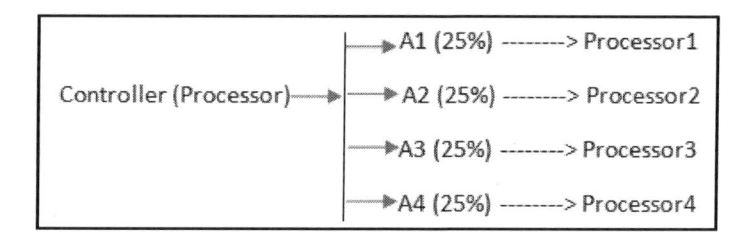

```
                              |──▶ A1 (25%) ────────▶ Processor1
Controller (Processor) ──▶────|──▶ A2 (25%) ────────▶ Processor2
                              |──▶ A3 (25%) ────────▶ Processor3
                              |──▶ A4 (25%) ────────▶ Processor4
```

In this arrangement, the total time that's taken to add all the numbers is reduced to (x/4 + d) or (x/number of processors +d), where d is the time that's taken to collate the sums from all the processors and add them to get the final results.

Some of the advantages of distributed systems are as follows:

- Systems can be scaled to any level without any hardware restrictions
- No single point of failure, which makes them more fault-tolerant
- Highly available
- Very efficient when handling big data problems

Distributed systems are often confused with parallel systems, but there are subtle differences between them. **Parallel systems** are an arrangement of multi-processors that are placed mostly in single, but sometimes in multiple, containers in close vicinity. **Distributed systems**, on the other hand, consist of multiple processors (each having its own memory and I/O devices) that are connected together via a network that enables data exchange.

Shared versus distributed memory model

To achieve high performance, the **multi-processor** and **multi-computer** architectures have evolved. With the multi-processor architecture, multiple processors share a common memory and communicate with each other by reading/writing to the shared memory. With multi-computers, multiple computers that don't share a single physical memory communicate with each other by passing messages. **Distributed Shared Memory** (DSM) deals with sharing memory in a physical, non-shared (distributed) architecture.

Let's look at each one and talk about their differences.

Shared memory model

In the case of shared memory models, multiple processors share a single common memory space. Since multiple processors share memory space, there needs to be some synchronization measures in place to avoid data corruption and race conditions. As we have seen so far in this book, synchronization comes with performance overheads. The following is an example representation of the shared memory model. As you can see, there are **n** processors in the arrangement, all of which have access to a commonly shared memory block:

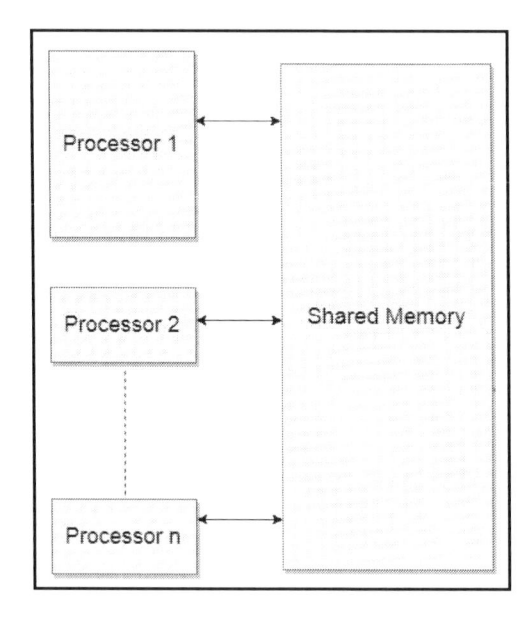

The features of the shared memory model are as follows:

- All the processors have access to the entire memory block. The memory block can be a single piece of memory composed of memory modules, as shown in the following diagram:

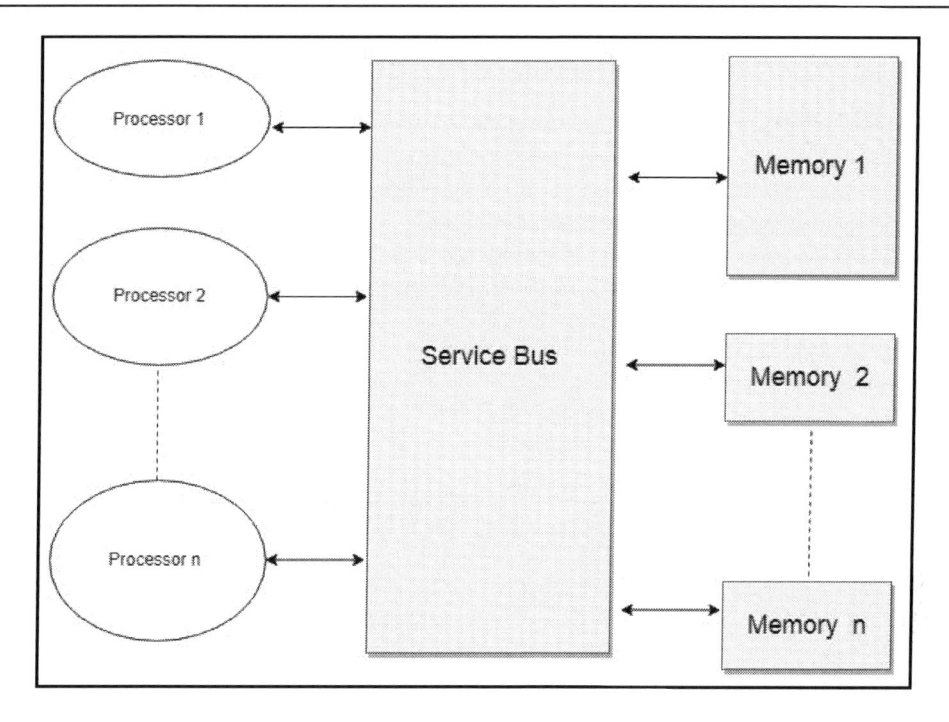

- Processors communicate with each other by creating shared variables in the main memory.
- The efficiency of parallelization largely depends on the speed of the service bus.
- Due to the speed of the service bus, the system can only be scaled up to n number of processors.

Shared memory models are also known as **symmetric multiprocessing (SMP)** models since all the processors have access to all the available memory blocks.

Distributed memory model

In the case of the distributed memory model, the memory space is no longer shared across processors. In fact, the processors don't share common physical locations; instead, they can be remotely placed. Each processor has its own private memory space and I/O devices. Data is stored across processors rather than in single memory. Each processor can work on its own local data, but to access data that's been stored in other processor memories, they need to connect via a communication network. Data is passed via **message passing** across processors using the *send message* and *receive message* instructions. The following is a diagrammatic representation of a distributed memory model:

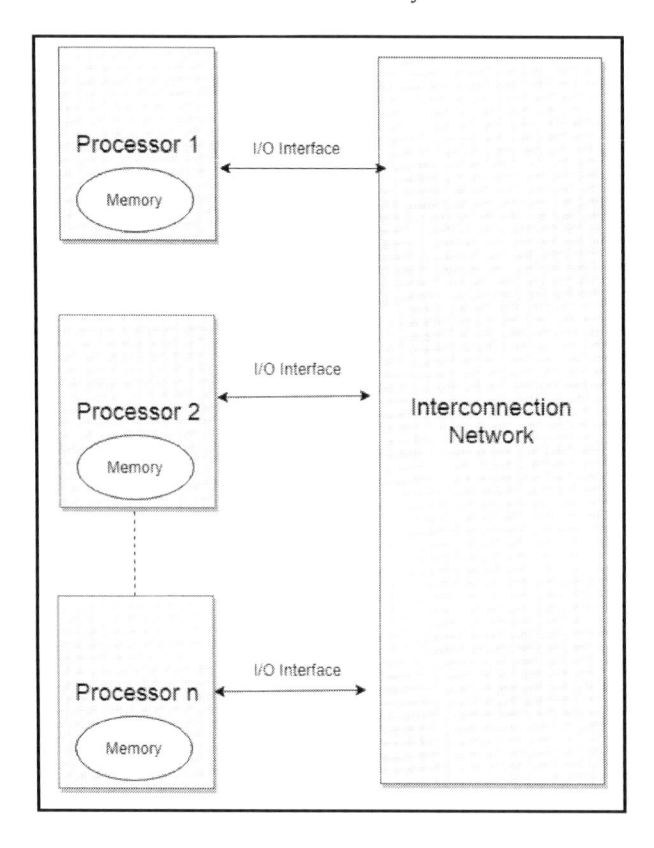

The preceding diagram depicts each processor, along with its own memory space and interaction with **communication networks** via I/O interfaces. Let's try to understand the various types of communication networks that can be used in distributed systems.

Types of communication network

Communication networks are the links that connect two or more nodes in a typical computer network. Communication networks are classified into two categories:

- Static communication networks
- Dynamic communication networks

Let's take a look at both.

Static communication networks

Static communication networks contain links, as shown in the following diagram:

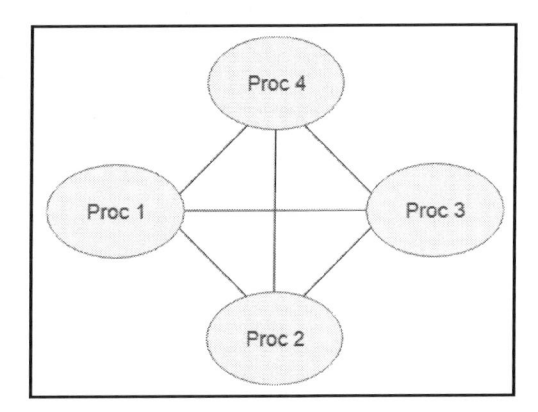

Links are used to connect nodes together, thereby creating a complete communication network where any node can talk to any other node.

Dynamic communication networks

Dynamic communication networks have links and switches, as shown in the following diagram:

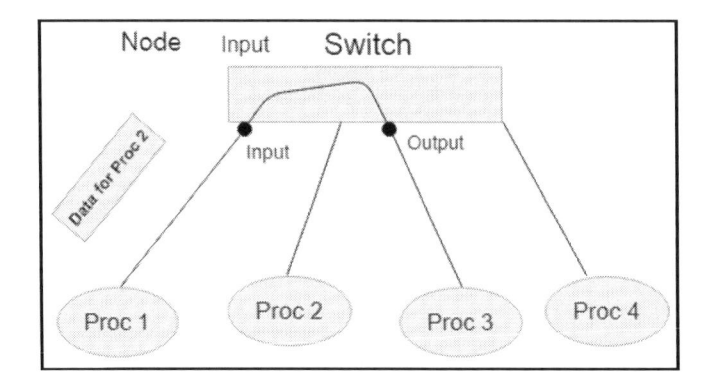

Switches are devices that have input/output ports, and they redirect input data to output ports. This means that pathways are dynamic. If one processor wants to send data to another, it needs to be done via a switch, as demonstrated in the preceding diagram.

Properties of communication networks

While designing a communication network, we need to consider the following characteristics:

- Topology
- Routing algorithm
- Switching strategy
- Flow control

Let's look at these characteristics in more detail.

Topology

Topology refers to how nodes (bridges, switches, and infrastructure devices) are connected. Some common topologies include crossbar, ring, 2D mesh, 3D mesh, higherD mesh, 2D torus, 3D torus, higherD torus, hypercube, tree, butterfly, perfect shuffle, and dragonfly.

In the case of the crossbar topology, every node in the network is connected to every other node (though they may not be connected directly). Thus, messages can be passed via a number of routes to avoid any conflicts. Here is a typical crossbar topology:

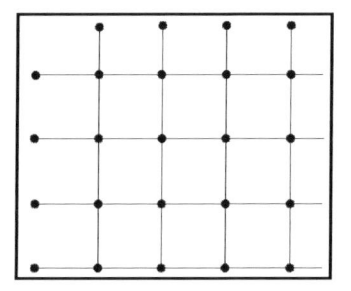

In the case of the mesh topology, or meshnet, as it's popularly called, nodes connect to each other directly without having a dependency on other nodes in the network. This way, all the nodes can relay information independently. The mesh can be partially or fully connected. Here is a typical fully connected mesh:

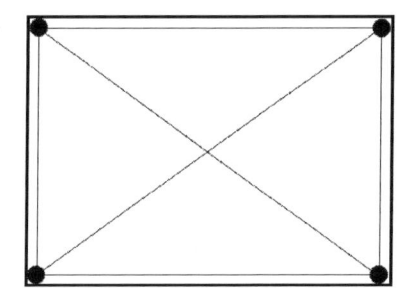

We will look at topology in more detail later in this chapter, in the *Exploring topologies* section.

Routing algorithms

Routing is a process via which a packet of information is sent across the network so that it reaches the intended node. Routing can be adaptive, that is, it responds to changes in the network topology by continuously taking information from adjacent nodes, or non-adaptive, that is, they are static and is where routing information is downloaded to nodes when the network is booted. Routing algorithms need to be chosen to make sure there are no deadlocks. For example, in 2D torus, all the pathways go from east to west and north to south to avoid any deadlock scenarios. We will look at 2D torus in more detail later in this chapter.

Switching strategy

Choosing an appropriate switching strategy can increase the performance of a network. The two most prominent switching strategies are as follows:

- **Circuit switching**: In circuit switching, the full path is reserved for an entire message, such as the telephone. To begin a call on a telephone network, a dedicated circuit needs to be established between the caller and callee and the circuit persists during the entire call duration.
- **Packet switching**: In packet switching, the message is broken into separately routed packets, such as the internet. In terms of cost benefits, it's far better than circuit switching as the cost of the link is shared across users. Packet switching is primarily used for asynchronous scenarios such as sending emails or file transfer.

Flow control

Flow control is a process by which a network makes sure that packets are transferred across the sender and received efficiently and without error. In the case of the network topology, the speeds of the sender and receiver can vary, which can lead to bottlenecks or loss of packets in some cases. With flow control, we can make decisions in case there's congestion on the network. Some strategies include storing data temporarily into buffers, rerouting data to other nodes, instructing source nodes to temporarily halt, discarding data, and so on. The following are some common flow control algorithms:

- **Stop and wait**: The entire message is broken into parts. The sender sends a part to the receiver and waits for an acknowledgement to come within a specific time period (timeout). Once the sender receives an acknowledgment, it sends the next part of the message.
- **Sliding window**: The receiver assigns a transmitting window for a sender to send messages. The sender has to stop transmitting when the window is full so that the receiver can process messages and advertise the next transmitting window. This approach works best when the receiver is storing data in a buffer and thus can only receive the buffer capacity.

Exploring topologies

So far, we've looked at some complete communication networks where each processor can communicate with the others directly, without the need for any switch. This arrangement serves well when there is a small number of processors but can become a real pain if the number of processors needs to be increased. There are various other performance topologies available that can be used. There are two important aspects while measuring the performance of a graph in a topology:

- **The diameter of the graph**: The longest path between the nodes.
- **Bisection bandwidth**: The bandwidth across the smallest cut that divides the network into two equal halves. This is important for networks where each processor needs to communicate with the others.

The following are examples of some network topologies.

Linear and ring topologies

These topologies work well with 1D arrays. In the case of the linear topology, all the processors are in a linear arrangement with one input and output flow, whereas in the case of the ring topology, processors form a loop back to the start processor.

Let's look at them in more detail.

Linear arrays

All the processors are in a linear arrangement, as shown in the following diagram:

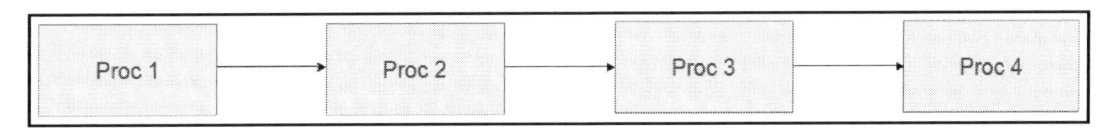

Proc 1 → Proc 2 → Proc 3 → Proc 4

This arrangement will have the following values for the diameter and bisection bandwidth:

- Diameter = n-1, where n is the number of processors
- Bisection bandwidth = 1

Ring or torus

All the processors are in ring arrangements and information flows from one processor to another, making a loopback to the originating processor. Then, this makes a ring, as shown in the following diagram:

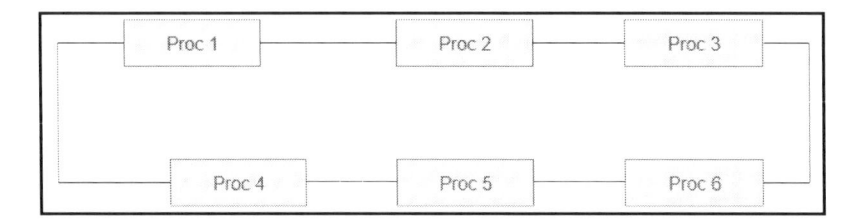

This arrangement will have the following values for the diameter and bisection bandwidth:

- Diameter = n/2, where n is the number of processors
- Bisection bandwidth = 2

Meshes and tori

These topologies work well with 2D and 3D arrays. Let's look at them in more detail.

2D mesh

In the case of the mesh, nodes connect to each other directly without having a dependency on other nodes in a network. All the nodes are in a 2D mesh arrangement, as shown in the following diagram:

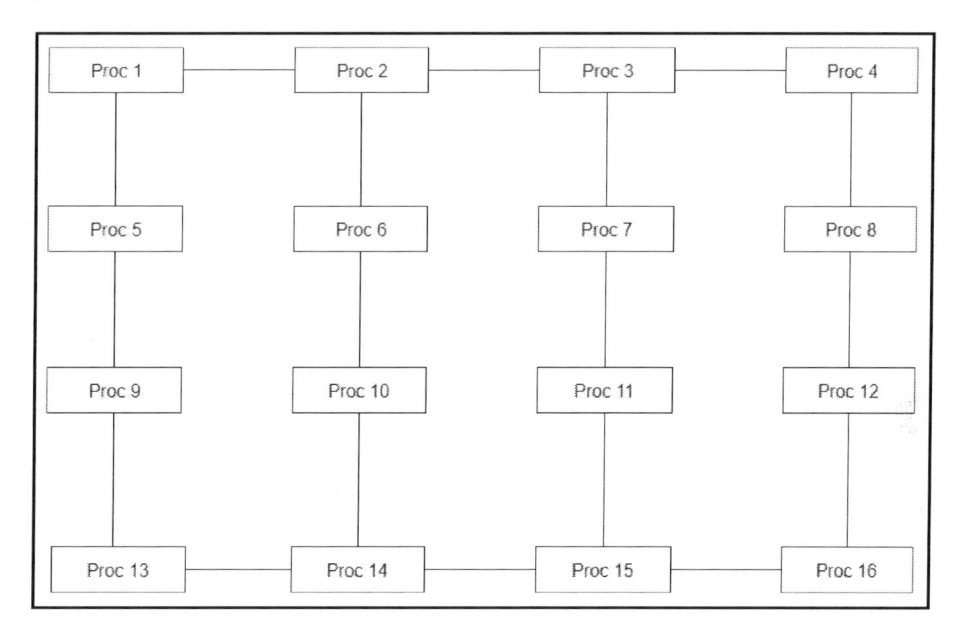

This arrangement will have the following values for the diameter and bisection bandwidth:

- Diameter = 2 * (sqrt (n) – 1), where n is the number of processors
- Bisection bandwidth = sqrt(n)

2D torus

All the processors are in a 2D torus arrangement, as shown in the following diagram:

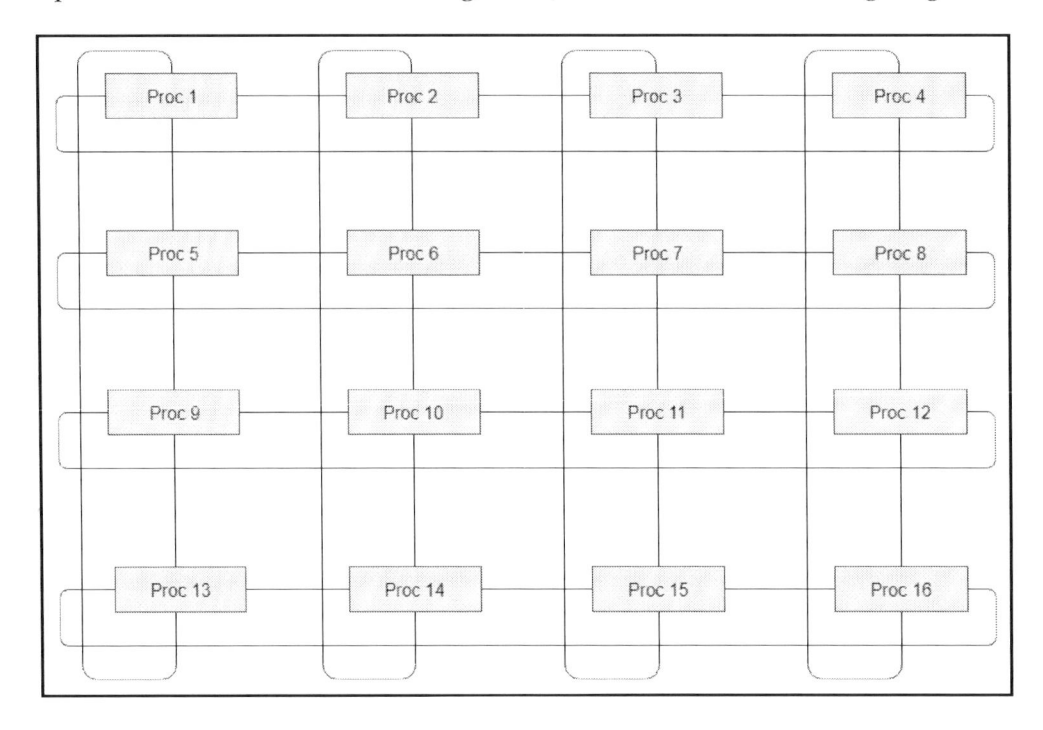

This arrangement will have the following values for the diameter and bisection bandwidth:

- Diameter = sqrt(n), where n is the number of processors
- Bisection bandwidth = 2 * sqrt(n)

Programming distributed memory machines using message passing

In this section, we will discuss how to program distributed memory machines using Microsoft's **message passing interface** (**MPI**).

MPI is a standard, portable system that has been developed for distributed and parallel systems. It defines the basic set of functions that are utilized by parallel hardware vendors to support distributed memory communication. In the following sections, we will discuss the advantages of using MPI over old messaging libraries and explain how to install and run a simple MPI program.

Why MPI?

An advantage of MPI is that MPI routines can be called from a variety of languages, such as C, C++, C#, Java, Python, and more. MPI is highly portable compared to old messaging libraries, and MPI routines are speed-optimized for each piece of hardware that they are supposed to run.

Installing MPI on Windows

MPI can be downloaded and installed as a ZIP file from https://www.open-mpi.org/software/ompi/v1.10/.

Alternatively, you can download the Microsoft version of MPI from https://github.com/Microsoft/Microsoft-MPI/releases.

Sample program using MPI

The following is a simple `HelloWorld` program that we can run using MPI. The program prints the processor number that the code is being executed on after a delay of two seconds. The same code can be run on multiple processors (we are able to specify the processor count).

Let's create a new console application project in Visual Studio and write the following code in the `Program.cs` file:

```
[DllImport("Kernel32.dll"), SuppressUnmanagedCodeSecurity]
public static extern int GetCurrentProcessorNumber();

static void Main(string[] args)
{
    Thread.Sleep(2000);
    Console.WriteLine($"Hello {GetCurrentProcessorNumber()} Id");
}
```

Distributed Memory Management

`GetCurrentProcessorNumber()` is a utility function that gives the processor number of where our code is being executed. As you can see from the preceding code, there is no magic – it runs as a single thread and prints `Hello` and the current processor number.

We will install `msmpisetup.exe` from the Microsoft MPI link we provided in the *Installing MPI on Windows* section. Once installed, we need to execute the following command from Command Prompt:

```
C:\Program Files\Microsoft MPI\Bin>mpiexec.exe -n 5 "path to executable "
```

Here, n signifies the number of processors that we want the program to run on.

The following is the output of the preceding code:

```
Hello 3 Id
Hello 7 Id
Hello 5 Id
Hello 6 Id
Hello 6 Id
```

As you can see, we can run the same program on multiple processors using MPI.

Basic send/receive use

MPI is a C++ implementation, and most of the documentation on the Microsoft website will only be available in C++. However, it's easy to create a .NET compiled wrapper and use it in any of our projects. There are some third-party .NET implementations available as well for MPI but, unfortunately, there is no support for .NET Core implementations as of now.

Here is the syntax of an `MPI_Send` function that sends a buffer of data to another processor:

```
int MPIAPI MPI_Send(
  _In_opt_ void         *buf, //pointer to buffer containing Data to send
           int          count, //Number of elements in buffer
           MPI_Datatype datatype,//Datatype of element in buffer
           int          dest, //rank of destination process
           int          tag, //tag to distinguish between messages
           MPI_Comm     comm //Handle to communicator
);
```

The method returns when the buffer can be safely reused.

Here is the syntax of an `MPU_Recv` function, which will receive a buffer of data from another processor:

```
int MPIAPI MPI_Recv(
    _In_opt_ void          *buf,
             int           count,
             MPI_Datatype  datatype,
             int           source,
             int           tag,
             MPI_Comm      comm,
    _Out_    MPI_Status    *status //Returns MPI_SUCCESS or the error code.
);
```

This method doesn't return until the buffer is received.

Here is a typical example of using the send and receive functions:

```
#include "mpi.h"
#include <iostream>
int main( int argc, char *argv[])
{
int rank, buffer;
MPI::Init(argv, argc);
rank = MPI::COMM_WORLD.Get_rank();
// Process 0 sends data as buffer and Process 1 receives data as buffer
if (rank == 0) {
buffer = 999999;
MPI::COMM_WORLD.Send( &buffer, 1, MPI::INT, 1, 0 );
}
else if (rank == 1) {
MPI::COMM_WORLD.Recv( &buffer, 1, MPI::INT, 0, 0 );
std::cout << "Data Received " << buf << "\n";
}
MPI::Finalize();
return 0;
}
```

When running via MPI, the communicator will send data that will be received by the receive function in another processor.

Collectives

Collectives, as the name suggests, is a communication method wherein all the processors in a communicator are involved. Collectives help us achieve these tasks. Two collective methods that are primarily used for this are as follows:

- `MPI_BCAST`: This **distributes** data from one (root) process to another processor in a communicator
- `MPI_REDUCE`: This **combines** data from all the processors within a communicator and returns it to the root process

Now that we understand collectives, we have come to the end of this chapter and ultimately the end of this book. Now, it's time to see what we have learned!

Summary

In this chapter, we discussed distributed memory management implementations. We learned about distributed memory management models, such as shared memory and distributed memory processors, as well as their implementation. In the end, we discussed what an MPI is and how it can be utilized. We also discussed communication networks and various design considerations for implementing efficient networks. Now, you should have a good understanding of network topologies, routing algorithms, switching strategies, and flow controls.

In this book, we have covered various programming constructs that are available in .NET Core 3.1 to achieve parallel programming. Parallel programming, if used correctly, can greatly enhance the performance and responsiveness of applications. The new features and syntaxes that are available in .NET Core 3.1 really make writing/debugging and maintaining parallel code easier. We also covered how we used to write multithreaded code before TPL came into being, for comparison's sake.

With new constructs for asynchronous programming (async and await), we learned how to take full advantage of non-blocking I/Os while the program flow is synchronous. Then, we discussed new features such as async streams and async main methods, which help us write async code more easily. We also discussed parallel tooling support in Visual Studio that can help us debug code better. Finally, we discussed how to write unit test cases for parallel code to make our code more robust.

Then, we wrapped up this book by introducing distributed programming techniques and how to use them in .NET Core.

Questions

1. _____ is an arrangement of multi-processors placed mostly in single containers but sometimes in multiple containers in close vicinity to each other.
2. In the case of the dynamic communication network, any node can send data to any other node.
    1. True
    2. False
3. Which of the following are characteristics of a communication network?
    1. Topology
    2. Switching strategy
    3. Flow control
    4. Shared memory
4. In the case of the distributed memory model, the memory space is shared across processors.
    1. True
    2. False
5. Circuit switching can be used for asynchronous scenarios.
    1. True
    2. False

Assessments

Chapter 1 – Introduction to Parallel Programming

1. 2
2. 2
3. 2
4. 2
5. 2

Chapter 3 – Implementing Data Parallelism

1. 2
2. 1
3. 2
4. 2
5. 2

Chapter 4 – Using PLINQ

1. 2
2. 1
3. 2
4. 2
5. 1

Chapter 5 – Synchronization Primitives

1. 3
2. 4
3. 3
4. 1
5. 1

Chapter 6 – Using Concurrent Collections

1. 4
2. 1
3. 1
4. 4

Chapter 7 – Improving Performance with Lazy Initialization

1. 2
2. 1
3. 2
4. 3

Chapter 8 – Introduction to Asynchronous Programming

1. 1
2. 1, 2, 3
3. 1, 2
4. 1

Chapter 9 – Async, Await, and Task-Based Asynchronous Programming Basics

1. 2
2. 1, 2, 3
3. 1
4. 1
5. 1
6. 2

Chapter 10 – Debugging Tasks Using Visual Studio

1. 3
2. 1
3. 2
4. 2
5. 3

Chapter 11 – Writing Unit Test Cases for Parallel and Asynchronous Code

1. 1
2. 2
3. 1
4. 3
5. 2

Chapter 12 – IIS and Kestrel in ASP.NET Core

1. 1
2. 1
3. 4
4. 1

Chapter 13 – Patterns in Parallel Programming

1. 1
2. 2
3. 3
4. 2

Chapter 14 – Distributed Memory Management

1. Parallel systems
2. 2
3. 4
4. 2

Other Books You May Enjoy

If you enjoyed this book, you may be interested in these other books by Packt:

Hands-On Software Architecture with C# 8 and .NET Core 3
Gabriel Baptista, Francesco Abbruzzese

ISBN: 978-1-78980-093-7

- Overcome real-world architectural challenges and solve design consideration issues
- Apply architectural approaches like Layered Architecture, service-oriented architecture (SOA), and microservices
- Learn to use tools like containers, Docker, and Kubernetes to manage microservices
- Get up to speed with Azure Cosmos DB for delivering multi-continental solutions
- Learn how to program and maintain Azure Functions using C#
- Understand when to use test-driven development (TDD) as an approach for software development
- Write automated functional test cases for your projects

Hands-On Design Patterns with C# and .NET Core
Gaurav Aroraa, Jeffrey Chilberto

ISBN: 978-1-78913-364-6

- Make your code more flexible by applying SOLID principles
- Follow the test-driven development (TDD) approach in your .NET Core projects
- Get to grips with efficient database migration, data persistence, and testing techniques
- Convert a console application to a web application using the right MVP
- Write asynchronous, multithreaded, and parallel code
- Implement MVVM and work with RxJS and AngularJS to deal with changes in databases
- Explore the features of microservices, serverless programming, and cloud computing

Leave a review - let other readers know what you think

Please share your thoughts on this book with others by leaving a review on the site that you bought it from. If you purchased the book from Amazon, please leave us an honest review on this book's Amazon page. This is vital so that other potential readers can see and use your unbiased opinion to make purchasing decisions, we can understand what our customers think about our products, and our authors can see your feedback on the title that they have worked with Packt to create. It will only take a few minutes of your time, but is valuable to other potential customers, our authors, and Packt. Thank you!

Index

.NET Core
  using, for unit testing 248, 249, 250
.NET, LINQ providers
  about 94
  LINQ to ADO.NET 94
  LINQ to datasets 94
  LINQ to entities 94
  LINQ to objects 94
  LINQ to SQL (DLINQ) 94
  LINQ to XML (XLINQ) 94
  Parallel LINQ (PLINQ) 94
.NET
  memory barriers 120

2

2D mesh arrangement 307
2D torus arrangement 308

A

aggregation 285, 286
APM patterns
  converting, into tasks 59, 60, 61
ASP.NET core 1.x
  Kestrel settings, modifying for 267
ASP.NET core 2.x
  Kestrel settings, modifying for 268
ASP.NET MVC core
  asynchronous code 271, 272, 274
AsUnOrdered() method
  used, for sequential execution 98, 99
async code, guidelines
  about 224
  async chain method, calling 224, 225
  async void, avoiding 224
  ConfigureAwait wherever possible, using 225

async code, performance
  measuring 221, 222, 223
async code
  used, for exception handling 213
async methods
  about 206, 207, 209, 210
  return types 210, 211
  with PLINQ 220
async streams 275, 276, 278
asynchronous code
  in ASP.NET MVC core 271, 272, 274
  setup, mocking with Moq 254, 255, 257
  used, for auditing 201
  used, for creating responsive UIs 201
  used, for logging 201
  used, for solving problems 201
  using, for CPU-bound applications 202
  using, for service calls 201
  writing 195, 196
  writing, with BeginInvoke method of Delegate class 196, 197
  writing, with IAsyncResult interface 198, 199
  writing, with Task class 197, 198
asynchronous delegates
  creating, with async keyword 211
asynchronous program execution 194, 195
Asynchronous Programming Model (APM) 202, 212
asynchronous programming
  avoiding 200, 201
  using 195
asynchronous services 270
attached task
  creating 67
AutoBuffered merge option
  using 100
await method 206, 207, 209, 210

B

BackgroundWorker
  about 27, 28, 30
  advantages 31
  disadvantage 31
barrier
  about 147
  case study 147, 149, 150
BeginInvoke method, of Delegate class
  used, for writing asynchronous code 196, 197
blocking
  versus spinning 126
BlockingCollection(T)
  creating 164, 165, 166
  using 164
Bulkheads pattern 270

C

Callback delegate
  used, for registering request cancellation 50, 51, 52
CancellationToken
  used, for canceling loops 86, 88
Central Processing Unit (CPU) 11
child tasks 66
chunk partitioning 82, 83
chunks 81
collectives 312
Common Language Runtime (CLR) 24
communication network, types
  about 301
  dynamic communication networks 302
  static communication networks 301
communication networks, properties
  about 302
  flow control 304
  routing algorithms 303
  switching strategy 304
  topology 302, 303
Component Object Model (COM) 14
concurrency 18
Concurrency Visualizer
  Cores view 244
  Threads view 243
  using 241, 242
  Utilization view 242
concurrent collections
  about 156
  BlockingCollection(T), using 164
  concurrent stack, creating 161, 162
  ConcurrentBag(T), using 162, 164
  ConcurrentQueue(T), using 157
  ConcurrentStack(T), using 161
  IProducerConsumerCollection(T) 156, 157
  problems, solving with concurrent queues 159, 160
  producer-consumer problem, solving with queues 158, 159
  Queue(T), versus ConcurrentQueue(T) 160
concurrent stack
  creating 161, 162
ConcurrentBag(T)
  using 162, 164
ConcurrentDictionary(TKey,TValue)
  using 167, 169
ConcurrentQueue(T)
  using 157
  versus Queue(T) 160
ConcurrentStack(T)
  using 161
constructs
  used, for avoiding code reordering 123
continuation tasks 63
Cores view 244
CountDownEvent
  about 147
  case study 147, 150
custom partitioning strategy
  chunk partitioning 82, 83
  creating 81
  range partitioning 82

D

debugging
  with Parallel Stacks windows 236
  with Parallel Watch windows 239, 240
  with VS 2019 232
dedicated thread pools 270, 271
degree of parallelism 79, 80, 81

Denial-of-Service (DoS) attack 209
detached task
  creating 66
Direct Memory Access (DMA) 195
distributed memory machines
  programming, with MPI 308
distributed memory model
  about 300, 301
  versus shared memory model 297
Distributed Shared Memory (DSM) 297
distributed systems 296, 297
dynamic communication networks 302

E

Event-Based Asynchronous Pattern (EAP)
  about 30, 202, 207
  converting, into tasks 61, 62, 63
EventWaitHandle
  about 136
  AutoResetEvent 136, 137
  ManualResetEvent 137, 139
exception handling, with async code
  about 213
  method, returning Task and throwing exception 213
exception handling, with lazy initialization pattern
  about 178
  no exceptions 178
  not caching exceptions 181
  random exception 178, 180
exceptions handling, for async methods
  scenarios 214, 215, 216, 217, 218, 219, 220
exceptions
  handling, with PLINQ 103, 104, 105
  throwing, with PLINQ 103, 104, 105

F

finished tasks
  results, obtaining from 47, 48
Floating-Point Operations Per Second (FLOPS) 160
flow control 304
flow control, algorithms
  sliding window 304
  stop and wait 304

Flynn classified computer architectures
  Multiple Instructions, Multiple Data (MIMD) 13
  Multiple Instructions, Single Data (MISD) 13
  Single Instruction, Multiple Data (SIMD) 13
  Single Instruction, Single Data (SISD) 13
fork/join pattern 287
FullyBuffered merge option
  using 101, 103

H

Hill Climbing algorithm 265, 266
hyper-threading (HT)
  about 11, 13
  Flynn's taxonomy 13

I

IAsyncResult interface
  used, for writing asynchronous code 198, 199
IIS threading model
  Hill Climbing algorithm 265, 266
  Starvation Avoidance algorithm 265
  working 264
Intellitest 257
interlocked operations
  about 119, 120
  constructs, used for avoiding code reordering 123, 124
  memory barriers, in .NET 120
  reordering 121
IProducerConsumerCollection(T) 156, 157

J

Just in Time (JIT) 120

K

Kestrel setting
  modifying, for ASP.NET core 1.x 267
  modifying, for ASP.NET core 2.x 268
Kestrel threading model 266, 267

L

lambda expressions
  creating, with async keyword 211
Last In First Out (LIFO) 161

[325]

lazy initialization pattern
  exception handling 178
lazy initialization
  concepts 172, 173, 175
  overhead, reducing 184, 186, 187
  with thread-local storage 182, 183
lazy pattern 289, 290, 291
LFENCE effect 122
lightweight synchronization primitives
  slim locks 143
linear topology
  about 305
  linear arrays 305, 306
LINQ providers
  in .NET 94
LINQ to ADO.NET 94
LINQ to datasets 94
LINQ to entities 94
LINQ to objects 94
LINQ to SQL (DLINQ) 94
LINQ to XML (XLINQ) 94
LINQ
  used, for implementing MapReduce pattern 282, 283, 284, 285
LINQPad
  about 96
  download link 96
lock 127, 128, 130
locking primitives
  about 124
  ReaderWriterLock 134
  thread state 125, 126
  working 124
loops
  canceling 83
  canceling, with CancellationToken 86, 88
  canceling, with Parallel.Break method 84, 85
  canceling, with ParallelLoopState.Stop 86

M

MapReduce pattern
  about 282
  implementing with LINQ 282, 283, 284, 285
memory barriers
  full memory barrier 123
  in .NET 120
  load (read) memory barrier 122
  store (write) memory barrier 122
  types 122
merge options, PLINQ
  about 99
  AutoBuffered merge option 100
  FullyBuffered merge option 101, 103
  NotBuffered merge option 99
mesh topology 306
message passing interface (MPI)
  about 308
  for program 309, 310
  installing, on Windows 309
  need for 309
  used, for programming distributed memory machines 308
MFENCE effect 123
microservice design approaches
  about 269
  asynchronous services 270
  dedicated thread pools 270, 271
  single thread-multiple process microservices 270
  single thread-single process microservices 269
microservices
  threading, best practices 269
Moq
  used, for mocking setup for async code 254, 255, 257
MPI_Send function 310, 311
MPU_Recv function 310, 311
Multi-Threaded Apartment (MTA) 223
multicore computing, process
  about 10
  operating system (OS) 11
multicore computing
  hyper-threading (HT) 11, 13
  multitasking 11
  multithreading 17, 18
  preparing for 10
  threads 14
Multiple Instruction, Multiple Data (MIMD) 13
multiple producer-consumer
  ConcurrentDictionary(TKey,TValue), using 167, 169

scenario 166, 167
multiple threads-single process 270
multitasking 11
multithreading
　versus multitasking 31
mutex 127, 130, 131

N

NotBuffered merge option
　using 99

O

Object Relational Mapping (ORM) 94
operating system (OS) 11
output
　creating, via Thread class 21

P

parallel and async code, unit test cases
　about 253
　result, checking 253, 254
Parallel LINQ (PLINQ)
　about 94
　order, preserving while parallel executions 97, 98
　used, for handling exceptions 103, 104, 105
　used, for throwing exceptions 103, 104, 105
　with async method 220
parallel LINQ queries
　versus sequential LINQ queries 106
parallel loops
　thread storage 88
parallel programming, with PLINQ
　disadvantages 108
parallel programming
　advantages 33
　disadvantages 33
　usage, scenarios 32
Parallel Stacks windows, views
　Tasks view 238, 239
　Threads view 237, 238
Parallel Stacks windows
　used, for debugging 236
　using 236
parallel systems 297

Parallel Watch windows
　used, for debugging 239, 240
Parallel.Break method
　used, for canceling loops 84, 85
Parallel.For method
　used, to move from sequential loops to parallel loops 77, 78
Parallel.ForEach method
　used, to move from sequential loops to parallel loops 78, 79
Parallel.Invoke method
　used, to move from sequential loops to parallel loops 75, 76
ParallelEnumerable class 95, 96
ParallelLoopState.Stop
　used, for canceling loops 86
parents tasks 66
partition local variable 90, 91
performance impact factor, PLINQ
　about 109
　degree of parallelism 109
　ForAll() method, versus Toarray() 111
　ForAll() method, versus ToList() 111
　merge option 109
　order of operation 110
　parallelism, forcing 111
　partitioning type 109
　PLINQ, versus parallelism 110
　sequences, generating 111, 112
PLINQ queries
　about 96, 97
　canceling 107, 108
　ParallelEnumerable class 95, 96
　writing 95
program execution, types
　about 192
　asynchronous program execution 194, 195
　synchronous program execution 192, 193

R

range partitioning 82
ranges 81
ReaderWriterLock class 134
ring topology 305, 306
routing algorithms 303

running tasks
  waiting on 52

S

semaphore
  about 127, 132, 133
  global semaphore 134
  local semaphore 133
sequential consistency model 120
sequential execution
  with AsUnOrdered() method 98, 99
sequential LINQ queries
  versus parallel LINQ queries 106
sequential loops, to parallel loops
  about 74, 75
  with Parallel.For method 77, 78
  with Parallel.ForEach method 78, 79
  with Parallel.Invoke method 75, 76
sequential
  creating, via Thread class 20
SFENCE effect 122
shared memory model
  about 298, 299
  versus distributed memory model 297
shared state pattern 292
single thread-multiple process microservices 270
Single-Threaded Apartment (STA) 223
slim locks
  about 143
  ManualResetEventSlim 146
  ReaderWriterLockSlim 144, 145
speculative processing pattern 287, 288
SpinLock object
  creating 151, 152
spinning
  versus blocking 126
SpinWait object
  creating 150
Starvation Avoidance algorithm 265
static communication networks 301
switching strategy
  about 304
  circuit switching 304
  packet switching 304
synchronization primitives

  about 118, 134
  categories 118
  EventWaitHandle 136
  interlocked operations 119
  lightweight synchronization primitives 143
  locking primitives 124
  SpinWait object, creating 150
  Thread.Join 135
  WaitHandles 140
synchronous program execution 192, 193
System.Lazy(T)
  about 175
  construction logic, encapsulating 175
  construction logic, passing as delegate 177
System.Threading.Tasks.Task class
  about 37
  Action delegate, using 38
  delegate, using 38
  lambda expressions syntax, using 38
System.Threading.Tasks.Task.Delay method 41
System.Threading.Tasks.Task.Factory.StartNew method
  about 39
  Action delegate, using 39
  delegate, using 39
  lambda expressions syntax, using 39
System.Threading.Tasks.Task.FromCanceled method 46
System.Threading.Tasks.Task.FromCanceled(T) method 46
System.Threading.Tasks.Task.FromException method 46
System.Threading.Tasks.Task.FromException(T) method 46
System.Threading.Tasks.Task.FromResult(T) method 45
System.Threading.Tasks.Task.Run method
  about 40
  Action delegate, using 40
  delegate, using 40
  lambda expressions syntax, using 40
System.Threading.Tasks.Task.Yield method 42, 43, 44

T

Task class
  used, for writing asynchronous code 197, 198
task exceptions
  handling 56
  handling, from multiple tasks 57, 58
  handling, from single tasks 56, 57
  handling, with callback function 58, 59
Task-Based Asynchronous Pattern (TAP)
  about 37, 212
  implementing, with compiler method using async keyword 212
  implementing, with manual method 212, 213
Task.Wait method 53
Task.WaitAll method 54
Task.WaitAny method 54, 55
Task.WhenAll method 55
Task.WhenAny method 55
tasks
  about 36, 37, 63
  APM patterns, converting into 59, 60, 61
  cancelling 48
  continuing, with Task.ContinueWith method 63, 64
  continuing, with Task.Factory.ContinueWhenAll 65
  continuing, with Task.Factory.ContinueWhenAll(T) 65
  continuing, with Task.Factory.ContinueWhenAny 65
  continuing, with Task.Factory.ContinueWhenAny(T) 65
  creating 37
  creating, with tokens 49
  EAPs, converting into 61, 62, 63
  starting 37
Test Explorer 257
thread local variable
  creating 89, 90
thread scheduler 17
thread states
  Aborted 125
  AbortRequested 125
  Background 125
  Running 125
  Stopped 125
  StopRequested 125
  Suspended 125
  SuspendRequested 125
  Unstarted 125
  WaitSleepJoin 125
thread storage
  in parallel loops 88
thread-local storage
  used, for lazy initialization 182, 183
Thread.Join 135
threads debugging 232, 234, 235
Threads view 243
threads, apartment states
  about 14, 16, 17
  Multi-Threaded Apartment (MTA) 15
  Single-Threaded Apartment (STA) 15
threads, Thread class
  advantages 23
  disadvantages 23
threads, ThreadPool class
  advantages 26
  avoiding 26
  disadvantages 26
threads, types
  background threads 14
  foreground threads 14
threads
  about 14
  creating, via Thread class 19, 23
  creating, via ThreadPool class 23, 24, 26
time slicing 18
tokens, status
  polling, via IsCancellationRequested property 49, 50
tokens
  creating 49
  used, for creating tasks 49
topologies
  exploring 305
topology 302, 303
torus topology 306

[329]

U

unit test cases, writing for async code
 problems 250, 251, 253
unit test cases
 writing, for parallel and async code 253
unit testing
 with .NET Core 248, 249, 250
Utilization view 242

V

VS 2019
 used, for debugging 232

W

WaitHandles 140, 141, 143
Windows Presentation Foundation (WPF) 208
Windows
 MPI, installing 309
work-stealing queues 68, 70

Printed in Great Britain
by Amazon